ROGER STRONSTAD

SPIRIT SCRIPTURE and THEOLOGY

A Pentecostal Perspective

Foreword by
Robert P. Menzies

WIPF & STOCK · Eugene, Oregon

NEW EXPANDED EDITION

Wipf and Stock Publishers
199 W 8th Ave, Suite 3
Eugene, OR 97401

Spirit, Scripture, and Theology, 2nd Edition
A Pentecostal Perspective
By Stronstad, Roger
Copyright©2018 APTS Press
ISBN 13: 978-1-5326-8031-1
Publication date 2/21/2019
Previously published by APTS, 2018

*Unless otherwise indicated, all Scripture quotations
are taken from the New American Standard Version.
Copyright ©, 1960, 1962, 1963, 1968, 1971, 1972, 1973, 1975, 1977
by the Lockman Foundation, Ramona, California.
Used by permission of the publishers.*

Publisher's Preface to the 2018 Edition

"Back by Popular Demand" would be a good reason to explain the new, expanded edition of this book. In truth, we were not planning to reprint the original edition, despite the fact that it had been well received, until we were requested to do so by Global University of the Assemblies of God in Springfield, Missouri, who indicated they would like to continue to use it in some of their courses. They also provided some financial assistance to help make this edition possible and we would like to express our gratitude for their generosity.

Professor Stronstad himself was quite eager for us to do this. While he opted not to revise the original manuscript, he added a chapter on prophecy at the end that greatly enhances the message of the book. In the years since the book's inception, the Pentecostal Movement has exploded in growth from over two hundred million in the early 1990s to over six hundred million today. Now, more than ever Dr. Stronstad's message, which brings strength and stability to Pentecostal distinctives, needs to be heard.

Also, thanks to digital technology that was not available when the book was originally published in 1995, we are now able to make this work available to a global market.

As always, we appreciate your patronage. Please feel free to let us know what you think by contacting us through our website, www.aptspress.org.

THE PUBLISHER

Contents

Acknowledgments		*vii*
Foreword to the 2018 Edition		*ix*
Foreword to the 1995 Edition		*xi*
Chapter 1	Trends in Pentecostal Hermeneutics	*1*
Chapter 2	The Hermeneutics of Lucan Historiography	*19*
Chapter 3	Pentecostal Experience and Hermeneutics	*39*
Chapter 4	"Filled with the Holy Spirit" Terminology in Luke-Acts	*61*
Chapter 5	Signs on the Earth Beneath	*79*
Chapter 6	The Holy Spirit in Luke-Acts	*115*
Chapter 7	Unity and Diversity: Lucan, Johannine, and Pauline Perspectives on the Holy Spirit	*137*
Chapter 8	The Rebirth of Prophecy: Trajectories from Moses to Jesus and His Followers	*159*

Acknowledgments

This book had its genesis in the invitation from Dr. H. Glynn Hall, President of the Assemblies of God Theological Seminary, Springfield, Missouri, to give the Guest Lectureship at the seminary for Fall, 1987. In cooperation with the Bible and Theology department, who sponsored the lectureship that year, it was agreed that I should develop four lectures relating to the two complementary themes in which I have a particular interest: Lucan and Pentecostal studies. The lectures, delivered October 13-16, 1987, were subsequently published virtually unchanged in *Paraclete*. They appear here by permission in a longer and revised form as chapters One, Two, Six and Seven. Chapter Three, "Pentecostal Experience and Hermeneutics," was read at the Twentieth Annual Meeting of the Society for Pentecostal Studies (1990) and was subsequently published in *Paraclete*. Chapter Four, "'Filled with the Holy Spirit' Terminology in Luke-Acts," was read at the Fourteenth Annual Meeting of the Society for Pentecostal Studies (1984) and was subsequently published in *The Holy Spirit in the Scriptures and the Church: Essays Presented to Dr. Leslie Thomas Holdcraft on His Sixty-Fifth Birthday*. Chapter Five, "Signs on the Earth Beneath," was read at the Twenty-First Annual Meeting of the Society for Pentecostal Studies (1991).

I would like to thank the faculty and students of the Assemblies of God Theological Seminary for their warm welcome and insightful interaction with the lectures. It is also my pleasant duty to express gratitude to those who helped me in the preparation of this manuscript: to Martha Schneeburger, Kris Potter, Valerie Rathjen, and my wife, Laurel, who typed various chapters at different stages in the history of the manuscript; and to Colleen Daher for proofreading the manuscript.

Roger Stronstad
Clayburn, British Columbia, Canada 1991

Foreword to the 2018 Edition

I am delighted to commend to you this very welcome, new edition of *Spirit, Scripture, and Theology: A Pentecostal Perspective*. This book is important for many reasons, but I shall name two. First, it represents the development of the central, seminal ideas that Roger first, and so powerfully, articulated in his groundbreaking book, *The Charismatic Theology of St. Luke* (1984). The articles in *Spirit, Scripture, and Theology* develop, albeit in different ways, the themes that made Roger's first book so compelling: the theological significance of biblical narrative; Luke's theological purpose; the vocational nature of the Spirit's empowering in Luke-Acts; the unity and diversity of the New Testament and, more particularly, the unique way in which Luke, John, and Paul contribute to a holistic biblical theology of the Spirit; and, finally, the distinctive emphases that mark the pneumatologies of Luke (service), John (salvation), and Paul (sanctification). All of these themes are touched upon, and developed, in a new chapter that now graces this updated edition, "The Rebirth of Prophecy: Trajectories from Moses to Jesus and His Followers."

The first edition of this book was published in 1995, just over a decade after *The Charismatic Theology of St. Luke* burst onto the scene. Now, with the addition of this new chapter, these essays collectively offer the reader an important vantage point from which to understand and assess the thinking of one of the most creative, and influential, Pentecostal scholars of our time. *The Charismatic Theology of St. Luke* has been described (and with good reason) as the most significant book written by a Pentecostal in the 20th century. With this mind, the value of the light that this new edition of *Spirit, Scripture, and Theology* sheds on the work of the Holy Spirit in the New Testament and, more specifically, Roger's approach to this crucial topic, can hardly be overestimated.

In addition to all of this, this new edition has special, personal significance for me. This significance is illustrated by the fact that my father wrote the Foreword for the first edition of this book. You see, my father and I were both friends of Roger and greatly admired his work. It is possible that my father, who was one of the first scholars, and theologians, of the modern Pentecostal Movement, encouraged, and in various ways, influenced Roger's reading of Luke-Acts and his approach to Pentecostal theology. In any event, I know without question that my father was profoundly impacted by Roger's insights into the New Testament and celebrated his writing and teaching ministry.

My father's admiration for Roger, and his creative insights, shaped the context for my first encounter with Roger. I remember with fondness sharing a week of discussion and fellowship with Roger in Fiji, where we were both teaching, just before I embarked on my PhD studies in 1985. Those conversations were a precious gift. Our friendship was rekindled when Roger visited the Asia Pacific Theological Seminary (Baguio City, The Philippines) in 1993. It is fitting that Roger delivered the inaugural series of lectures in the annual William Menzies Pentecostal Lectureship, which continues at APTS to this day. Roger's lectures on that occasion were brilliant and featured themes developed in this book. As you read this book you will learn what I have discovered through personal interaction: Roger has a special gift for bringing clarity to complex issues, and for articulating in clear language concepts that most find difficult to comprehend. Pedagogically speaking, he is a master. This book illustrates that fact.

I thank the Lord for Roger's writings, ministry, and friendship. They have significantly shaped my own theological convictions, and those of countless other Pentecostals around the world. I pray that this new edition of *Spirit, Scripture, and Theology* will make Roger's insights accessible to an even larger audience, and that it will encourage each reader to "fan into flame" the gift that God has given them.

Robert P. Menzies
Palm Sunday, 2017

Foreword to the 1995 Edition

The modern Pentecostal Movement began in humble surroundings nearly a century ago. The great revivals of those early days were marked by earnest meditation on the teachings of the Bible—frequently requiring the discarding of time-worn traditions as the Bible was read through new lenses by people who had been baptized in the Spirit. The early Pentecostals experienced something quite similar to what they read occurred in the early church. For many years, the Pentecostals, isolated from the main currents of Christianity, quietly continued their perceived mission of reaching the lost world for Christ. Pentecostals insisted that what they had experienced was the "Bible pattern." However, their argumentation was not very persuasive to evangelical Christians. But the unchurched flocked to these humble assemblies—especially on the frontiers of Christianity. By mid-century, many evangelicals acknowledged that their Pentecostal brothers were really quite sound, except for their insistence on the special features of Pentecostal theology. Then, about a generation ago, a veritable explosion of interest in the person and work of the Holy Spirit occurred. It became known as the "charismatic renewal." Spiritual phenomena, such as divine healing, speaking in tongues, and a whole panoply of gifts of the Spirit—once largely the province alone of Pentecostals—now became more widely practiced. Religious presses cranked out an avalanche of books on the work of the Holy Spirit. Still, although large numbers of people were experiencing Pentecostal realities, earnest evangelicals still struggled with the biblical theology underlying such practices. Following traditional hermeneutical guidelines, evangelicals frequently shook their heads, saying, "We admire the enthusiasm of you Pentecostals, but we fail to see the biblical warrant." The simple testimony of earnest Pentecostals, such as "This is the pattern we see in the Book of Acts," was simply not very convincing. But that is changing.

It was while I was serving as editor of *Pneuma, The Journal of the Society for Pentecostal Studies* that I first became aware of the work of

Roger Stronstad. That was more than fifteen years ago. I saw to it that several of his articles appeared in that periodical. His insights, I felt, were worth sharing with those interested in Pentecostal theology. Later, I met Roger on his home turf at Western Pentecostal Bible College, Abbotsford, British Columbia, Canada, where he was serving on the faculty. I learned then of his M.A. thesis which he had submitted at Regent College, Vancouver. In time that thesis was edited for publication. It appeared in 1984 as *The Charismatic Theology of St. Luke* (Peabody, MA: Hendrickson Publishers). I think it is not an exaggeration to claim that that book became the forerunner of a new generation of Pentecostal literature.

Professor Stronstad provided in that volume a persuasive argument for the biblical validity of Pentecostal theology. He demonstrated that Luke's theological methodology is in harmony with Jewish theological practice. He further demonstrated that Luke discloses, not only in Acts, but in the Gospel as well, intentional themes regarding the work of the Holy Spirit that have strong Old Testament roots. Of special significance is his insistence that Luke must be seen as a theologian in his own right, requiring his emphases to be considered as a distinct complement to the pneumatology of Paul.

Stronstad's provocative ideas were an important inspiration in the subsequent doctoral work of Robert P. Menzies, who studied with I. Howard Marshall at Aberdeen University. His, *The Development of Early Christian Pneumatology,* published in 1991 by the Sheffield Academic Press, England, is another important step forward in Pentecostal scholarship, yet another contribution from a new generation of scholars.

To draw together his thinking on the theme of Pentecostal methodology, Professor Stronstad called upon some previously-published articles. These include the four papers delivered in a lectureship series at the Assemblies of God Theological Seminary, Springfield, Missouri, September, 1987, and subsequently published in *Paraclete.* The manuscript also contains a paper read at the Society for Pentecostal Studies, Gordon-Conwell Theological Seminary, Wenham, Massachusetts, in 1984, and later published as a chapter in a Festschrift in honor of Dr. Leslie Thomas Holdcroft. Professor Stronstad seized the opportunity, while gathering the above- mentioned previously-published materials together for publication in book form to include some of his more recent reflections on Pentecostal hermeneutics.

Of fresh interest is Chapter Three, "Pentecostalism, Experiential Presuppositions and Hermeneutics." Stronstad makes a persuasive case for the validity of Pentecostal experience as a matrix for good biblical theology, or at least a clearer understanding of the work of the Holy Spirit. He challenges the assumptions of evangelical hermeneutics that disdain the role of experience. Stronstad confronts the inherently rationalistic tendencies found in much current evangelical theology. Although it is likely that all will not be equally impressed with his argumentation, it is equally likely that future Pentecostal and evangelical theologians will feel the need to respond to the provocative and challenging concepts Stronstad has so clearly articulated.

At Asia Pacific Theological Seminary, when an annual lectureship was instituted in February 1993, the faculty had little hesitation in extending to Professor Stronstad the honor of serving as the featured speaker at the initial lecture series. Only occasionally do truly creative minds appear, and even less frequently do they appear within the evangelical and Pentecostal sphere. It is even more rare to find fresh thinking matched by spiritual fervor. Schools do well to model before students the mix of scholarship and piety exhibited by men such as Roger Stronstad. It is with great pleasure that I commend to you the pages that follow.

William W. Menzies
Asia Pacific Theological Seminary
Baguio City, Philippines
September, 1993

CHAPTER ONE

TRENDS IN PENTECOSTAL HERMENEUTICS

On January 1, 1901, just one year after the birth of the twentieth century, the Pentecostal Movement was born. The world was the maternity ward for the new century; the small Midwest town of Topeka, Kansas, was the ward for the birth of the new movement. The twentieth century was born to public celebration; in contrast, the Pentecostal Movement was born in the individual experience of a member of a small private prayer meeting at Bethel Bible School. Though the Pentecostal Movement began in humble obscurity, now, just one decade shy of its centenary, and numbering an estimated 193,679,200 Pentecostals/charismatics,[1] it has grown to become a major force within Christendom and in the world.

The Classical Pentecostal Tradition: A "Pragmatic" Hermeneutic

Charles F. Parham: Origins of the "Pragmatic" Hermeneutic

As Martin Luther is the fountainhead of Lutheranism, John Calvin that of Reformed Theology, and John Wesley that of Methodism, so Charles F. Parham, who bequeathed to Pentecostalism its distinctive hermeneutic, theology, and apologetics, stands as the fountainhead of Pentecostalism. Parham was not the first to speak in tongues. In one

---

[1] R.D. Barrett, "Statistics, Global," in *Dictionary of Pentecostal and Charismatic Movements*, edited by Stanley M Burgess and Gary B. McGee (Grand Rapids: Zondervan Publishing House, 1988), 812-13.

sense that honor goes to Miss Agnes N. Ozman.[2] In another sense, the birth of the Pentecostal Movement was the climax to the growing swell of charismatic experiences among various revival and Apostolic Faith movements.[3] What makes Charles F. Parham the Father of Pentecostalism, and Topeka, Kansas, the locus of modern Pentecost, is not the uniqueness of this experience, but the new hermeneutical/ Biblical understanding of this experience.

Charles F. Parham bequeathed to the Pentecostal Movement its definitive hermeneutics, and consequently, its definitive theology and apologetics. His contribution arose out of what he perceived to be the problem of the interpretation of the 2nd Chapter of Acts and his conviction that Christian experience in the twentieth century, "... should tally exactly with the Bible, [but] neither sanctification nor the anointing that abideth . . . tallied with the 2nd Chapter of Acts."[4] Consequently he reports, "I set the students at work studying out diligently what was the Bible evidence of the baptism of the Holy Ghost that we might go before the world with something that was indisputable because it tallied absolutely with the Word."[5] He tells the results of their investigation in the following words:

> Leaving the school for three days at this task, I went to Kansas City for three days of services. I returned to the school on the morning preceding Watch Night service in the year 1900. At about 10:00 o'clock in the morning I rang the bell calling all the students into the

---

[2] Mrs. Charles F. Parham, *The Life of Charles F. Parham Founder of the Apostolic Faith Movement* (Joplin, MO.: Hunter Printing Company, 1930), 52-53, 65-68.

[3] J. Philip Newell, "Scottish Intimations of Modem Pentecostalism: A.J. Scott and the 1830 Clydeside Charismatics," *Pneuma*, Vol. 4, No. 2 (1982), 1-18. Newell begins his article with the following report:

On 28 March 1830, Mary Campbell, a young devout Scotts woman from Clydeside, during an act of communal prayer in her own home, spoke in "an unknown tongue." Mary and those with her believed this to be a resurgence of the Apostolic gift of tongues.

On the history of the Catholic Apostolic church of the same period see Larry Christenson, "Pentecostalism's Forgotten Forerunner," in *Aspects of Pentecostal-Charismatic Origins*, edited by Vinson Synan (Plainfield, N.J.: 1975); "Revival in Cherokee County, North Carolina," *Pneuma*, Vol. 5, No. 2 (1983): 1-17; Donald W. Dayton, "From 'Christian Perfection' to the 'Baptism of the Holy Ghost,'" Melvin E. Deiter, 'Wesleyan. Holiness Aspects of Pentecostal Origins: As Mediated Through the Nineteenth-Century Holiness Revival," and William W. Menzies, "The Non-Wesleyan Origins of Pentecostal Movement," in Vinson Synan's, *Aspects*, 40-98.

[4] Parham, *Life*, 52.

[5] Ibid.

Chapel to get their report on the matter in hand. To my astonishment they all had the same story, that while there were different things occurring when the Pentecostal blessing fell, that the indisputable proof on each occasion was, that they spoke with other tongues.[6]

In Parham's report we find the essential distinctives of the Pentecostal Movement, namely, 1) the conviction that contemporary experience should be identical to apostolic Christianity, 2) the separation of the baptism of the Holy Spirit from sanctification (as Holiness Movements had earlier separated it from conversion/incorporation), and 3) that tongues speaking is the indisputable evidence, or proof, of the baptism in the Holy Spirit.

The discovery that tongues speaking was the indisputable biblical proof of the baptism in the Holy Spirit was confirmed the next day, January 1, 1901, in the experience of one of the students at Bethel Bible School; namely, Miss Agnes N. Ozman. She testified:

> The spirit of prayer was upon us in the evening. It was nearly seven o'clock on this first of January that it came into my heart to ask Bro. Parham to lay his hands upon me that I might receive the gift of the Holy Spirit. It was as his hands were laid upon my head that the Holy Spirit fell upon me and I began to speak in other tongues, glorifying God. I talked several languages, and it was clearly manifest when a new dialect was spoken.[7]

Agnes Ozman was the first one, but not the last one, to speak in tongues in the Bible school. By January 3, 1901, other students, and soon even Parham, himself, had spoken in tongues. When questioned about her experience, Miss Ozman, ". . . pointed out to them the Bible references, showing [she] had received the baptism according to Acts 2:4 and 19:1-6."[8]

Thus, in the momentous days which bridged the Christmas season of 1900 and the New Year 1901, tongues was identified as the biblical

---

[6]Ibid.
[7]Ibid., 66.
[8]Ibid.

evidence of the baptism in the Spirit and was confirmed by contemporary (twentieth century) experience. This identification of biblical tongues and contemporary charismatic experience was both populist and pragmatic. This pragmatic hermeneutic passed into the infant Pentecostal Movement as "oral tradition."[9] This tradition was subsequently "received" by church councils and codified in doctrinal statements. As a result of this codification of Parham's hermeneutics and theology for the majority of its brief history, Pentecostal hermeneutics has existed in an analytical vacuum. In fact, Pentecostal hermeneutics has relied on exposition rather than investigation and analysis. Nevertheless, this pragmatic hermeneutic became the bulwark of Pentecostal apologetics, and the pillar of classical Pentecostalism, which, though it might be articulated with greater clarity, finesse and sophistication, remained inviolate until recently.

Carl Brumback: Exemplar of the Classical Pentecostal Hermeneutic

Just as a wind-driven fire sweeps across tinder-dry prairie, so, in the decades following the momentous events at Bethel Bible School, the winds of the Spirit swept the flames of Pentecost upon spiritually dry hearts. The infant Pentecostal revival advanced, and grew, rapidly becoming more international than the table of nations of that first Christian Pentecost (Acts 2:9-11). The revival quickly spread from Kansas and Missouri to Texas, to California,[10] and from there to the ends of the earth. Contrary to the expectations, and wishes, of most in the fledgling movement, it coalesced into various denominational structures. By mid-century it was cautiously admitted into mainstream Evangelicalism.[11] Through that kaleidoscope of variety (which characterized Pentecostalism locally, nationally, and even internationally), one aspect stood constant—the pragmatic hermeneutics which looked to Pentecost as the pattern for contemporary experience.

---

[9]William G. MacDonald, "Pentecostal Theology: A Classical Viewpoint," in *Perspectives on the New Pentecostalism*, edited by Russell P. Spittler (Grand Rapids: Baker Book House, 1976), 59.

[10]William W. Menzies, "The Revival Spreads to Los Angeles (1901-1906)," Ch. 3, in, *Anointed to* Serve (Springfield, MO: 1971), 41-59.

[11]Ibid. "Cooperation: From Isolation to Evangelical Identification," ch. 9, 177-227.

Writing about midway between the beginning of the Pentecostal Movement and the present, one expositor declared: ". . . we believe that the experiences of the one hundred and twenty in Acts 2:4—'And they were all filled with the Holy Ghost and began to speak with other tongues, as the Spirit gave them utterance'—is the Scriptural pattern for believers of the whole church age."[12]

This affirmation was penned by Carl Brumback, whom I selected at random as an exemplar of Pentecostal hermeneutics.[13] This affirmation of Pentecostal hermeneutics, however, could have been written in any decade of the Movement's history, or by anyone within the Movement. This is because Pentecostal hermeneutics is traditional, and, therefore, essentially both timeless and anonymous.

In his book, *"What Meaneth This?": A Pentecostal Answer to a Pentecostal Question,* Brumback never tires of asserting this Pentecost-as-pattern hermeneutical stance. For example, ". . . the baptisms or fillings with the Holy Spirit, as recorded in Acts," he writes, "should likewise be the standard for believers today"; furthermore, ". . . in apostolic days speaking with tongues was a constant accompaniment of the baptism with the Holy Ghost, and should be in these days as well"; moreover, "speaking in tongues formed the pattern for every similar baptism or charismatic enduement"; and, finally, "the tongues of Pentecost . . . set the pattern for future baptisms in the Holy Spirit."[14]

For Pentecostals, then, tongues is normative for their experience, just as it was normative in the experience of the apostolic church, as recorded in Acts. Though normative, tongues is not the purpose of the baptism. For Pentecostals, generally, and Brumback, in particular, Jesus established the purpose of the baptism, or filling, with the Spirit in Luke 24:49— " . . . but you are to stay in the city until you are clothed with power from on high." Again, in Acts 1:8 He said, " . . . but you shall receive power when the Holy Spirit has come upon you."

---

[12]Carl Brumback, *"What Meaneth This?" A Pentecostal Answer to a Pentecostal Question* (Springfield, MO.: Gospel Publishing House, 1947), 192.

[13]For example, compare the following two expositions of Pentecostal theology: Frank Linblad, *The Spirit Which Is from God* (Springfield, MO.: 1928), and L. Thomas Holdcroft, *The Holy Spirit: A Pentecostal Interpretation* (Springfield, MO.: Gospel Publishing House, 1979), coming from the same publisher as Brumback's *"What Meaneth This?"*

[14]Brumback. *"What Meaneth This?"* 186-87, 198-200.

Conceding that there are opposing views to the meaning of these promises, Brumback nevertheless insists, " . . . that the *primary* (we do not say the *only*) purpose of the baptism at and since Pentecost was and is the enduement of believers with 'power from on high.'"[15] This gift of power, of course, is to enable and/or empower the witness or service of believers.

This brief survey of Brumback's Pentecost-as-pattern hermeneutic is an example of Pentecostal hermeneutics at the midpoint of the Movement's history, and is a restatement of the pragmatic hermeneutics of the students of Parham's Bethel Bible School more than a generation earlier. As with Parham's students, there is the same conviction that the experience of both apostolic and contemporary Christianity should be identical; that the baptism is for service and for neither salvation nor sanctification; and that tongues is the invariable initial evidence of the baptism with the Holy Spirit.

One striking peculiarity of Brumback's discussion to those who read it forty years later is that this pragmatic Pentecost-as-pattern hermeneutic is simply assumed to be self-evident and self-authenticating. Nowhere does he analyze or explain this hermeneutic; he simply asserts it. Nowhere does he betray any self awareness that, in a book of Pentecostal apologetics, he needs to discuss, defend, and justify his hermeneutical base for developing "a contemporary Pentecostal answer to that ancient Pentecostal question."

Up to the 1970s, classical Pentecostals have remained confidently, if not always quietly, impervious to criticism of its pragmatic Pentecost-as-pattern hermeneutic. While it remains confident, classical Pentecostalism is no longer impervious to the hermeneutical debate. In the 1970s and '80s, Pentecostals have begun to address the hermeneutical issues, and to articulate new hermeneutical approaches, while at the same time, attempting to remain true both to their experience and to their tradition. Several factors of varying importance have produced this new attitude. First, the Movement itself has matured; it is no longer a young movement struggling to shape its identity and to survive in a hostile world. Second, Pentecostalism is now more widely accepted and is fully integrated into mainstream Evangelicalism. As a result, it is less defensive than it was in earlier generations. Third, the neoPentecostal or Charismatic movement

---

[15]Ibid., 197.

has shown classical Pentecostals a variety of alternative hermeneutics, worship and lifestyles. Finally, Pentecostal leadership, at least in its Bible colleges and seminars, is now seminary and university trained. As a result, this leadership is trained in critical methodology and skilled in scholarly dialogue. Consequently, the classical Pentecostal Movement has now brought its pragmatic hermeneutic to the intellectual market place, to buy and to sell. The market place is fraught with great danger for the unwary merchant, but also promises great spiritual gains for the wise merchant.

When discussing the pragmatic hermeneutic of classical Pentecostals, because one is discussing the exposition of a tradition, one can choose almost any exemplar from any age as representative of the movement. When discussing the current debate, however, because one is no longer discussing a tradition, one must look at individuals and their particular contribution to the debate. In the 1970s and '80s the work of three Pentecostal scholars demand attention: Dr. Gordon D. Fee, professor of New Testament at Regent College, Vancouver, B.C.; Dr. Howard M. Ervin, professor of Old Testament at Oral Roberts University, Tulsa, Oklahoma; and Dr. William W. Menzies, president, Asia Pacific Theological Seminary, Baguio, Philippines. In contrast to the pragmatic hermeneutic espoused by classical Pentecostals, these scholars espouse a genre, pneumatic, and holistic hermeneutic, respectively.

Gordon D. Fee: A "Genre" Hermeneutic

Dr. Gordon Fee has moved to fill the analytical vacuum of classical Pentecostalism with perhaps more vigor than any other contemporary scholar. His analysis of Pentecostal hermeneutics and his proposals for new directions in hermeneutics are found in several articles, including the following: "Hermeneutics and Historical Precede—a Major Problem in Pentecostal Hermeneutics,"[16] "Acts—The Problem of Historical Precedent,"[17] and "Baptism in the Holy Spirit: The Issue of Separability

---

[16]Gordon D. Fee, "Hermeneutics and Historical Precedent - A Major Problem in Pentecostal Hermeneutics," in *Perspectives on the New Pentecostalism,* edited by Russell P. Spittler (Grand Rapids, MI: Baker Book House, 1976), 118-132.

[17]Gordon D. Fee and Douglas Stuart, "Acts - The Problem of Historical Precedent," in *How to Read the Bible for All its Worth: A Guide to Understanding the Bible,* (Grand Rapids, MI.: Zondervan, 1982), 87, 102.

and Subsequence."[18] As a son of the Pentecostal Movement and a scholar of international reputation, Fee's credentials are impeccable. His primary contribution to the hermeneutical debate is to advocate a "genre" hermeneutic as an alternative to the pragmatic hermeneutic of classical Pentecostals.

As a general principle Fee advocates "It should be an axiom of biblical hermeneutics that the interpreter must take into account the literary genre of the passage he is interpreting, along with the question of text, grammar, philosophy, and history."[19] So with the Acts, upon which Pentecostal theology is based: " . . . it is *not* an epistle, nor a theological treatise. Even if one disregards its historical value, he cannot, indeed must not, disregard the fact that it is cast in the form of historical narrative."[20] The significance of fully appreciating that Acts is cast in the form of historical narrative, " . . . is that in the hermeneutics of biblical history the major task of the interpreter is to discover the author's [I would add, the Holy Spirit's] *intent* in recording that history."[21] Three principles emerge from this view with regard to the hermeneutics of historical narrative:

1. The Word of God in Acts which may be regarded as normative for Christians is related primarily to what any given narrative was intended to teach.
2. What is *incidental* to the primary intent of the narrative may indeed reflect an author's theology, or how he understood things, but it cannot have the same didactic value as what the narrative was *intended* to teach has.
3. Historical precedent, to have normative value, must be related to *intent*. That is, if it can be shown that the purpose of a given narrative is to *establish* precedent, then such precedent should be regarded as normative.[22]

---

[18]Gordon D. Fee, "Baptism in the Holy Spirit: The Issue of Separability and Subsequence," *Pneuma*, Vol. 7, No. 2, (1985): 87-99.
[19]Fee, "Hermeneutics,"124.
[20]Ibid.
[21]Ibid., 125
[22]Ibid., 126.

Having discussed the hermeneutical use of historical narrative in general, Fee then gives three specific principles for the use of historical precedent:

1. The use of historical precedent as an analogy by which to establish a norm is never valid in itself.
2. Although it may not have been the author's primary purpose, historical narratives do have and, sometimes, "pattern" value.
3. In matters of Christian experience, and even more so in Christian practice, biblical precedents may be regarded as repeatable patterns—even if they are not to be regarded as normative.[23]

On the basis of his guidelines for the use of historical precedent, Fee then discusses the relationship between the Pentecostal distinctives (the baptism in the Holy Spirit with speaking in tongues as its evidence, and distinct from, and subsequent to, conversion) and historical precedent. Fee asserts, "... for Luke (and Paul) the gift of the Holy Spirit was not some sort of adjunct to Christian experience, nor was it some kind of second and more significant part of Christian experience. It was rather the chief element in the event (or process) of Christian conversion."[24]

Furthermore, "The question as to whether tongues is the initial physical evidence of the charismatic quality of life in the Spirit is a moot point."[25] In fact, "... to insist that it is the only valid sign seems to place far too much weight on the historical precedent of three (perhaps four) instances in Acts."[26]

"What then," Fee asks, "may the Pentecostal say about his experience in view of the hermeneutical principles suggested in this paper?"[27] To his question Fee gives a fivefold answer, concluding:

> Since speaking in tongues was a repeated expression of this dynamic, or charismatic, dimension of the coming of the Spirit, the contemporary Christian may expect this, too, as part of his

---
[23]Ibid., 128-29.
[24]Ibid., 130.
[25]Ibid.
[26]Ibid., 131.
[27]Ibid.

experience in the Spirit. If the Pentecostals may not say one must speak in tongues, he may surely say, why not speak in tongues? It does have repeated biblical precedent, it did have evidential value at Cornelius' household (Acts 10:45-46), and—in spite of much that has been written to the contrary—it does have value both for the edification of the individual believer (I Cor. 14:2-5) and, with interpretation, for the edification of the church (I Cor. 14:5, 26-28).[28]

Fee's subsequent articles overlap with, repeat, clarify, and add new emphases to his discussion. They do not, however, substantially modify the genre hermeneutics which he espoused in his first article. As one who has approached the subject from within the classical Pentecostal Movement, his discussion demands both respect and careful scrutiny. There is much in what he writes with which we can agree. For example, he is correct in observing that "hermeneutics has simply not been a Pentecostal thing."[29] He correctly insists that Acts be interpreted as historical narrative, and not as a theological treatise.[30] He is also correct to caution Pentecostals not to elevate an incidental element in the narrative to a position of primary theological importance. Finally, he correctly affirms that the *intent* of the author determines the normative value of the narrative.[31]

When discussing the hermeneutical issues which confront Pentecostals as they interpret Acts, Fee writes with passion and conviction. He is both a crusader and an iconoclast. On the one hand, as a crusader, he effectively champions a "genre" hermeneutic. Surprisingly, however, he does not extend his "genre" hermeneutic to its proper limits. He writes as if there is one hermeneutic for the Gospel of Luke and another for the Acts of the Apostles. Yet H. J. Cadbury's landmark study, *The Making of Luke-Acts,* decisively demonstrated that both the Gospel of Luke and the Acts of the Apostles must be studied as a literary unit.[32] This Fee fails to do. To discuss the hermeneutics of Acts

---

[28]Ibid., 132.
[29]Ibid., 121.
[30]Ibid., 125.
[31]Ibid.
[32]Henry J. Cadbury, *The Making of Luke-Acts* (Second Edition; London: S.P.C.K., 1958), 1-11. Cf; W.C. Van Unnik, "Luke-Acts, A Storm Center in Contemporary Scholarship," in *Studies in Luke-Acts,* edited by L.E. Keek and J.L. Martyn (London: S.P.C.K., 1968), 18-22.

post-Cadbury from the perspective of a pre-Cadbury stance, as he does, is similar to attempting to explain a playwright's style and methodology and purpose for his two-act play, after having viewed only the second act.[33] Fee is correct about genre. Pentecostals, and, indeed, interpreters from every theological tradition need to interpret Acts according to its genre as historical narrative, but it must be studied as part of the literary unit, Luke-Acts, and not Acts separated and isolated from the study of the Gospel of Luke. To understand the message of Luke, half measures will not do.

On the other hand, Fee writes as an iconoclast, tearing down the hermeneutical pillars upon which the structure of Pentecostal doctrine is built. He objects to Spirit Baptism being distinct from conversion.[34] This objection is difficult to understand until one remembers that Fee believes that the gift of the Spirit (as a charismatic experience) is part of the conversion event (or process).[35] As a consequence, while Fee remains a Pentecostal experientially, and even advocates the probability of speaking in tongues when the Spirit is received, his hermeneutic is no longer Pentecostal in any nonnative sense of the word, for he has positioned Spirit baptism with conversion rather than with vocation.

Howard M. Ervin: A "Pneumatic" Hermeneutic

As we have observed, Gordon D. Fee espouses a "genre" hermeneutic for Pentecostals. In his essay, "Hermeneutics: A Pentecostal Option,"[36] Howard M. Ervin proposes a different approach to Pentecostal hermeneutics, namely, a "pneumatic" hermeneutic. Fee is a

---

[33]In regard to the unwarranted separation of Luke and Acts, Cadbury writes, "Professor Edward Meyer, who complains of this separate treatment of Luke and Acts, says it is unreasonable as though we treated as separate works the account concerning Tiberius' *Annals* and that concerning Claudius and Nero, or if we divided the several decades of Livy, or separated the first part of Polybius (Books 1-29), in which we worked over older presentation of the subject from the latter part (Books 30-40), where he arranged the material for the first time, working independently as one who lived at the time and participated in the events" (7).

[34]Fee, "Hermeneutics," 120-21; 129-31; "Baptism," 87ff.

[35]Ibid., 96, 130.

[36]Howard M. Ervin, "Hermeneutics: A Pentecostal Option," *Pneuma*, Vol. 3, No. 2 (1981): 11-25. Reprinted with slight alterations under the same title in *Essays on Apostolic Themes: Studies in Honor of: Howard M. Ervin*, edited by Paul Elbert (Peabody, MA.: Hendrickson Publishers, 1985), 23-35.

native son in the Pentecostal Movement. Ervin is not a native son, but is, as it were, a resident alien in the Movement. It was as the pastor of seventeen years at Emmanuel Baptist Church, Atlantic Highlands, New Jersey, that he attended a Full Gospel Business Men's Fellowship International meeting in Miami, Florida. In a prayer meeting there both David Du Plessis and Dennis Bennett prayed for him and he received his personal Pentecost, speaking in tongues as the Spirit gave utterance.[37] Fee's preoccupations are predictably those of a native son: historical precedent, separability and subsequence. In contrast, Ervin's concerns are those of a naturalized son: the epistemology of the Word and experience.

Ervin launches his discussion, "Hermeneutics: A Pentecostal Option," with the observation that "Fundamental to the study of hermeneutics, as to any academic discipline, is the question of epistemology."[38] For Western Man two ways of knowledge are axiomatic: sensory experience and reason. Not only for Orthodoxy, but also for Pietism and Neo-Orthodoxy, the result is a perennial dichotomy between faith and reason. He sums up the consequences of this epistemological problem in these words: "The consequence for hermeneutics has been in some quarters a destructive rationalism (neo-Orthodoxy), in others a dogmatic intransigence (Orthodoxy), and yet in others a non-rational mysticism (Pietism)."[39]

In the face of this epistemological deadlock, "What is needed," he writes, "is an epistemology firmly rooted in the Biblical faith with a phenomenology that meets the criteria of empirically verifiable sensory experience (healing, miracles, etc.) and does not violate the coherence of rational categories."[40] For Ervin, a pneumatic epistemology not only meets these criteria but it also ". . . provides a resolution of (a) the dichotomy between faith and reason that existentialism seeks to bridge, though at the expense of the pneumatic; (b) the antidote to a destructive rationalism that often accompanies a critical-historical exegesis; and (c)

---

[37]Charles Farah, Jr. and Steve Durasoff, "Biographical and Bibliographical Sketch," in *Essays,* edited by Elbert, xi.
[38]Ervin, "Hermeneutics," 11.
[39]Ibid., 12.
[40]Ibid.

a rational accountability for the mysticism by a piety grounded in *sola fidei*."[41]

The ground for a pneumatic hermeneutic lies in the nature of Scripture as the absolute, ultimate and transcendent Word of God. This word, ". . . is fundamentally an ontological reality (the incarnation)."[42] A precondition for understanding that Word, ". . . is man's ontological re-creation by the Holy Spirit (the new birth)."[43] However, while the new birth bridges the distance between the creator and the creature it does not erase it. Therefore, "This distance renders the word ambiguous until the Holy Spirit, who 'searches even the depth of God' (I Corinthians 2:10), interprets it to the hearer."[44] Thus, "It is a word for which, in fact, there is no hermeneutic unless and until the divine *hermeneutes* (the Holy Spirit) mediates an understanding."[45]

The Pentecostal Movement, Ervin observes, has contributed to this "pneumatic" hermeneutic. He writes, "The contribution to hermeneutics of the present charismatic, or Pentecostal, renewal of the Church is its insistence upon the experiential immediacy of the Holy Spirit. There are direct contacts with non-material reality that informs a Pentecostal epistemology, hence its hermeneutics."[46] Furthermore,

> Pentecostal experience with the Holy Spirit gives existential awareness of the miracles in the Biblical world view. These events are no longer "mythological" (the view of Neo-Orthodoxy), but "objectively" real. Contemporary experience of divine healing, prophecy, miracles, tongues, and exorcism are empirical evidence of the impingement of a sphere of non-material reality upon our time-space existence with which one can and does have immediate contact. Awareness of and inter-action with the presence of this spiritual continuum is axiomatic in a Pentecostal epistemology that affects decisively its hermeneutic.[47]

---

[41]Ibid.
[42]Ibid., 17.
[43]Ibid.
[44]Ibid.
[45]Ibid., 16, *cf.* 18, 22-21.
[46]Ibid., 23.
[47]Ibid., 24.

Though his essay is entitled, "Hermeneutics: A Pentecostal Option," Ervin contributes little to the subject of Pentecostal hermeneutics. Apart from a few paragraphs at the end of his essay, he writes primarily about epistemology and not about hermeneutics. It is unfortunate that he failed to explore his "pneumatic" hermeneutic in greater depth, for the pneumatic, or vertical, dimension is a vital dimension in Pentecostal hermeneutics. After all, it is the Spirit, who is both non-temporal and immanent, who establishes both the existential and pre-suppositional continuum between the word, written in the past and that same word in the present.

In his essay, "Hermeneutics and the Spiritual Life," Dr. Bruce Waltke reminds us of this deficit in hermeneutics. He observes, "Most textbooks on hermeneutics and exegesis written by evangelicals in the past decade emphasize and refine the grammatico-historical method and neglect the role of the Holy Spirit and spiritual qualification of the interpreter."[48] He continues, "The Spirit, if mentioned, is demoted to the secondary role of applying the text." Furthermore, this is, " . . . the widespread neglect of the most important factor in exegesis." Ervin's "pneumatic" hermeneutic points to the rehabilitation of the role of the Holy Spirit in the interpretation of Scripture. Because of the immediacy of the Holy Spirit in their experience, Pentecostals are in a unique position to contribute significantly to addressing this neglect of the role of the Holy Spirit in hermeneutics. This is the time for Pentecostals to get as serious about the role of the Holy Spirit in the interpretation of Scripture as they are about His role in their Christian experience and service.

William W. Menzies: A "Holistic" Hermeneutic

Dr. William W. Menzies is a third Pentecostal scholar who is contributing significantly to the discussion of Pentecostal hermeneutics. His current thinking on the subject is summarized in the recent article, "The Methodology of Pentecostal Theology: An Essay in Hermeneutics."[49] In contrast to Gordon Fee, who focuses upon the genre

---

[48]Bruce Waltke, "Hermeneutics and the Spiritual Life," *Crux*, Vol. xxiii, No. 1, 5.

[49]William W. Menzies, "The Methodology of Pentecostal Theology: An Essay on Hermeneutics," in *Essays . . .* , edited by Elbert, 1-14.

of Biblical literature, and Ervin, who focuses upon epistemology, Menzies focuses upon theology. As Menzies understands it, ". . . the current charismatic theological issue" today is the connection between such phenomena as tongues and the baptism in the Spirit.[50] For Menzies, the heart of this theological battle today is the bedrock issue of *hermeneutics* or *methodology*.[51] Whereas Fee proposes a "genre" hermeneutic and Ervin proposes a "pneumatic" hermeneutic, Menzies proposes a "holistic" hermeneutic for interpreting the Biblical foundation for Pentecostal theology.

Menzies' "holistic" hermeneutic has three levels: 1) the inductive level, 2) the deductive level, and 3) the verification level. The inductive level is the scientific exegesis of Scripture. He sees three kinds of inductive listening: 1) *declarative;* that is, those texts, "whose transparency renders their meaning relatively unambiguous," 2) *implicational,* for some important truths, such as the doctrine of the Trinity, " . . . are *implied* in Scripture, rather than stated in categorical declarations of an overt kind," and 3) the *descriptive,* which is the real battleground. In this battleground, "The book of Acts is the burning issue in the entire debate."[52] This is Fee's issue of genre, and, as Menzies observes, is the real crux of the debate. If it can be demonstrated that Luke did not intend to teach theology by what he *described,* then "there is no genuine basis for a Pentecostal theology at all."[53] This realization constrains Menzies to reject Fee's guidelines for historical precedent and normativeness, and he concludes, contra Fee, that the biblical data implies normativeness, rather than mere repeatability.[54]

In Menzies' "holistic" hermeneutic the deductive level complements the inductive level. If the inductive level is exegesis, then the deductive level is that of biblical theology. It integrates, ". . . disparate and sometimes disconnected passages into a meaningful whole."[55] It proceeds on "the principle of the analogy of faith."[56] In regards to the peculiar theology of Acts, Menzies concludes, "the concepts of

---

[50]Ibid., 4.
[51]Ibid.
[52]Ibid., 5-6.
[53]Ibid., 6.
[54]Ibid., 8-10.
[55]Ibid., 10.
[56]Ibid., 11.

subsequence and a normative, accompanying sign of tongues (is) meaningful."[57]

Finally, Menzies' "holistic" hermeneutic includes the verification Level. This is the level of contemporary experience. Menzies believes that, "if a biblical truth is to be promulgated, then it ought to be demonstrable in life."[58] In other words, though experience does not establish theology, it does verify or demonstrate, theological truth. Thus, on the day of Pentecost, "the apostles, led of the Spirit, instructed the disciples in the connection between revelation and experience. 'This is that,' announced Peter (Acts 2:16)."[59]

Menzies' "holistic three level hermeneutic—inductive, deductive, and verification—has much to commend it. For example, it integrates the analytical, the synthetic, and the existential processes. Moreover, it integrates the exegetical, the theological, and the applicational dimensions of biblical interpretation. Applying this "holistic" hermeneutic to the book of Acts, Menzies finds that he can reaffirm four aspects of Pentecostal hermeneutics and theology; namely: 1) Pentecost as pattern, 2) the theological normativeness of this pattern, 3) subsequence, and 4) the sign of tongues.

At the conclusion of this survey on trends in Pentecostal hermeneutics, and as the Pentecostal Movement has entered its tenth decade, and ultimately approaches its centenary, we remind ourselves that the "pragmatic" hermeneutic of our founding Fathers has served the Movement well in its preaching and teaching directed toward those who stood within the Movement. It is no longer adequate for apologetics directed to those outside classical Pentecostalism, whether they are charismatic or non-charismatic. For this reason, the decades-long era of the analytical vacuum of the "pragmatic" hermeneutics of classical Pentecostalism has now been forever, and irreversibly, ended.

Fee, Ervin and Menzies have drawn attention to important components in an overall Pentecostal hermeneutic. Thus, as Fee reminds us, the distinctive genre of (Luke) Acts as historical narrative must be factored into the hermeneutical equation. Moreover, as Ervin reminds us, the experience of the pneumatic establishes a continuum between the contemporary Pentecostal and the ancient biblical world. Finally, as

---

[57]Ibid., 12.
[58]Ibid., 13.
[59]Ibid.

Menzies reminds us, both theology and hermeneutics are complex processes that properly combine inductive, deductive and verification levels. Fee, Ervin and Menzies have proven to be seminal strategists in the development of the new Pentecostal hermeneutic, but each has a partial, or fragmentary, focus. Though Menzies' "holistic" hermeneutic comes the closest; ninety years after the Pentecostal Movement began, it has not yet fully articulated the hermeneutical basis for its understanding of Acts. This is the urgent hermeneutical agenda which still confronts contemporary Pentecostalism.

CHAPTER TWO

THE HERMENEUTICS OF LUCAN HISTORIOGRAPHY

*I*n chapter one, "Trends in Pentecostal Hermeneutics," we observed that Pentecostal hermeneutics is inseparably linked to the message of the book of Acts. We also observed that four hermeneutical strategies control the interpretation and application of Lucan pneumatology within Pentecostalism: 1) pragmatic, 2) genre, 3) pneumatic and 4) holistic (which includes genre within it). Since Luke-Acts constitutes 25 per cent of the bulk of the New Testament, a bulk which is greater than the combined writings of any other author, the problem of genre is of immense importance, not only for Pentecostalism, but also for New Testament studies as a whole. In spite of its immense bulk, however, Luke-Acts is traditionally assigned a lesser place in the hermeneutics and theology of the New Testament. All too often interpreters fail to permit Luke to have an independent voice. For example, in regards to genre, the Gospel of Luke is often read as though it were Mark. Similarly, in regards to pneumatology, Luke is often read as though he were Paul.

In this discussion of the hermeneutics of Lucan historiography we will: 1) examine and clarify the genre of Luke-Acts as historical books, 2) survey two contrasting approaches to Lucan historiography, and 3) submit an alternative approach to the hermeneutics of Lucan historiography.

The Literary Genre of Luke-Acts[1]

For the most part the literary genre of the books of the New Testament is easily identifiable. Paul and others, for example, wrote twenty or so epistles which are identified as such by their prescript, the circumstantial character of their content, and their subscript. John wrote the Apocalypse, or Revelation (Rev. 1:1), which also has stylistic affinities with the epistle (1:4), and which he designates as a prophecy (22:7, 10). The anonymous author of the epistle to the Hebrews identified it as a "word of exhortation" (13:22), which might simply describe its hortatory content, but which is more likely to identify it as a synagogue style homily (cf. Acts 13, 15). Mark wrote, "the Gospel of Jesus Christ" (1:1). Though it has some similarities with contemporary biographies, memoirs and acts, the Gospel of Mark is a new, distinctly Christian, literary genre.[2] Though the first volume of Luke's two volume work is traditionally identified as the Gospel of Luke, and his second volume as the Acts of the Apostles, Luke, himself identifies his work as historical narrative. This, at once, separates his genre from the epistles, the apocalypse and the homily, and also somewhat distances his work from the gospel genre. This is particularly significant if, as most scholars believe, Mark's Gospel is one of the sources which Luke used for his account "about all that Jesus began to do and teach."

In the prologues which preface each of his two volumes (Luke 1:1-4, Acts 1:1-5), Luke gives both stylistic and verbal clues to the identity of the genre of Luke-Acts. Luke's first clue is stylistic; he conforms to the conventions of his literary models. On the one hand, following the custom of dedicating books to distinguished persons, Luke addresses his work to Theophilus. On the other hand, at the beginning of his second

---

[1]In his discussion of Luke-Acts and the genre of historical narrative, which was not yet published when this chapter was first written, David E. Aune arrives at similar conclusions to those which I am arguing in this chapter; namely, 1) Luke follows Hellenistic literary models, 2) Luke-Acts is a literary unit, and, as a corollary Luke (i.e., the gospel) cannot be forced into Mark's literary mold, and 3) that with varying emphasis historical narrative did have an instructional-paradigmatic-normative purpose. cf., "Luke-Acts and Ancient Historiography," and "the Generic Features of Luke-Acts and the Growth of Apostolic Literature, "in *The New Testament in Its Literary Environment* (Philadelphia: The Westminster Press, 1987).

[2]Ralph P. Martin, *New Testament Foundations, Volume 1: The Four Gospels* (Grand Rapids: Wm. B. Eerdmans, 1975), 16-20.

volume his preface recapitulates the first volume. The book *Against Apion* by Josephus, the Jewish historian and contemporary of Luke, is an interesting parallel. Just as Luke addresses Luke-Acts to his literary patron, the most excellent Theophilus *(kratiste Theophile,* Luke 1:3), so Josephus addresses *Against Apion* to his literary patron, the most excellent Epaphroditus *(kratiste andron Epaphrodite,* 1.1). Similarly, just as Luke recapitulates book one in his second prologue, writing, "The first account *(proton logon)* I composed, Theophilus, about all that Jesus began to do and teach . . ." (Acts 1:1), so Josephus also recapitulates book one of *Against Apion,* writing, "In the first volume *(proterou Bibliou)* of this work, my most esteemed Epaphroditus, I demonstrated the antiquity of our faith . . . (11.1). In writing Luke-Acts, then, Luke, no less than Josephus, is following the style of his literary models.

In his two prologues Luke not only conforms to the style of his literary models, but he also identifies his writings by two terms, *diegesis* and *logos* (Luke 1:1, Acts 1:1), which place Luke-Acts in the tradition of historical writing, both sacred and secular. In his prologue to his overall work (Luke 1:1-4), Luke classifies his writings as *diegesis,* i.e., account or narrative. This is a *hapax legomena,* i.e., used but once in the New Testament. Therefore, we must examine other Greek literature for help in determining its meaning. The word is used from Plato onwards, including the first century Jewish writers, Philo and Josephus. However, in the light of Luke's demonstrable dependence on the Septuagint, we do not have to go further afield than this translation of the Hebrew Scriptures into Greek. There it has a variety of meanings: tale[3] (Deut. 28:37), byword (2 Chron. 7:20), riddle (Ezek. 17:2) and discourse (Sir. 8:8-9). More relevant to Luke's usage, the anonymous author of 2 Maccabees describes the five books of Jason of Cyrene, which he proposes to epitomize into a single book, as "narratives of history" *(tes historias diegemasin,* 2 Macc. 2:24). Moreover, *diegesis,* "is used *ter* in the letter of Aristeas to Polycrates (1, 8, 322) to describe the 'narrative' he has to unfold."[4] It is this latter usage of Aristeas, and, especially, 2 Maccabees

---

[3]Henry George Liddell and Robert Scott, *A Greek-English Lexicon* (9th ed. with a Supplement; London: Oxford University Press, 1968)), 427.
[4]James Hope Moulton and George Milligan, *The Vocabulary of the Greek Testament* (Grand Rapids: Wm. B. Eerdmans, 1963), 161.

which most closely approximates its meaning in Luke's prologue; namely, to imply a full narrative.

In his prologue to Acts (1:1-5) Luke identifies what he has written earlier as his "first account" *(proton logon,* 1:1). In his commentary on the Greek text of Acts, F. F. Bruce informs us, *"logos* is used for a division of a work which covered more than one papyrus roll. . . . Lk. and Ac. covered one papyrus roll each."⁵ As used here by Luke, however, *logos* means more than simply, "first papyrus roll." It also points to the genre of Luke-Acts. In similar contexts, such as in the earlier historian, Herodotus, for example, *logos* means either a complete historical work (Her. 2.123; 6.19; 7.152), or else one section of such a work (Her. 1.75; 2.38 et al.). In language similar to Luke's, Herodotus writes about, "the first book of my history" *(en to(i) proto(i) ton logon,* 5.36), or, "the beginning of my history" *(en toisoi protoisi ton logon,* 7.93). Thus, in these contexts, not only does *logos* mean papyrus roll, but it also means narrative history, whether viewed in whole, or in its parts.

In the Septuagint, moreover, *logos* often translates the Hebrew *dabar,* which can mean either "word" or "affair, thing,"⁶ to mean both "act" and "chronicle." Concerning David, for example, we read: "Now the acts of King David *(logoi tou basileos Dauid),* from first to last, are written in the chronicles of Samuel the Seer *(en logois Samouel tou blepontos),* in the chronicles *(logon)* of Nathan the prophet, and in the chronicles *(logon)* of Gad the seer" (1 Chron. 29:29).

Similarly, the acts *(logoi)* of Rehoboam, and other kings, are written in the chronicles of the prophets (2 Chron. 12:15 et al.). Indeed, as designating the "record of X" *logoi* is synonymous with *praxeis,* and as designating the "record of Y" *logoi* is synonymous with *biblio(i)* (2 Chron. 13:22).

Obviously, this evidence means that the genre of Luke-Acts is historical narrative. In terms of style and vocabulary, Luke-Acts has affinities with the histories of Josephus and Herotodus, on the one hand, and, in the Septuagint, with the Hellenistic Jewish history, written by

---

⁵F. F. Bruce, *The Acts of the Apostles: The Greek Text with Introduction and Commentary* (2nd ed.; Grand Rapids: Wm. B. Eerdmans, 1952), 65.

⁶William L. Holladay, *A Concise Hebrew and Aramaic Lexicon of the Old Testament* (Grand Rapids: Wm. B. Eerdmans, 1971), 67.

Jason of Cyrene and epitomized in 2 Maccabees, as well as with the sacred history, First and Second Chronicles.

During what we call the intertestamental period, two streams of historical tradition flowed together, like the waters of two tributary streams, to become the river of Jewish-Hellenistic historiography. The sacred stream of Israelite historiography, in its Hebrew and Greek texts, mixed and merged with the secular stream of Greco-Roman historiography, represented by Herodotus and Thucydides and their successors. Josephus and Luke, two contemporary historians, became the quintessential development of this historical tradition. Josephus writes the history of the Jews, and, as a sometime participant and first-hand observer, reports the demise of the Judaism of the Second Temple Era. Luke, on the other hand, writes the history of the followers of Jesus and their converts. Like Josephus, a sometime participant and first-hand observer in the history which he writes, Luke reports the birth of Christianity within Judaism and its subsequent penetration of the Roman Empire. Ironically, Josephus reports and laments the earlier passing of prophetic inspiration within Judaism. In contrast Luke reports, indeed, exults in, that renewed outburst of prophetic inspiration, which begins within Judaism, and, in his generation, extends to the ends of the earth. Though their historical and theological orientations are different, Luke, as much as the great historian Josephus, is a historian of the first order, and his writings equally belong to the tradition of Jewish Hellenistic historiography.

To sum up, Luke is a historian and Luke-Acts is history. This means that we can no longer continue to classify Luke's first account simply as a Gospel, and Luke as an Evangelist. Luke, himself, does not give us these options. Whereas Mark claims to have written a Gospel, Luke claims to have written a history. Thus, Mark is an evangelist, but Luke is not; Luke is a historian, but Mark is not. Therefore, to identify Luke's first book as a Gospel, as is traditionally done, is to read Luke as though he were Mark. The church must begin to read Luke, the so-called Gospel as well as the Acts, much more consistently as the historian of redemptive history.

If it is advisable to jettison the traditional twofold classification of Luke's writings, into Gospel and Acts (and for the sake of hermeneutical clarity I suggest that it is necessary), then Luke's terms *diegesis* and *logos* furnish us with several options. In terms of content, Luke's first account *(proton logon)* is the Acts of Jesus and his second account is the Acts of the Apostles. In terms of form, Luke's two volumes are either the Narratives of Jesus and the Narratives of the Apostles, or else the Chronicles of Jesus and the Chronicles of the Apostles. Though the traditional division of Luke-Acts into Gospel and History is deeply entrenched, perhaps as solidly entrenched as the proverbial Rock of Gibraltar, these alternatives have two advantages. In the first place, they compel us to recognize the unity of genre, as Luke intended us to, and, in the second place, they compel us to recognize the unity-continuity of the historical and theological themes of both volumes.

Approaches to Historical Narrative

Those who spar academically over the use, or abuse, of the narratives of Acts for Pentecostal theology sit in one of two corners. The Pentecostals, with their pragmatic hermeneutic are in one corner; their opponents, who advocate scientific methodology, are in the other corner. As we have seen, Pentecostals look to the book of Acts for their theology and the biblical pattern for their twentieth century experience. Thus, "The doctrines of the Holy Spirit that are popularly known as 'Pentecostal' are those that apply to contemporary experience that is in the pattern of Acts chapter 2 and subsequent New Testament practice."[7] Though this hermeneutic seems self-evident to Pentecostals, some hard-hitting criticisms have been aimed at Pentecostal pragmatism. The heaviest blow is that this pragmatic Pentecost-as-pattern hermeneutic is considered to be a "general disregard for scientific exegesis and carefully thought out hermeneutics."[8]

This is not the knock-out punch many think it to be. The use of the narratives of Acts by Pentecostals may apparently fall short of scientific exegesis; it may be unsophisticated, and perhaps, even somewhat popular and naive. It is, however, reminiscent of the Pauline principle of interpreting historical narrative. To identify the Pentecostal interpretation of historical narrative with the Pauline principle is not

---

[7]L. Thomas Holdcroft, *The Holy Spirit: A Pentecostal Interpretation* (Springfield: Gospel Publishing House, 1979), 90.

[8]Fee, "Hermeneutics," 121.

mere conceit. In other words, just as Paul believed that "all Scripture [that is, the narratives of Genesis as well as the Laws of Deuteronomy] is inspired by God and profitable for teaching . . . [and] for training in righteousness" (2 Tim. 3:16), so Pentecostals similarly believe that all Scripture [that is, the narratives of Acts as well as the theology of Romans] "is inspired by God and profitable for teaching . . . (and) for training in righteousness." Moreover, just as Paul believed that "whatever was written in earlier times [the Old Testament] was written for our instruction" (Rom. 15:4), so Pentecostals similarly believe that whatever was written in earlier times (in Acts, as well as in the Gospels or the Epistles) was written for our instruction. Furthermore, just as Paul believed that the experiences of Israel "happened to them as an example *(tupos)*, and they were written for our instruction" (1 Cor. 10:11), so Pentecostals similarly believe that some of the experiences of the apostles happened to them as an example, and they were written by Luke in Acts for our instruction.

Admittedly, this may appear to be a popular and naive approach to the interpretation of historical narrative. It emphasizes the "art" of hermeneutics more than it does the "science" of hermeneutics. It is the approach of the person in the pew more than it is the approach of the professor at the podium. But if it is a naive approach, it is a naivete which has apostolic precedent, a naivete which is sanctioned by Paul's similar treatment of historical narrative in the Old Testament. A *caveat* is in order here. Though Pentecostals take it on the chin for their approach to the interpretation of historical narrative, scientific exegesis in itself is far too rationalistic, narrow and limited a methodology. As Dr. Bruce Waltke in his article, "Hermeneutics and the Spiritual Life," observes, "The scientific method... is appropriate for understanding the text, but it is inappropriate for the principle aim of Christian understanding of Scripture, *the knowledge of God.*"[9] Thus, in spite of its implied disadvantages of naivete and its danger of excesses, the Pentecostal hermeneutics of historical narrative has this advantage over scientific exegesis: it definitely brings the Christian to the (experiential) knowledge of God.

---

[9]Waltke, "Hermeneutics and the Spiritual Life," 7.

The second approach to the hermeneutics of historical narrative either strips historical narrative of all didactic or instructional value, or else it radically limits its normativeness for contemporary Christian experience. John R.W. Stott typifies the former approach. In response to what he calls, "a recrudescence of 'Pentecostalism' in non-Pentecostal churches,"[10] Stott wrote his booklet, *The Baptism and Fullness of the Holy Spirit*. In this booklet, he outlines three introductory points for dealing with the issues raised by this "recrudescence of Pentecostalism":

> First, the purpose of God . . . is to be discerned in Scripture, not in the experience of particular individuals or groups. Secondly, this revelation of the purpose of God in Scripture should be sought in its *didactic,* rather than in its *historical* parts. More precisely, we should look for it in the teaching of Jesus, and in the sermons and writings of the apostles, and not in the purely narrative portions of the Acts. Thirdly, our motive . . . is practical and personal, not academic or controversial.[11]

In the sense that it reinforced many in their opposition to Pentecostalism, Stott's booklet was widely influential and frequently reprinted. In spite of its popularity, however, it was impotent to stem the "recrudescence of Pentecostalism in non-Pentecostal churches," namely, the neo-Pentecostal or Charismatic Movement. Indeed, a decade after the publication of *The Baptism and Fullness of the Holy Spirit* it was rumored that Stott had fallen victim to Pentecostalism, and he published a re-written and expanded version to correct this false rumor in 1975. Significantly, the second edition of *Baptism and Fullness* maintains the cornerstone principles of the first edition; namely, Stott's antithesis toward charismatic experience and his opposition to the use of historical narrative for didactic purposes.[12]

Gordon D. Fee is an example of a scholar who radically limits the normative or precedent value of historical narrative. Fee outlines his

---

[10]John R. W. Stott, *The Baptism and Fullness of the Holy Spirit* (Downers Grove: Inter-Varsity Press, 1964), 7.
[11]Ibid., 8-9.
[12]Stott, *Baptism and Fullness*, 13-17.

principles most fully in chapter 6, "Acts - The Problem of Historical Precedent," in *How to Read the Bible for All Its Worth*. His main thesis, "... is that unless Scripture explicitly tells us we must do something, what is merely narrated or described can never function in a normative way."[13] This assumption, and it can never be more than an assumption, echoes Stott's denial that historical narrative might have any didactic value. Fee hedges this general assumption by giving three specific principles:

1. It is probably never valid to use an *analogy* based on biblical precedent as giving authority for present day actions.
2. Although it may not have been the author's primary purpose, biblical narratives do have illustrative and, sometimes, "pattern" value. . . . A warning is in order here. For a biblical precedent to justify a present action, the principle of the action must be taught elsewhere, where it is the primary intent so to teach.
3. In matters of Christian experience, and even more so of Christian practice, *biblical precedents may sometimes be regarded as repeatable patterns—even if they are not to be regarded as normative.*[14]

Fee also insists "It is a general maxim of hermeneutics that God's Word is to be found in the intent of Scripture. This is an especially crucial matter to the hermeneutics of historical narrative."[15]

For the remainder of this chapter it will be my purpose to demonstrate a different approach to the interpretation of historical narrative from that which is typified in the principles of Stott and Fee. I will demonstrate that, for Luke, historical narrative can, and does, have a didactic purpose or instructional intentionality. Therefore, I will not here engage in a critical dialogue with the hermeneutics of historical narrative which are espoused by Stott, Fee, and others, especially since I

---

[13]Fee and Stuart, *How to Read the Bible for All Its Worth*, 97.
[14]Ibid., 101.
[15]Ibid., 98.

have done it elsewhere.¹⁶ Nevertheless, before moving on, I must object to the absolutely false dichotomy which Stott makes between the so-called *didactic* and *historical* parts of Scripture. F. F. Bruce includes Luke-Acts within the compass of his discussion when he boldly states, "History writing in antiquity had a *didactic* quality and aim."¹⁷ Similarly, Fee's assertion that what is narrated, or described, can never function in a normative way equally fails to understand ancient historiography in particular. In his discussion of the function of Luke-Acts, David E. Aune properly affirms, "Luke-Acts provided historical definition and identity as well as theological legitimation for the author's conception of *normative* Christianity."¹⁸

Clearly, that hermeneutics of historical narrative which Stott, Fee and others espouse—despite their embracing much that every thoughtful Pentecostal must endorse—is to be rejected. Nevertheless, to the extent that their hermeneutic has the salutary effect of keeping Pentecostals and others from the all too common tendency to allegorize, moralize and/or spiritualize historical narrative, their structures are to be heeded, if not applauded. But, more importantly, there is an alternative, more productive approach to the hermeneutics of Lucan historiography. This approach recognizes that Luke modelled his historiography after the pattern of biblical-Jewish Hellenistic historiography, and, therefore, that he used narrative in different ways. On the one hand, Luke uses narrative to introduce key theological themes. On the other hand, once having established those themes, he uses narrative to establish, illustrate, and reinforce those themes through specific historical episodes.

The Hermeneutics of Lucan Historiography: A Modest Proposal

In regards to the style of the Old Testament histories, I intend to demonstrate that Christians need to read Luke-Acts in the same way that they read the histories of Israel. This is because Luke modeled his twofold

---

¹⁶Roger Stronstad, *The Charismatic Theology of St. Luke* (Peabody: Hendrickson Publishers, Inc., 1984), 5-9.
¹⁷F. F. Bruce, "The First Church Historian," in *Church, Word, and Spirit,* edited by James E. Bradley and Richard A. Muller (Grand Rapids: Wm. B. Eerdmans, 1987), 13.
¹⁸David E. Aune, *The New Testament in its Literary Environment* (Philadelphia: The Westminster Press, 1987), 137.

narrative of the origin and expansion of Christianity along the lines of Old Testament historical narrative. The Old Testament narratives are episodic and function, either individually or in combination, as exemplary, typological, programmatic and paradigmatic elements in the narratives. In fact, when we, as Christians, read the narratives of Luke-Acts in regards to genre in the same way that we read the narratives of Israel, then our understanding of historical narrative will be radically different from what Fee himself advocates.

In general, the histories of Scripture, in both the Old Testament and the New Testament, not only consist of the reports of dialogues, speeches, and a variety of figures of speech, such as parables, they also, and more commonly, consist of episodes. An episode is an event or incident which is complete in itself, but which also forms part of the whole. The narrative is the report of these dialogues, speeches and episodes. Some narratives are formulaic. The histories of the kings of Israel, for example, are often little more than the formula: X did evil in the sight of the Lord and walked in the sins of his father Jeroboam. Furthermore, the six major episodes in the book of Judges are narrated according to the fourfold formula: sin, servitude, supplication and salvation (Jud. 2:11-23). Most narratives, however, report the episodes in their historical particularity. Whether formulaic or historically particular, the narratives give the pertinent facts. According to the author's purpose, or intent, they give the reader the who? what? when? and where? of the episode. The narratives also, implicitly or explicitly, give the historical and theological explanation of the narrative: the how? and the why? In addition to the episode itself, and its narration, there are also the questions: Why did the author record the event, that is, what historical and theological message does the author intend to convey? How does the individual episode fit into the overall structure of the narrative? When viewed from the perspective of authorial literary-historical-theological intent, the episodes, or narratives, primarily function in one of four ways. They may have an exemplary, typological, programmatic or paradigmatic literary-historical-theological function.

Why were some episodes included in the narrative and others excluded from the narrative? Most commonly the answer to this question is that the episode simply illustrates, or is a specific example of the author's theme. For example, in his prologue, the author of Judges describes the history of Israel as a generations-long cycle of sin, servitude, supplication and salvation (Jud. 2:11-23). Beginning with the judge Othniel, the body of the narrative gives six specific examples to illustrate this cycle of history. Similarly, the author of the two books of Samuel gives two examples each of Saul's disobedience (1 Sam. 13, 15), of David's loyalty (1 Sam. 24, 26), and David's kindness (2 Sam. 9-10). The second example illustrates or reinforces the first example. As these examples illustrate, many episodes were included in the narrative for their exemplary function.

Other narratives exhibit a typological relationship between episodes. In a typological relationship, there is a historical correspondence or pattern between two or more historically independent episodes. The parting of the Red Sea by Moses (Ex. 14), and the Jordan River by Joshua (Josh. 3-4), are examples of this, made explicit by the author of Joshua himself (Josh. 4:14, 23). Similarly, there is a typological relationship in the transfer of the Spirit from one leader to another, that is, the transfer of the Spirit from Saul to David (1 Sam. 16:13-14), and from Elijah to Elisha (2 Kings 2:9ff.). The vantage point of typology is retrospective, that is, it looks back to a historically analogous and relevant episode from earlier times. Of course, it is God, who is the Lord of history, who gives the typological correspondence between the past and the present, and shapes his narrative accordingly.

While some narratives exhibit exemplary and typological functions, others exhibit a programmatic function. Such a narrative contains a strategic announcement or episode which is programmatic for the whole. The programmatic elements point to the wider reality, or else point to the unfolding of future events. Thus, in contrast to the retrospective vantage point of a typological narrative, the vantage point of a programmatic narrative is often anticipatory or prospective. For example, the transfer of the Spirit from Moses to the seventy elders of Israel (Num. 11:25ff.) has two programmatic elements. On the one hand, this report of the Spirit informs the reader of something that he is not told elsewhere in the narrative: that Moses was a charismatic leader who administered Israel by the power of the Spirit. On the other hand, the transfer of the Spirit from Moses to the elders anticipates, or is programmatic, of the future time when "all the Lord's people were prophets, that the Lord would put His Spirit upon them" (Num. 11:29).

The transfer of the Spirit from Elijah to Elisha (2 Kings 2:9ff.) is a further example of the programmatic function of the narrative. In other words, apart from the historian's report of the transfer of the Spirit, the reader would never have known that each of these two prophets was charismatic. Yet, as the narrative reports, Elisha requests a double portion of Elijah's Spirit (2 Kings 2:9) and the sons of the prophets recognize that the Spirit of Elijah rested upon Elisha (2 Kings 2:15). Thus, Elijah's ministry, with its miraculous manipulation of nature, raising the dead and multiplying of food (1 Kings 17:1, 16, 22) is programmatic for the subsequent ministry of Elisha, his successor (2 Kings 2:14; 4:34, 42).

Finally, some narratives have a paradigmatic function. That is, a paradigmatic narrative is one that has normative features for present or future ministries. For example, just as Moses ministers in the Spirit, so the elders as his colleagues, must also minister in the Spirit. Moreover, just as Elijah ministered in the power of the Spirit, so Elisha as his successor, must also minister in the power of the Spirit. However, because of the wide diversity of leadership in Israel (for example, the sacerdotal, the political and the prophetic), and also because of the change in leadership offices as Israel's history advances (for example, elders, judges, kings) the paradigmatic function is rare in Old Testament narratives.

In summing up, some observations are in order. In the first place, it is evident that there are few so-called "purely narrative portions" in the histories of Israel. Rather, the narratives have a complex function. This is as true if the function is simply illustrative or exemplary as it is if the function is either typological, programmatic or paradigmatic. Secondly, as the examples of the Moses and Elijah narratives show, any given narrative may have a combination of functions. In other words, the narratives seldom function simply as types, programs or paradigms. Thirdly, because history advances, an episode which may have a programmatic or paradigmatic function when it is first reported, may develop a typological function from the vantage point of subsequent history. Fourthly, statistically insignificant elements, such as the single reports that Moses, David, Elijah and Elisha have the Spirit, have a significance which transcends the merely quantitative because they are programmatic. I have briefly, if inadequately, examined this data of Old Testament historiography because it lays the foundation for an examination of Lucan historiographical principles. In general, Luke modelled his historiography after Old Testament historiography. In particular, the fourfold function of Old Testament narratives, with all of its complexity, combinations, transformations of perspective, and statistical dynamics, is also to be found in the Lucan narratives.

Luke conceived his two-part narrative of the origin and spread of Christianity to be the sequel to the sacred history of Israel. As he, himself, tells us in his prologue to both books of his history that he wrote as a historian, "having investigated everything carefully from the beginning" (Luke 1:3), so that Theophilus his patron, "might know the exact truth about the things you have been taught" (Luke 1:4). On his own terms, Luke expected to be treated as a reliable witness to the events which he reported. Though he was bound by the facts which he had investigated, like every good historian, he also included or excluded data according to his purposes. He also presented the information according to both the design or structure, and the literary genre which he chose. Thus, it was that Luke radically altered the design and the "Gospel" genre of his sources, among whom Mark is probably to be numbered, to a history. He did so by adding the birth narrative, expanding the inauguration narrative, adding the narrative telling of the spread of Christianity as a sequel to the narrative of Jesus, and then setting the whole story into the chronological and geographical framework of Judaism under Imperial Rome. Three primary influences shaped the final product: Luke's sources, his purpose(s), and his historiographical model in the histories of Israel, both sacred and secular.

Luke designed his two-part history with great care and precision. The thematic structure of his first book has the following elements: a beginning, specifically the birth and anointing of Jesus; a subsequent inaugural sermon at Nazareth, followed by the complementary confirmatory miracles of casting out demons and healing the sick; success and widespread popular acclaim; growing opposition from the Pharisees and leaders of the Jews; travel throughout Galilee, Perea and Judea; arrest and threefold trial before the Sanhedrin, Pilate and Herod; and the consummation of his redemptive ministry in the Cross. Luke's second book, the history of the spread of Christianity, follows the same thematic design. It begins with Peter's inaugural sermon on the day of Pentecost. It continues with the subsequent confirmatory miracle of the healing of the lame man at the Beautiful gate; success and widespread popular acclaim, yet also growing opposition from the Sanhedrin and ultimately from the Diaspora Jews; the travel narratives, or missionary journeys, of Peter and Paul; the arrest of Paul and his threefold trial before Felix, Festus and Agrippa; and consummation in Paul's arrival and two-year ministry at Rome.

As part of his careful design Luke strategically invests his inauguration narratives with the typological, programmatic, and paradigmatic functions of his historiographical models. The histories which follow these inauguration narratives are primarily the development, illustration, and examples of the programmatic elements in these inauguration narratives.

Luke launches his history of Jesus with an infancy narrative (Luke 1:5-3:38) which prefaces his first book. With its episodes of angelic visitations, outbursts of prophecy, and nativity scenes, Luke's infancy narrative contains a variety of typological, programmatic elements. For example, in announcing the future birth of John, the angel casts his ministry in the typological pattern of Elijah (1:17). Furthermore, Luke portrays a clear typological correspondence between John and Jesus. John, who is filled with the Holy Spirit while yet in his mother's womb, will be a prophet of the Most High (1:15, 76). Similarly, Jesus, who is conceived by the power of the Holy Spirit, will be the Son of the Most High (1:32, 35). Though John is the son of Zacharias, and Jesus is the Son of God, the activity of the Holy Spirit, nevertheless, creates a genuine typological correspondence between these two infants, whose births herald the dawning of the messianic age.

In addition to those typological correspondences, the infancy narratives also give programmatic anticipations of what is to follow. In the words of Paul Minear, "There is an observable kinship between the Canticles in the opening chapters, the opening 'Keynote addresses' of John and Jesus (chaps. 3, 4), and the sermons of Acts ... Luke's thought gravitates toward and is oriented around strategic speeches, citations and hymns."[19]

---

[19]Paul S. Minear, "Luke's Use of the Birth Stories," in *Studies in Luke-Acts*, ed. By L. E. Keck and J. L. Martyn (London: S.P.C.K., 1968), 116.

Moreover, these programmatic elements are not limited to strategic speeches, citations, and hymns; they are also to be found in the charismatic activity of the Holy Spirit. In the infancy narrative, John, Elizabeth, and Zacharias are filled with the Holy Spirit. This is programmatic for the gift of the Spirit in Acts, beginning with the disciples on the day of Pentecost and ending with the disciples at Iconium (Acts 2:4, 13:52). This outburst of charismatic activity is also paradigmatic, for just as it means "prophetic inspiration" in the infancy narrative, it also means "prophetic inspiration" in the Acts.

The typological, programmatic, and paradigmatic elements which are found in the infancy narrative are also to be found in the three episodes which collectively inaugurate the public ministry of Jesus. Paradoxically, just as Elijah is a type for the public ministry of John the Baptist, so his rejection in Israel and subsequent ministry to the widow woman of Zarephath, is a type of Jesus' rejection by his homepeople and subsequent ministry to strangers (Luke 4:22-30). In addition, the charismatic ministries of Elijah and Elisha are types of the miraculous charismatic ministry of Jesus. Therefore, when Jesus raised the dead, as his charismatic precursors had done earlier, the people exclaimed, "a great prophet has arisen among us" (Luke 7:16), and his reputation which reached Herod's ears was that, "Elijah had appeared" (Luke 9:8). Furthermore, both Isaiah and the Isaianic charismatic servant-prophet are types of the parabolic teaching (Luke 8:9-10, Isa. 6:10) and charismatic anointing of Jesus (Luke 3:22, Isa. 42:1, Luke 4:18-19, Isa. 61:1). Finally, Moses is a type of Jesus, for Jesus is the prophet like unto Moses (Luke 9:35; Acts 3:22, 7:37; Deut. 8:15).

In addition, Luke intends his report of the Spirit's anointing, leading, and empowering of Jesus to be programmatic of his entire ministry. This echoed the programmatic function of the Moses and Elijah narratives (Num. 11:16 ff., 2 Kings 2:1ff.). In other words, just as the single, almost incidental reference to the Spirit in the lives of these two charismatic prophets points to a widespread charismatic ministry, so Luke's references to the Spirit in the inauguration narrative signify that from his baptism to his ascension the entire ministry of Jesus is charismatic. The programmatic function of these episodes explains why Luke will later report Jesus' defense for casting out demons in the words, "if I cast out demons by the finger of God...," whereas Matthew reports, "if I cast out demons by the Spirit of God . . . " (Luke 11:20, Matt. 12:28). Because Matthew's inauguration narrative lacks the programmatic report of the empowering of the Spirit, he must specify that the "finger of God" is the empowering of the Spirit. Luke need not do this, for his readers understand that every miracle that Jesus performs is done by the empowering of the Spirit.

Luke also invests a paradigmatic significance to the gift of the Spirit in the inauguration narrative. In other words, the ministry of Jesus, anointed, led, and empowered by the Spirit is a paradigm for the ministry of the disciples, who will be baptized, led, and empowered by the Spirit. That is, just as the ministry of Jesus, as the Christ, must be charismatic and inaugurated by the anointing of the Spirit, so the ministry of his disciples, heirs, and successors to his own ministry must be both charismatic (Acts 1:8) and inaugurated by the baptizing-filling of the Spirit (Acts 1:5, 2:4).[20] Though it is often denied, Luke intends the charismatic experience and ministry of Jesus to be normative for the charismatic experience and ministry of the disciples. Therefore, as Luke reports it, in the ongoing history of salvation, at Pentecost the ministry of the charismatic Christ is transferred to a necessarily charismatic community of disciples.

In common with his infancy and inauguration narratives (Luke 1:5-4:44), Luke's Pentecost narrative also has typological, programmatic elements. For example, the paradigmatic inaugural "anointing" of Jesus is, from the later perspective of Pentecost, a type of inaugural "Spirit baptism-filling" of the disciples. Similarly, the earlier transfer of the Spirit from Moses to the seventy elders is a type of the transfer of the Spirit from Jesus to the hundred and twenty disciples. Moreover, the Pentecost narrative is not only programmatic for the geographic (Acts 1:8, 2:9-11), social, and temporal extension of the Gospel and the gift of the Spirit, but, as for the charismatic ministry of Jesus, is also

---

[20]In the chapter "New Directions in Lucan Theology: Reflections on Luke 3:21-22 and Some Implications," in *Faces of Renewal: Studies* in *Honor of Stanley M. Horton*, edited by Paul Elbert, 123, Ben Aker draws a similar conclusion, advancing Pentecostal precedent theology from the disciples to Jesus. He writes "... it (Lk. 3:21, 22) removes the theological precedent of the disciples' experience in Jerusalem in Acts 2 and places it at Jordan and upon Jesus' anointing with the Spirit. What happened to the disciples on the day of Pentecost, then, was patterned after Jesus' experience at Jordan."

programmatic for the charismatic ministry of the disciples. In other words, having informed his readers that the disciples are empowered by the Spirit, Luke will not continue to tell his readers that the signs and wonders which the apostles performed are performed by the empowering of the Spirit. That is to be understood from the Pentecost narrative onwards. Finally, just as the charismatic experience of Jesus is a paradigm for the charismatic experience of the disciples, so the charismatic experience of the disciples on the day of Pentecost is a paradigm for the charismatic experience of other disciples, of whom the believers at Samaria, Saul of Tarsus, the household of Cornelius, and the disciples at Ephesus are examples. In more general terms, the charismatic-prophetic gift of the Spirit on the day of Pentecost is paradigmatic for the experience of the eschatological people of God. For Luke, from Pentecost onwards God's people have become a charismatic community, a parenthood of all believers. According to Luke this is normative Christianity.

This discussion of historical narrative and the historiographical methodology which served as Luke's model for his own history, particularly the inauguration narratives (Luke 1:5-4:44; Acts 1-2), leads to one inescapable conclusion; namely, that Luke had a didactic or catechetical, or instructional, rather than a merely informational, purpose for his history of the origin and spread of Christianity. This conclusion, which is based on the function of the two inauguration narratives, confirms the authorial intent which is stated in the first prologue (Luke 1:1-4). As Luke explains it in a series of parallel phrases to his literary patron, Theophilus, the "word," that is the narrative or chronicle *(logos,* 1:2) of the acts *(logoi,* 1:4) (of Jesus) had been handed down by eyewitnesses. Many had then compiled a narrative *(diegesis)* of these events *(pragmata)*. Having carefully investigated both the word, or *logos*, of the eyewitnesses and the narrative, which he alternately identified with the *diegesis* of the Many and the *logos* of the tradition (Luke 1:1, Acts 1:1). The significance of Luke's purpose, as he states it in the prologue, is that if the narratives, whether oral or written, about the events *(pragmata)* or acts *(logoi)* (of Jesus) were the basis for the earlier instruction of Theophilus, whether that instruction was evangelistic, apologetic, or pastoral; then Luke's own narrative, which is a carefully investigated, accurate, and reliable transmission of the earlier *logos*, is also the literary vehicle for instruction. If this is true for the events *(pragmata)* and acts *(logoi)* of his first book, his *proton logon*, then it must similarly be true for its sequel. In other words, the Acts of the Apostles, as surely as the Gospel, must also be intended for the instruction of Theophilus, and, not only for Theophilus, but also for the wider audience of Christians who would subsequently read Luke's history.

To be valid, any hermeneutic of Lucan historiography must recognize Luke's historiographical heritage in Jewish-Hellenistic historiography, and be sensitive to his own stated aims and methodology, particularly as it is to be discovered in his prologues and inauguration narratives. This hermeneutic will set the parameters for the contemporary understanding of Luke's genre, methodology and instructional intent. Exegesis proper, and the biblical and systematic theology which builds upon it, will determine the actual content of that instruction. Included in this content is the unexpected and unprecedented place of the Holy Spirit in the unfolding events of Jesus and his successors. In a way which is unparalleled in the New Testament, Luke, the historian of redemptive history, is also the historian of the Spirit. Not only this, but, because historical narrative is Luke's vehicle of instruction, he is also a theologian of the Spirit, par excellence. Indeed, his teaching on the Spirit is as essential as either the teaching of John or Paul. When examined, it will be discovered that Luke has a charismatic pneumatology which is the sequel to the charismatic pneumatology of Old Testament times, is ontological-trinitarian, and is functional or vocational. This is the subject of chapter six, "The Holy Spirit in Luke-Acts."

CHAPTER THREE

PENTECOSTAL EXPERIENCE AND HERMENEUTICS

Writing about the Holy Spirit a century ago, the German theologian Hermann Gunkel contrasted the experience of the Holy Spirit in the so-called primitive church of Apostolic times with the church of his own day. Of the experience of the Spirit in the Apostolic church he observed, "... at issue are concrete facts, obvious to all, which were the object of daily experience and without further reflection were directly experienced as effected by the Spirit."[1] But what was true of the primitive church's daily experience of the Spirit was not true of the church in Gunkel's own day. He admits, "We who live in a later age and do not as a matter of course have analogous experiences on which to draw can only grasp the primitive, apostolic view of the Spirit by proceeding from his activities as reported to us and by attempting to conceive the Spirit as the power calling forth these activities."[2] Thus, Gunkel sees the church of his day to be handicapped in its ability to understand the Apostolic witness to the Holy Spirit because it lacked any analogous experience of the Spirit.

In the century between the time when Gunkel wrote and the present, the modern Pentecostal Movement was born, and in the twentieth century millions of Christians now, as a matter of course, do have analogous experiences on which to draw for understanding the primitive church's experience of the Holy Spirit. Concerning the Pentecostal

---

[1] Hermann Gunkel, The *Influence of the Holy Spirit*, trans. by Roy A. Harrisville and Philip A. Quanbeck II (Philadelphia: Fortress Press, 1979), 13.
[2] Ibid., 14.

Movement and its understanding of the apostolic witness to the Holy Spirit, the Baptist theologian, Dr. Clark H. Pinnock writes, "...we cannot consider Pentecostalism to be a kind of aberration born of experimental excesses but a 20th century revival of New Testament theology and religion. It has not only restored joy and power to the church but a clearer reading of the Bible as well."[3] Now, in writing that Pentecostals have restored a clearer reading of the Bible, that is, Acts, to twentieth century Christendom, Pinnock is not saying, on the one hand, that the Pentecostal's charismatic experience, which he labels the baptism in the Holy Spirit, makes him a better interpreter of Acts in areas that are of necessity a matter of academic research, such as, the correctness of the titles which Luke gives to various officials, matters of Roman law, chronology, geography, etc. On the other hand, Pinnock is saying that the charismatic experience of the Pentecostal (ministering in the power of the Holy Spirit, speaking in other tongues as the Spirit gives utterance, being led by the Spirit) enables him to understand Luke's record of the activity of the Holy Spirit in Acts better than the non-Pentecostal. On this twofold issue of Pentecostal experience and Pentecostal theology it is not surprising that Pinnock's conclusions have not carried the day. Indeed, it is precisely here—Pentecostal experience and theology—that, with the exception of those rare outsiders such as Pinnock, Pentecostals run afoul of their critics.

This issue of Pentecostal experience, which is a stigma and stumbling block to many non-Pentecostals, needs to be addressed. In his "Introduction" to his book, *Showing the Spirit: A Theological Exposition of I Corinthians 12-14*, D. A. Carson gives the caricature which many non-charismatics draw of charismatics and, presumably, also of classical Pentecostals. He writes,

> The charismatics, they (non-charismatics) think, have succumbed to the modern love of "experience," even at the expense of truth. Charismatics are thought to be profoundly unbiblical, especially when they evaluate their experience of tongues to the level of theological and spiritual shibboleth. If

---

[3]Clark H. Pinnock, "Foreword," to *The Charismatic Theology of St. Luke*, by Roger Stronstad (Peabody, MA: Hendrickson Publishers, 1984), viii.

they are growing, no small part of their strength can be ascribed to their raw triumphalism, their populist elitism, their promise of short cuts to holiness and power . . . [they are] devoid of any real grasp of the Bible that goes beyond mere prooftexting.[4]

Though Carson distances himself from this caricature, it is, nevertheless, pertinent to our subject because it portrays Pentecostals as both in love with "experience" and also as "profoundly unbiblical." Similarly, another scholar asserts, "the Pentecostal tends to exegete his own experience."[5] Further, from John Calvin to Benjamin B. Warfield and their contemporary successors, those in the Reformed tradition have adopted a cessationist theology of the charismata.[6] Leon Morris is a typical contemporary exemplar of this tradition. He writes,

> The early Church knew quite well what all these gifts were. They exulted in the exercise of them. But, in view of the fact that they disappeared so speedily and so completely that we do not even know for certain exactly what they were, we must regard them as the gift of God for the time of the Church's infancy. They did not last very long, and in the providence of God evidently, they were not expected to last very long.[7]

The arguments against contemporary, that is, twentieth century, Pentecostal experience cut both ways. When Leon Morris admits that the charismata died out in the early church he is, as surely as every Pentecostal is accused of doing, exegeting his own experience and the experience of earlier generations of non-Pentecostals. And if one is to exegete his experience there can be no question about which experience, Pentecostal or non-Pentecostal, is the better experience to exegete for it is the unanimous witness of the Gospels, the Acts, and the Pauline

---

[4]D. A. Carson, *Showing the Spirit: A Theological Exposition of I Corinthians 12-14* (Grand Rapids: Baker Book House, 1987), 12.

[5]Fee, "Hermeneutics," 122.

[6]John Mark Ruthven, "On the Cessation of the Charismata: The Protestant Polemic of Benjamin B. Warfield," Ph.D. dissertation, Marquette University Graduate School, 1989.

[7]Leon Morris, *Spirit of the Living God: The Bible's Teaching on the Holy Spirit* (London: Inter-Varsity Press, 1960), 63-64.

epistles that Jesus, the Apostles, and the early Church generally were all charismatic in their ministry.

So great is the antipathy toward charismatic experience in many sectors of the contemporary church that Pentecostals from the turn-of-the-century beginnings of the movement have been forced to address the "stigma" of their experience. At times many Pentecostals have flaunted the emotional dimension of their experience, no doubt primarily because so many non-Pentecostals stridently denied its legitimacy. More productively, others have articulated the theoretical place of Pentecostal experience in a consistent Pentecostal theology and hermeneutic. For example, representing the classical Pentecostal viewpoint, William G. MacDonald describes Pentecostal theology as an "experience-certified theology." Responding to the criticism that Pentecostalism has an over-emphasis on experience in the form of emotionalism, he asks, "Does this holy experience result in an experience-centered theology?" He answers, "Hardly. The better way to label it is this: Christ-centered, experience-certified theology."[8] In the essay, "The Methodology of Pentecostal Theology: An Essay on Hermeneutics," William W. Menzies develops Pentecostalism as an "experience-certified theology" more fully. For Menzies, "If a biblical truth is to be promulgated, then it ought to be demonstrable in life. This is precisely what the modern Pentecostal revival has been reporting to the larger church world."[9] Thus, according to Menzies, the verification level of Pentecostal experience is not only legitimate, but it is a necessary element in a Pentecostal hermeneutic in the threefold chain: 1) inductive level, 2) deductive level, and 3) verification level. According to MacDonald and Menzies, then, experience is the final element in theology and hermeneutics, certifying or verifying the theological enterprise.

While it is valid to assign to Pentecostal experience a certification or verification function, it is an inadequate or incomplete description of the place of experience in Pentecostal hermeneutics, for experience also enters the hermeneutical enterprise at the beginning of the task, that is, as a presupposition, and not merely as a certification/verification. Thus, if Pinnock's observation, with which we began this lecture, is correct;

---

[8]MacDonald, "A Classical Viewpoint," 64.
[9]Menzies, "The Methodology of Pentecostal Theology," 13.

namely, that Pentecostals have restored a clearer reading of the Bible (that is, Acts) to the church (and a growing number of Christians are coming to similar conclusions) then it is primarily because Pentecostals bring a valid experiential presupposition to the interpretation of Acts, rather than because they do superior historico-grammatico exegesis of Acts.[10] In other words, their charismatic experience is an experiential presupposition which enables them to understand the charismatic life of the apostolic church, as Luke reports it, better than those contemporary Christians who lack this experience.

Presuppositions and the Hermeneutical Task

In a justifiably famous essay written several decades ago, Rudolph Bultmann asked, "Is exegesis without presuppositions possible?"[11] The answer to this question for Bultmann, and, indeed, as it must be for all exegetes, is a resounding no. It is not possible to do exegesis, theology, hermeneutics, historical studies, etc., independent of, and apart from, the influence of presuppositions. The illusory pursuit of presuppositionless exegesis has been aptly called, "the Principle of the Empty Head."[12] Nevertheless, though there can be no Biblical interpretation without presuppositions, Oscar Cullmann gives a timely warning, namely, "The fact that complete absence of presuppositions is impossible must not excuse us from striving for objectivity altogether, going so far as to regard such striving primarily as an outmoded standpoint, and making a necessary fact into a virtue."[13] What is true for exegesis is equally true for hermeneutics. Presuppositions have as integral a place in the theory and

---

[10] It is a great irony of Pentecostalism that a movement which is founded upon a particular interpretation of Acts has produced so little exegetical scholarship on Acts. For example, F. F. Bruce's newly revised commentary on Acts in the New International Commentary series lists no commentaries by Pentecostals in his select Bibliography. In fact, in the English language only the two commentaries, by Stanley M. Horton in the Radiant and Complete Biblical Library series, and the more recent commentary, *The Acts of the Apostles: Introduction, Translation, and Commentary,* by French L. Arrington (Peabody, MA: Hendrickson Publishers, 1988) merit serious consideration.

[11] R. Bultmann, "Is Exegesis without Presuppositions Possible?" ET in *Existence and Faith,* ed. and tr. S.M. Ogden (London: Hodder and Stoughton), 289ff.

[12] Quoted from Graham N. Stanton, "Presuppositions in New Testament Criticism," in *New Testament Interpretation: Essays on Principles and Methods,* edited by I. Howard Marshall (Grand Rapids: Wm. B. Eerdmans, 1977), 66.

[13] Oscar Cullmann, *Salvation in History,* trans. by Sidney G. Sowers (New York: Harper & Row Publishers, 1967), 67.

practice of hermeneutics as they do in exegesis. This is true for all kinds of presuppositions, including appropriate experiential presuppositions.

The Validity of Experiential Presuppositions

As stated earlier, my thesis is that charismatic experience, in particular, and spiritual experience, in general, gives the interpreter of relevant Biblical texts an experiential presupposition which transcends the rational or cognitive presuppositions of scientific exegesis, and, furthermore, results in an understanding, empathy, and sensitivity to the text, and priorities in relation to the text which other interpreters do not, and cannot, have. Admittedly, to state this thesis as badly as I have done no doubt smacks of that elitism which so many non-Pentecostals find so abhorrent about Pentecostalism. Yet I do not intend it to be elitist, nor would it be right to take it in that way. As provocative and inflammatory as this thesis might be to many non-Pentecostals, its validity is not only demonstrable, but it is also legitimized by the place of experiential presuppositions in many other aspects of Christian scholarship.

Though they may use different terminology, those scholars who reflect upon the exegetical and theological enterprise invariably insist upon the necessity of at least one experiential presupposition, namely, saving faith. For example, concerning Biblical exegesis, Oscar Cullmann writes, "When it comes to interpreting the witness of faith, this, of course, means that I must know from my own experience what faith is."[14] Similarly, Protestant evangelical theology has always insisted that theology must be done from a position of Christian experience. Hence, "The creative task of theology is, first of all, the task of the redeemed, who, through the prior grace of God, have returned to the Father by the Son, and through the inner working of the Holy Spirit have been put into tune with the mind of Christ."[15] Now, while no one will deny that a non-Christian may do first rate linguistic, historical and related studies which can be of great, even indispensable help to the Christian exegete or theologian, it is proper to affirm that only the redeemed, only those

---

[14]Ibid.
[15]Philip Edgecumbe Hughes, *Creative Minds* in *Contemporary Theology* (Grand Rapids: Wm. B. Eerdmans Publishing Company, 1966), 25.

whose faith is the same as the apostles, can do Biblical exegesis and theology. In other words, saving faith is the necessary experiential prerequisite, or experiential presupposition, for understanding the Biblical message, exegetically and theologically.

Biblical scholars and theologians not only affirm saving faith as an experiential presupposition, but often make similar claims for various specialized and additional dimensions of experiential knowledge. For example, concerning the study of topography, Sir William Ramsay, classicist, archaeologist, and New Testament scholar writes,

> Topography is the foundation of history. No one has familiarized himself with Attic history in books and afterwards ascended Pentelicus and seen history spread forth before him in the valleys and mountains and sea that have moulded it will ever disbelieve in the value of topography as an aid to history.... If we want to understand the Ancients, especially the Greeks, we must breathe the same air as they did and saturate ourselves with the same scenery and the same nature that wrought upon them. For this end correct topography is a necessary though humble servant.[16]

While in this quotation Ramsay is writing specifically about understanding Attic history, his proposition is equally applicable to the history of Asia Minor of New Testament times, in which he specialized, and even to the history of the Palestine of Old and New Testament times. In another area of Biblical studies (the interpretation of the parables) as a further example, a first-hand knowledge of the contemporary peasant culture of the Near East, and other tools, "must be used in addition to the standard critical tools of scholarship."[17] There is no need to multiply further examples. Whether we are considering exegesis, theology, history, the parables, or any other aspect of Biblical scholarship, there are appropriate and legitimate experiential presuppositions which give their

---

[16] Quoted from W. Ward Gasque, *Sir William M. Ramsay: Archaeologist and New Testament Scholar*, Baker Studies in Biblical Archaeology (Grand Rapids: Baker Book House, 1966), 18-19.

[17] Kenneth E. Bailey, *Poet and Peasant and Through Peasant Eyes: A Literary-Cultural Approach to the Parables of Luke* (Grand Rapids: Wm. B. Eerdmans Publishing Company, 1976, 1980), 43.

possessor a better understanding of the Bible than those who do not possess them.

Not only are there a variety of appropriate and legitimate experiential presuppositions which have their place in the formal and academic study of the Bible, but there are also those which have their place in a more popular understanding of the Bible. In general terms, the Christian who has experienced the miraculous, whatever his theological tradition might be, will understand the Biblical record of the miraculous better than those whose world view either denies the miraculous altogether and, therefore, explains the Biblical record in rationalistic terms, or else restricts it to the past and rejects its applicability to the present. More specifically, the Christian who has been healed will understand the record of Jesus' healing ministry, or that of the apostles, better than the one who has never experienced it.[18] In other words, he knows he experienced the power of the Spirit of God, which was operating through Jesus rather than a psychosomatic suggestion. Similarly, the one who has witnessed demonic possession knows that the New Testament is describing a spiritual condition rather than epilepsy or some form of mental disorder. Moreover, the one who has seen a little food multiplied into much food knows that the report of Jesus feeding the 5,000 involves much more than that others simply followed the example of the boy, each one sharing his own meal with his neighbor, so that all were fed. What is true for these examples is also true for

---

[18]Healings are too commonplace to need documentation. For a report on demonic activity see the article, "I See the King of Hell," by Harrison Forman in David V. Plymire, *High Adventure in Tibet* (Springfield, MO: Gospel Publishing House, 1959), 2-9. For an example of the multiplication of food, specifically vitamins, see Corrie Ten Boom, *The Hiding Place* (Minneapolis: Chosen Books, 1971), 202-03. A portion of Corrie's experience of the multiplying vitamins is worth quoting in full,

> And still, every time I tilted the little bottle, a drop appeared at the tip of the glass stopper. It just couldn't be! I held it up to the light, trying to see how much was left, but the dark brown glass was too thick to see through. "There was a woman in the Bible," Betsie said, "whose oil jar was never empty". She turned to it in the Book of Kings, the story of a poor widow of Zarephath who gave Elijah a room in her home. "The jar of meal wasted not, neither did the cruse of oil fail, according to the word of Jehovah which he spoke by Elijah."

Well-but-wonderful things happened all through the Bible. It was one thing to believe that such things were possible thousands of years ago, another to have it happen now, to us, this very day. And yet it happened, this day, and the next, and the next, until an awed little group of spectators stood around watching the drops fall onto the daily rations of bread.

Pentecostal experience. The Christian in this century who has been filled with the Spirit, and has ministered in the power of the Spirit, will understand Luke's charismatic history and theology on both the academic and popular levels better than those who have not.

To sum up, it is abundantly evident that Pentecostals are not alone in bringing experiential presuppositions to the interpretation of the Bible. Every Christian brings the experience of saving faith to his reading of the Bible. In addition, some bring a specialized experiential knowledge, whether it be of topography, or culture, or any number of relevant experiences. Finally, some Christians bring the experience of the miraculous to their study of the Bible. All of this (and much more could be added) in principle legitimizes the Pentecostal practice of bringing his charismatic experience as a pre-understanding, or presupposition, to the interpretation of Luke-Acts. Therefore, unless there is conclusive evidence that the charismatic experiential presuppositions of the Pentecostal lead to a wrong understanding of Luke-Acts, then the comparable role of experiential presuppositions by other Christians in their interpretation of the Bible must also be conceded to Pentecostals.

Of course, the charismatic experiential presuppositions of the Pentecostal do not, in themselves, guarantee a better understanding of Luke-Acts any more than does the mere application of traditional Protestant principles of interpretation. That is, just as the principles of Protestant Biblical interpretation can, and often do, lead to a rationalizing of the text at the expense of its contemporary spiritual dynamics, so the experiential dynamics of the Pentecostal are susceptible to subjectifying the text at the expense of its objective historical particularity. Therefore, since neither traditional Protestant Biblical hermeneutics nor Pentecostal experiential presuppositions, in themselves and independently of each other, can lead to the best understanding of Luke-Acts, then it is incumbent upon every interpreter to unite, as in a marriage of equal but complementary partners, both the cognitive presuppositions of traditional Protestantism and the experiential presuppositions of Pentecostalism.

Cognitive and Experiential Presuppositions

The Bible is the written record of God's past revelation, which, nevertheless, the interpreter experiences not merely as a historical document, but as a contemporary Word from God to us. The understanding of this historical-contemporary Word, then, involves both cognitive and experiential presuppositions; that is, the understanding of the Bible is as much pectoral as it is cerebral. On the one hand, the cognitive dimension is necessary in order that the interpreter may understand languages which are not his own, cultures which are radically different from his culture, and the history of other peoples which is not his history. On the other hand, whereas experience can never be the basis of theology, experience is the contemporizing of history. Thus, the understanding of the Bible, generally, and Luke-Acts, particularly, involves a hermeneutical cycle. In this cycle the record of the experience of the divine by God's people in the past addresses the experience of God's people in the present, and the present experience of the divine informs the understanding of the past. In this way the divine word as a historical document becomes a living Word—a Word which, like God Himself, is, was, and is to come. Thus, the record of the past historicizes experience, and the present encounter with that record contemporizes history.

Whether the interpreter is Lutheran, Calvinist, Methodist or Pentecostal, he follows a similar set of hermeneutical principles. These include what are commonly called general principles of hermeneutics, such as the priority of the Biblical languages, the accommodation of revelation, progressive revelation, etc. They also include specific principles, which apply to the various genre to be found in the Biblical literature: historical narrative, law, poetry, epistle, apocalypse, etc. However, because the subject of this chapter is an analysis of the place of experiential presuppositions in the Pentecostal's understanding of the Bible, and, further, since evangelicals, to a greater or lesser extent, hold these cognitive principles in common, it is not my purpose here to do more than alert the listener to the place of cognitive presuppositions as the necessary context and complement to experiential presuppositions.

Experiential Presuppositions

As we have already demonstrated, it is not the case that Pentecostals have experiential presuppositions, and that non-Pentecostals do not. Neither is it the case that non-Pentecostals have cognitive presuppositions, whereas Pentecostals do not. Rather it is the case that every interpreter, Pentecostal and non-Pentecostal alike, brings both cognitive and experiential presuppositions to his interpretation of the text. Since both Pentecostal and non-Pentecostal evangelicals stand in agreement on the fundamental cognitive presuppositions, the primary issue for the interpreter is which range of experiential presuppositions he brings to his interpretation of the Bible.

Though there are a growing number of exceptions, non-Pentecostal evangelicals often bring negative and hostile experiential presuppositions to the interpretation of the Biblical data on the charismatic activity of the Holy Spirit, such as is reported in Luke-Acts or discussed in I Corinthians 12-14. In contrast, Pentecostals bring positive and sympathetic experiential presuppositions to the interpretation of these and other relevant texts.

Negative Experiential Presuppositions

Though the rapid and extensive growth of Pentecostalism has caused many non-Pentecostals to adopt a more neutral, or even sympathetic attitude toward Pentecostalism than is consistent with their own theological and ecclesiastical tradition, many non-Pentecostal evangelicals, particularly in the Reformed tradition, continue to color their interpretations of texts relevant to Pentecostalism with experiential presuppositions which are negative and hostile. These fall into two not always mutually exclusive camps: 1) those who adopt a minimalist position on Biblical and contemporary charismatic experience, and 2) those who adopt a rejectionist position.

The Minimalist Position

With a somewhat softened antipathy toward charismatic experience many interpreters adopt a minimalist position on charismatic experience. This finds a variety of expressions. For example, interpreters sometimes label this experience as *abnormal*[19] and urge Christians to be content with normal growth into Christian maturity. Along similar lines, charismatic experience such as "tongues", it is asserted, was, ". . . always associated with spiritual immaturity, not with spiritual maturity and stability . . . it was a gift for the immature rather than the profound."[20] Others, while accepting the legitimacy of Luke's charismatic theology, regard it as secondary rather than primary.[21] Further, others emphasize the statistical scarcity of those passages where Luke reports the charismatic activity of the Spirit. Thus, "the few historical accounts in Acts, in comparison with other Scriptures provide a flimsy foundation indeed upon which to erect a doctrine of the Christian life."[22]

In the same way that the criticism against the Pentecostal's exegeting his experience cuts both ways, so these criticisms designed to minimize charismatic experience, both Biblical and contemporary, also cut both ways. First, since it is the consistent testimony of the New Testament that Jesus, the disciples and their converts, both Jews and Gentiles, were charismatic in experience, then this is normal, not abnormal, Christianity. Indeed, based on the New Testament standard, and what better standard is there, it is contemporary non-Pentecostal/non-charismatic Christianity, and not Pentecostalism which is abnormal. Second, if "tongues" is always associated with spiritual immaturity and not with profundity, then tens of millions of Pentecostals will be content to identify themselves with the Apostle Paul (who regularly spoke in "tongues") in his own spiritual immaturity. Third, when interpreted on his own terms, Luke describes the activity of the Spirit in relation to charismatic activity, or service alone, rather than in terms of salvation or sanctification. Therefore, this charismatic activity must be interpreted to be primary to Luke's theology, rather than secondary. Fourth, the appeal

---

[19]Stott, The *Baptism and Fullness*, 33, 48-49, 68.

[20]Leon Morris, *Spirit of the Living God*, 66.

[21]James D. G. Dunn, *Baptism in the Holy Spirit: A Re-examination of the New Testament Teaching of the Gift of the Spirit in Relation to Pentecostalism Today*, Studies in Biblical Theology, Second Series, 15 (London: SCM Press Ltd., 1970), 54; Stott, *Baptism and Fullness*, 71.

[22]Frank Farrell, "Outburst of Tongues: The New Penetration," *Christianity Today* (September 13, 1963), 5.

to statistics totally disregards Luke's narrative strategy, whereby he selects programmatic episodes for his narrative history. Moreover, such an objection to the Pentecostal's appeal to those few narratives in Acts is self-defeating, for if theological truth is a matter of statistics, then the doctrine of the virgin birth, which is explicitly reported by Matthew and Luke alone (along with a few other isolated references), must be assigned a minimal place in New Testament Christology. Moreover, if a significant theological truth cannot be established on the basis of up to five references, then, all other considerations aside, doctrines such as infant baptism and predestination must be dismissed out of hand. Further, on the basis of statistics alone, the doctrine of justification by faith, since it is taught only in Romans and Galatians, must be displaced by other themes, such as union with Christ (*en christou*) as the center of both Pauline and Lutheran and Reformed Theology. Clearly, the theological importance and validity of doctrines such as the virgin birth, infant baptism, justification by faith and Pentecostal theology can never be reduced, as is done by opponents of Pentecostal theology, to the statistical frequency of the Biblical data upon which these doctrines are based. With equal clarity, each of these minimalist stances which are adopted against Pentecostal theology and experience, stand discredited. The fact that these criticisms cut both ways, specifically, that they turned against their proponents to favor rather than to minimize Pentecostalism, shows that they are specious and spurious; shows, indeed, that they are nothing more than a case of special pleading rather than legitimate criticism.

The Rejectionist Position

Within non-Pentecostal evangelicalism many competent Biblical scholars still reject Pentecostal theology. To a Pentecostal it appears that this position carries with it a resolute contempt for charismatic experience, both Biblical and contemporary. This contempt for charismatic experience is usually justified on the basis of a dispensational interpretation,[23] in which the virtual disappearance of charismatic

---

[23] A. M. Stibbs and J. I. Packer, *The Spirit Within You: The Church's Neglected Possession*, Christian Foundations (London: Hodder and Stoughton, 1967), 33; Leon Morris, *Spirit of the Living God*, 63ff.

experience throughout church history is applied to the nature of Biblical revelation. In other words, when the canon was complete, the written word allegedly displaced the need for that charismatic experience which was characteristic of the apostles, who were the living word. Thus, the claim by every Pentecostal that he has received a charismatic empowering, and by virtue of his experience, has a clearer understanding of the Biblical data on the charismatic experience of Christians in New Testament times, is to be rejected out of hand.

To illustrate this "rejectionist" position, we can turn once again to Leon Morris, a highly competent and widely respected Biblical scholar, as a typical representative. Writing about 1 Corinthians 12:28, for example, Morris observes that concerning the apostles and prophets, "we need not feel that their main functions are hid from us," adding, "but it is not so with all the gifts."[24] Of these gifts, such as helps and governments, he observes "We *know* nothing about these gifts or their possessors. They have vanished without leaving a visible trace."[25] Concerning the gift of tongues he writes, "We are somewhat in the dark about this gift."[26] Responding to people today, that is, the Pentecostals, who hold that some of the *charismata* are a necessity for Christians who are loyal to the New Testament he observes:

> ... historically all the gifts disappeared quite early in the history of the church ... And, as we have pointed out already, some of the gifts disappeared so completely that to this day we do not know what they were. Even the gift of "tongues" comes under this heading ... We cannot feel that the Spirit of God would have allowed this state of affairs to develop and to continue if the gift were so important.[27]

Additionally, he affirms, " ... we must regard them [the *charismata*] as the gift of God for the time of the church's infancy."[28] Moreover, the needs of the church today, " ... do not necessarily require the charismata

---

[24]Morris, *Spirit of the Living God*, 63.
[25]Ibid.
[26]Ibid., 64.
[27]Ibid., 65-66.
[28]Ibid., 63.

of New Testament days,"²⁹ and furthermore, as an alternative to these "spectacular gifts," " . . . the Spirit is at work in appointing the regular ministry of the church."³⁰

Clearly, Morris restricts the charismata to New Testament times, admits to an agnosticism about the gifts, denies that the experience of the Pentecostals and charismatics is what the Christians of Apostolic times experienced, and asserts that the charismata are neither desirable nor necessary in the contemporary church. The spiritual and theological cost of this position is very great. It is, moreover, devoid of any genuine exegetical basis. In addition, it is proven false by the fact that in this century several hundred million Pentecostals and charismatics have experienced "tongues" and the full range of New Testament charismata. Most damning of all, it simply exegetes his own negative experience. For centuries Reformed Christendom has placed Protestant Christianity under the tyranny of its negative experiential presuppositions. Unhappily for Morris, and all who believe as he does, the gifts of the Spirit are so important that the Spirit of God has not allowed the state of affairs, so cherished by Morris, to continue. In part, and in this context, the Pentecostal revival is the Spirit's answer to the negative experiential presuppositions of Reformed theology. In terms of the charismatic experience, then, Reformed theology is a theology of denial, whereas Pentecostal theology is a theology of affirmation.

Positive Experiential Presuppositions

In terms of charismatic experience, whereas many non-Pentecostals subscribe to a theology of denial; Pentecostals subscribe to a theology of affirmation. This is because Pentecostals bring positive, sympathetic, and affirmative experiential presuppositions to their understanding of appropriate Biblical texts. To a greater or lesser extent, the Pentecostal has been filled with the Spirit and has spoken in other tongues as the Spirit gave utterance, has been led by the Spirit, has ministered in the power of the Spirit, and has exercised one or more of the charismata in his ministry in the church and to the world. When he works back from

---

²⁹Ibid., 64.
³⁰Ibid., 66.

his positive charismatic experiences to the text, he understands with Luke that these experiences are normative Christianity, that this is Luke's primary rather than secondary emphasis, that Luke's reports of the charismatic activity are not incidental or isolated, but are programmatic and paradigmatic and that, for Luke, it is an eschatological reality, that is, for this age until it is consummated by the coming of Christ.

To sum up, in the interpretation of Scripture—as much in hermeneutics as in exegesis and even in application—cognitive and experiential presuppositions co-exist like a marriage of equal and complementary partners. In contrast to an all too common practice in Protestant hermeneutics, what God has joined together in the nature of man must not be torn asunder in Biblical studies.

Pentecostal Hermeneutics: A Modest Proposal

Thus far I have discussed the validity of experiential presuppositions in Biblical hermeneutics. For the discussion to be complete, however, I need to move on from analysis to synthesis. Though I do not presume to speak for the Pentecostal Movement, the following is a proposal of what I, as a Pentecostal, believe to be the essential elements of a Pentecostal hermeneutic. As I see it, a Pentecostal hermeneutic will have a variety of cognitive and experiential elements. On the one hand, it will be experiential, both at the presuppositional and verification levels. On the other hand, it will also be rational, respecting the literary genre of the relevant Biblical data and incorporating historico-grammatico principles of exegesis. Not only will a Pentecostal hermeneutic be both experiential and rational, but it will also be pneumatic, recognizing the Spirit as the illuminator as well as the inspirer of Scripture. While the definitive Pentecostal hermeneutic necessarily lies in the future, the hermeneutical program which follows advances Pentecostal hermeneutics one step closer to that goal.

Pentecostal Hermeneutics and Experiential Presuppositions

As we have already seen, when it comes to charismatic experience Pentecostalism is a theology of affirmation rather than of negation. Of necessity, therefore, a Pentecostal hermeneutic will have experiential presuppositions. At the irreducible minimum these will be two: 1) saving faith, and 2) charismatic experience. In other words, just as the Pentecostal understands the overall record of faith, that is, the Bible, from his experience of faith, so he understands the more limited record of the charismatic activity of the Spirit, that is, Luke-Acts, from his charismatic experience of the Spirit. Thus, in a positive way the Pentecostal moves back to the Bible from his experience, which is both saving and charismatic.

To include charismatic experience as one element in Pentecostal hermeneutics is not to open a Pandora's box of subjectivism or emotionalism. On the one hand, the objective reality of the Bible remains inviolate. On the other hand, though they are in one sense inseparable, experience and emotion are not identical. Though it may or may not be expressed in emotional terms, charismatic experience is a spiritual reality and not an emotion. The fact that some Pentecostals have sometimes sought the experience for the sake of the emotion, and that some non-Pentecostals have rejected the experience because of the emotionalism, must not be allowed to prejudice anyone against this spiritual experience.

Further, in defending the legitimacy of charismatic experiential presuppositions, I am not implying that they guarantee sound interpretation. In other words, by virtue of his charismatic experience the Pentecostal is not an infallible interpreter. This is because experiential presuppositions do not stand alone, do not stand in independence from either cognitive presuppositions or historico-grammatico principles. Rather, experiential presuppositions are but one, albeit important and complementary, element of hermeneutics. Though they do not guarantee sound interpretation, they give an important pre-understanding of the text. This pre-understanding guards the interpreter from the all too common tendency for Western man to reduce the spiritual reality of the Bible to rationalistic propositions. It also makes it more likely that the interpreter will recognize charismatic emphases in the text which non-Pentecostals/non-charismatics might miss. Finally, in appropriate cases it actually gives a better understanding of the text. For example, someone who has been filled with the Spirit and has spoken in tongues understands that tongues-speaking is better than the interpreter who has never spoken in tongues.

Pentecostal Hermeneutics and the Pneumatic

Having completed the task of inspiring Scripture during the Apostolic age, the Holy Spirit did not then simply abandon his Word to the custody of the Church, becoming, as it were, a *Deus absconditus*. Though the church is the custodian of the Word, the Word remains God's Word, not simply in the sense that it has its origin in God (*theopneustos*, 2 Tim. 3:16), but also in the sense that it is spiritual (*pneumatikos*, Rom. 7:14). Because it is spiritual, the task of interpretation, and, therefore, hermeneutics, necessarily transcends the human; it transcends the creatureliness and finitude of human experience, intellect and knowledge. As Paul writes, "But a natural man does not accept the things of the Spirit of God; for they are foolishness to him, and he cannot understand them, because they are spiritually appraised" (*pneumatikos anakrinetai*, I Cor. 2:14).

Because Scripture is spiritual, and because it must be spiritually appraised, it can only be understood with the contemporary help of the Spirit. This ever present and immanent Spirit bridges the temporal gap between inspiration (in the past) and interpretation (in the present). Though Paul, in his First Epistle to the Corinthians, is writing about revelation through the Spirit (I Cor. 2:10), and I am speaking about the interpretation through the Spirit, the interpreter (he who is spiritual—*pneumatikos*, I Cor. 2:15), because of the Spirit, can say with Paul, "But we have the mind of Christ" (I Cor. 2:16). Therefore, just as there is no revelation which does not bear the stamp of the Spirit, so there can be no interpretation worthy of the name which does not bear the imprint of the living Spirit upon it. In other words, just as Scripture, in terms of its inspiration, is self-authenticating, that is, it commends itself as the Word of God, so Biblical interpretation, in spite of the finitude of the interpreter should also be self-authenticating, that is, it should commend itself as sound, not simply because interpreters may share similar methodology, but because it is spiritually appraised.

Chapter 3   *Pentecostal Experience and Hermeneutics*   57

Pentecostal Hermeneutics and Literary Genre

After several centuries of developing awareness of the literary genre of the Bible, Biblical scholars are now sensitive, both hermeneutically and exegetically, to the full range of the literary genre which is to be found in the Bible. For it to be worthy of the name, a sound Pentecostal hermeneutic will be genre sensitive. In particular, and in common with hermeneutics generally, a Pentecostal hermeneutic demands that I Corinthians be interpreted as an epistle and the Luke-Acts be interpreted as historical narrative. Of course, this means that Luke-Acts is to be interpreted as historical narrative according to the canons of Biblical, Jewish-Hellenistic and Greco-Roman historiography, and not according to the canons of contemporary historiography. Positively, a number of considerations follow from this. In the first place, Luke-Acts is to be interpreted as a literary unit. Luke's prefaces (Luke 1:1-4, Acts 1:1-5) leave the interpreter no option. In the second place, the interpreter must recognize that different episodes in the narrative have different functions. In Luke-Acts, episodes may have an exemplary, typological, programmatic or paradigmatic function. This being so, the interpreter will not, for example, make an exemplary narrative normative for contemporary Christian experience, but he will make a paradigmatic narrative normative for Christian experience. In the third place, interpreters must concede that historical narrative can have a didactic purpose. What was generally true for Jewish-Hellenistic and Greco-Roman historiography is claimed by Luke for his two-volume history of the origin and spread of Christianity (Luke 1:1-4). In other words, in the history that he wrote, Luke purposed to instruct his patron, Theophilus (and, by extension, every reader of Luke-Acts), just as surely as Paul, through the letters that he wrote, purposed to instruct his readers.

Negatively, a number of considerations also follow. Firstly, Acts is not to be interpreted independently of Luke, that is, as if Luke was a different literary genre than Acts, or as if Acts was written from a different theological perspective than Luke. Secondly, Luke's narrative is not merely episodic, and, therefore, merely descriptive in purpose. There is nothing novel about insisting that Luke-Acts must be interpreted as historical narrative. Both Pentecostals and non-Pentecostals agree on that. What is novel is the observation that Luke intended to instruct the church about normative Christianity, which is, in part evangelistic and charismatic. Pentecostals have always been more certain about this than most non-Pentecostals have been.

Pentecostal Hermeneutics and the Rational

If charismatic experience and the illumination of the Spirit constitute the experiential and the pneumatic elements of a Pentecostal hermeneutic, then respect for literary genre and Protestant Biblical hermeneutics constitute the rational element of a Pentecostal hermeneutic. Now, in affirming the place of charismatic experiential presuppositions in a Pentecostal hermeneutic, I am not shifting the foundation of exegesis and theology from divine revelation to an experience. Further, in affirming the place of the pneumatic, I am not saying that the Spirit gives the interpreter knowledge independently of study and research. Moreover, in affirming the place of literary genre in hermeneutics I am not giving form ascendency over content. Charismatic experience, the illumination of the Spirit, a sensitivity to literary genre, each have their essential and proper place in hermeneutics; but individually and collectively, that place can never be more than complementary to the place of grammatico-historico exegesis and the hermeneutical principles upon which it is built.

Because man is a creature made in God's image, understanding the Bible is always a matter of the mind, of the human intellect. It is this human rationality which distinguishes man from other creatures, and it is in the Word that the human mind encounters the divine mind. Thus, interpretation must necessarily be a matter of rationality as well as experience and spiritual perception. If non-Pentecostals sometimes inflate the place of rationality in understanding the Bible at the expense of experience, Pentecostals must not fall into the opposite error, namely deprecating the rational in favor of the experiential. In theory the Pentecostal is as committed to the rational element in hermeneutics as every other evangelical. Of equal importance, the Pentecostal needs to be as committed in practice as he is in theory. In other words, because his mind is just as important as his experience, the Pentecostal must be committed to serious and sober Biblical studies. This is a commitment to diligent and disciplined study, to honing analytical and synthetic skills, to exegesis and theology. Thus, the rational element in Pentecostal hermeneutics is demanded by the nature of man, is the necessary complement to the experiential and the pneumatic elements in hermeneutics, and guards against the excesses of religious enthusiasm.

Pentecostal Hermeneutics and Experiential Verification

Christianity is not merely a historical religion, such as Israelite religion, but it is a present spiritual and experiential reality. This is as potentially true for charismatic experience as it is for saving faith. As we have demonstrated in Pentecostal hermeneutics, charismatic experience gives the interpreter a pre-understanding of the relevant Biblical texts, such as Luke-Acts. Just as importantly, however, charismatic experience also completes the hermeneutical task. In other words, just as the practice of hermeneutics results in sound exegesis and theology, so sound exegesis and theology will be integrated into contemporary experience; that is, doctrine in its fullness, including Pentecostal theology, becomes a matter of Christian experience. Therefore, Pentecostal hermeneutics has a verification level as well as inductive and deductive levels, and Pentecostal theology is an experience-certified theology.

In conclusion, a Pentecostal hermeneutic has five components: 1) charismatic experiential presuppositions, 2) the pneumatic, 3) genre, 4) exegesis, and 5) experiential verification. The five components include the experiential, the pneumatic and the rational dimensions.

Thus, a Pentecostal hermeneutic is a holistic hermeneutic, which differs from Protestant Biblical hermeneutics at two significant points; namely, charismatic experiential presuppositions and experiential verification.

CHAPTER FOUR

"FILLED WITH THE HOLY SPIRIT" TERMINOLOGY IN LUKE-ACTS

From one perspective the history of the relationship between God and man is the history of successive steps from transcendence to immanence. The Tabernacle-Temple metaphor signifies this progress: in the Old Testament the transcendent glory of the Lord God dwelt within the Tabernacle; in the New Testament the Son "tabernacled" among men as a man; and finally, the Spirit now dwells within the "temple"—the body of believers. John, Paul, and Luke are the major New Testament theologians of this "immanent" Spirit. For John, the Spirit is the agent of the new birth and the *alter ego* to Jesus. For Paul, the Spirit is the agent of cleansing, sanctification and justification, one who, moreover, is the source of those *charismata* by which God's people minister in the world and among themselves. In contrast to John and Paul, however, Luke has a narrower, though complementary, perspective on the Holy Spirit. For Luke's record the Spirit does not function in relation to salvation or sanctification, but he functions exclusively in relation to service.

Among the many terms which Luke uses to describe this charismatic, or dynamic, activity of the Spirit, the term "filled with the Holy Spirit" takes pride of place. Its meaning, however, is disputed. The Reformed tradition interprets it primarily as moral power, and only secondarily as charismatic power. The Wesleyan tradition interprets it in holiness terms. Finally, the Pentecostal tradition interprets Luke's "filled with the Holy Spirit" terminology to mean charismatic power. This confusion among the Protestant traditions demands a new evaluation of the Lukan data.

Select Lexical Data

In the New Testament the cognate verbs *pleroo* and *pimplēmi* lie behind the English verbal phrase "filled with the Holy Spirit." Both *pleroo* and *pimplēmi* mean "to fill, fulfill."[1] The term "filled with the Holy Spirit" translates *pleroo* two times (Acts 13:52, Eph. 5:18). Moreover, "filled with the Holy Spirit" translates *pimplēmi* eight times (Luke 1:15, 41, 67, et al.). The following select lexical data sets these verbs in their biblical context.

Pleroo occurs eighty-six (86) times in the New Testament. Luke (25x) and Paul (23x) use it about equally. Each uses this verb one time in reference to the Holy Spirit. In his Acts of the Apostles Luke reports that the disciples at Iconium "were continually filled with joy and with the Holy Spirit" (Acts 13:52). Luke also uses the cognate noun *pleres* to describe Jesus, the seven deacons, Stephen, and Barnabas as "full of the Holy Spirit." In his Epistle to the Ephesians Paul, on the other hand, gives the imperative "be filled with the Spirit" (Eph. 5:18).

Pimplemi makes its first biblical appearance in the Greek translation of the Hebrew Bible, the Septuagint (LXX). The compound *empimplemi* is more common than the simple form, and it is this form which yields the Septuagintal phrase "X was 'filled' with the Spirit" *(eneplesa pneumatos* plus variants). This term occurs five times: God fills the artisans, who not only make Aaron's priestly garments, but who also work on the Tabernacle with "the spirit of perception" or with "a divine spirit of wisdom and understanding" (Ex. 28:3, 31:3, 35:31). For these artisans, the Spirit of wisdom is the Spirit who imparts wisdom: a wisdom which is manual skill or craftsmanship. Similarly, as successor to Moses,

---

[1] For full lexical and theological information see Henry George Liddell and Robert Scott, *A Greek-English Lexicon* (9th ed. with a Supplement; London: Oxford University Press, 1968), 1405, 1419-20; W. F. Arndt and F. W. Gingrich, *A Greek-English Lexicon of the New Testament and Other Early Christian Literature* (2nd ed; Chicago: The University of Chicago Press, 1979), 658, 670-71; Gerhard Delling, *"pimplēmi, empimplemi; pleroo"* in *Theological Dictionary of the New Testament*, VI, ed. by Gerhard Freidrich, trans. by Geoffrey W. Bromiley (Grand Rapids: William B. Eerdmans, 1968), 128-34, 286-98; R. Schippers, *"pleroo"* in *The New International Dictionary of New Testament Theology*, I, edited by Colin Brown (Grand Rapids: Zondervan Publishing House, 1975), 733-41.

Joshua is "filled with the Spirit of wisdom" (Deut. 34:9). Finally, the enigmatic, "shoot . . . from the stem of Jesse," upon whom rests the sevenfold Spirit of the Lord, will also be filled "with the spirit . . . of the fear of the Lord" (Isa. 11:1-3). Of these occurrences, the first four are in the aorist passive followed by the genitive (of content), while the latter, as befits an announcement, is in the future tense.

Pimplēmi occurs twenty-three (23) times in the New Testament. In contrast to the wide distribution of *pleroo* throughout the New Testament (with the exception of Matt. 22:10, 27:48) *pimplēmi* is exclusive to the Lukan literature. Luke uses it to mean "to fulfill." Thus, not only is Scripture "fulfilled" (Luke 21:22), but also various periods of time, such as the priestly course, circumcision, purification and pregnancy, are "fulfilled" (Luke 1:23, 2:21-22, 1:57, 2:6). Luke also uses *pimplēmi* to mean "to fill," both literally and metaphorically. On the one hand, it can describe the great catch of fish which "filled both of the boats" (Luke 5:7). On the other hand, it describes the reactions of both rage and fear to Jesus (Luke 4:28, 5:26), and either wonder and amazement, or jealousy and confusion to the Gospel (Acts 3:10, 5:17, 13:45, 19:29). Finally, and most importantly, it describes persons who are "filled with the Holy Spirit" (Luke 1:15, 41, 67; Acts 2:4; 4:8, 31; 9:17; 13:9). Along with the single occurrence of *pleroo* in respect to the term "filled with the Holy Spirit," it is this latter use of *pimplēmi* which is the subject of this study.

Luke's use of *pimplēmi* has a number of specific characteristics. With the exception of his description of the disciples "filling" their boats with fish (Luke 5:7), in every other occurrence *pimplēmi* is in the passive voice. Furthermore, with the exception of the announcement that John "will be filled with the Holy Spirit" (Luke 1:15), *pimplēmi* is always in the aorist tense. With equal consistency, *pimplēmi* plus genitive always describes the content which fills the object or person.[2] Thus, the phrase "X 'was filled' with the Holy Spirit" *(eplēsthē pneumatos hagiou* plus variants), has no semantic peculiarities, but it is consistent with the way Luke regularly uses *pimplēmi*.

Luke has a rich and comprehensive pneumatology. The terminology by which he describes the presence and activity of the Holy Spirit is

---

[2]Delling, *"pimplēmi, empimplēmi" TDNT* VI, 128.

equally rich and varied. The following verbal phrases, listed in order of increasing frequency, illustrate this wealth of expression.

1x to lead *(agō)*	Luke 4:1
1x to clothe *(enduō)*	Luke 24:49 (power = Holy Spirit)
2x to fall upon *(epi/ piptō)*	Acts 10:44, 11:15
3x to baptize *(baptizō)*	Luke 3:16; Acts 1:5, 11:16
4x to come upon *(ep/erchomai)*	Luke 1:35, 2:27; Acts 1:8, 19:6
5x to give *(didōmi)*	Luke 11:13; Acts 2:4, 8:18, 11:17 (gift = Holy Spirit); 15:8
5x to receive *(lambanō)*	Acts 2:38; 8:15, 17; 10:47; 19:2
5x to speak *(pro/legō)*	Acts 1:16, 8:29, 11:12, 13:2, 21:11
9x to fill *(pimplēmi pimplēmi,* 8x; *pleroo,* 1x)	Luke 1:15, 41, 67; Acts 2:4; 4:8, 31; 9:17; 13:9, 52

Note: these references are included irrespective of whether the Holy Spirit is in the subject or predicate.

This distinctive Lukan terminology is virtually absent in the Johannine and Pauline literature. Of equal significance, characteristic Johannine terminology, such as "the Spirit of Truth" and "the Paraclete," and typical Pauline terminology, such as, "the fruit of the Spirit," "gifts of the Spirit," and "seal of the Spirit" is absent in the Lukan literature.

Summary

From this lexical data, we are justified in the following preliminary conclusions: 1) the distinctively Lukan term "filled with the Holy Spirit" has a Septuagintal antecedent; 2) in the New Testament the term *eplēsthē pneumatos hagiou* is exclusively Lukan, and is distributed between the Gospel and Acts on a ratio of 3/5; 3) the cognate term *eplerounto . . . pneumatos hagiou,* which also occurs but one time in the Pauline literature, supplements this uniquely Lukan term; 4) statistically, "filled with the Holy Spirit" is Luke's most frequent term, on a ratio of 9/5 to its closest rivals; 5) thus, "filled with the Holy Spirit" is not only Luke's most characteristic term to describe the presence and activity of the Holy Spirit, but it is unrivalled as the center of his pneumatology. Having surveyed this lexical data, and established some preliminary conclusions, we may now proceed to the interpretation of the "filled with the Holy Spirit" terminology in Luke-Acts.

In this chapter I wish to demonstrate the thesis that the term "filled with the Holy Spirit" describes neither Christian behavior nor Christian service in general, but that it specifically describes prophetic inspiration and vocation. In developing this thesis, I will 1) discuss my hermeneutical program, 2) interpret the lexical data, and 3) relate the term to the larger context of Luke's charismatic theology.

A Hermeneutical Program

The lexical data which we have summarized appears to be uncomplicated and problem free. However, the literature on the subject, which represents different ecclesiastical and theological presuppositions, yields a wide variety of interpretations, some of which are mutually exclusive and contradictory. According to this literature, the term "filled with the Holy Spirit" describes either sanctification, that is, ethical or moral behavior, or service, whether it be prophecy, preaching or apostolic mission. There are, moreover, differences as to 1) whether it is related to the Old Testament activity of the Spirit of God, or whether it is uniquely Christian, and 2) whether it is a temporary or a permanent possession—differences which are sometimes resolved by assuming that "filled with the Holy Spirit" has a different meaning in the Gospel than it does in the Acts. It is hoped that the following hermeneutical program will be the correct key to the resolution of these competing and sometimes contradictory interpretations.

Luke's Terminology Is Modelled after the Septuagint

Though it is not unchallenged, there is a growing scholarly consensus that Luke is heir to the Septuagint. This indebtedness is true for his historiography. In his *Acts and the History of Earliest Christianity,* Martin Hengel concludes, "Luke is evidently influenced by a firm tradition with a religious view of history which essentially derives from the Septuagint. His imitation of the Septuagint shows that he wants quite deliberately to be in this tradition."[3]

Similarly, in his *Luke: Historian and Theologian*, I. Howard Marshall writes, "His [Luke's] style of writing, which is frequently reminiscent of the Septuagint, demands that he also be compared to Jewish Historians."[4] Marshall's comment reminds us that Luke's indebtedness to the Septuagint extends beyond his historiography to his style. Conceding that "Luke may well have had the skill to write what looks like a deliberate LXX style," Nigel Turner comments, "alternatively, his may have been part of the style of a Jewish kind of Greek."[5] He concludes, "To us it seems doubtful whether such an artist would inadvertently leave any so-called 'pools' of Semitisms, if his natural language were not Semitic Greek."[6] Thus, whether his style is either "imitative" of the Septuagint, or "natural" Semitic-Biblical Greek, Luke is clearly heir to the Septuagint in matters of historiography and style.

Luke's stylistic indebtedness, in particular, extends to his terminology by which he describes the presence and activity of the Holy Spirit.[7] The following chart illustrates that the majority of Luke's terms are paralleled in the Septuagint to describe the presence and activity of the Spirit of God.

LUKE-ACTS		SEPTUAGINT	
1x	to lead (*agō*)	5x	Ezek. 8:3; 11:1, 24; 37:1; 43:5
1x	to clothe (*enduō*)	3x	Jud. 6:34, 1 Chron. 12:18, 2 Chron. 24:20
2x	to fall upon (*epi/piptō*)	1x	Ezek. 11:5
3x	to baptize (*baptizō*)		

---

[3]Martin Hengel, *Acts and the History of Earliest Christianity*, trans. by John Bowden (Philadelphia: Fortress Press, 1980), 51-52.
[4]I. Howard Marshall, *Luke: Historian and Theologian*, Contemporary Evangelical Perspectives (Grand Rapids: Zondervan Publishing House, 1970), 55.
[5]Nigel Turner, *Style*, Vol IV of *A Grammar of New Testament Greek*, edited by James Hope Moulton (Edinburgh: T & T Clark, 1976), 56.
[6]Turner, *Style*, 57.
[7]Roger Stronstad, "The Influence of the Old Testament on the Charismatic Theology of St. Luke," *Pneuma*, Vol. 2, No. 1 (1980); 44ff. For a full discussion of the subject see my *Charismatic Theology of St. Luke* (Peabody: Hendrickson Publishers, Inc., 1984).

| 4x | to come upon (ep/erchomai) | 2x | Ezek. 2:2, 3:24 |
| 5x | to give (didōmi) | 3x | Num. 11:29, Neh. 9:20, Isa. 42:1 |

LUKE-ACTS		SEPTUAGINT
5x	to receive (lambanō)	7x (ana/ lambanō) Ezek. 2:2; 3:12, 14; 8:3; 11:1, 24
5x	to speak (pro/legō)	2x Ezek. 3:34, 11:5
9x	to fill (pimplēmi - plēroō)	5x (em/pimplēmi) Ex 28:3, 31:3, 35:31; Isa. 11:3

A comparison of the appropriate verbs between the Septuagint and Luke-Acts shows that the Septuagint has a wider variety than Luke-Acts on a ratio of 23/9.[8] It is of great significance, however, that with the exception of the verb *baptizō* all nine Lucan terms are paralleled in the Septuagint. Of greatest significance, moreover, is the fact that Luke's most characteristic term, "filled *(pimplemi)* with the Holy Spirit," is paralleled in the Septuagintal term "filled *(pimplēmi)* with the Spirit."

Not only does Luke, and Luke alone in the New Testament, use this Septuagintal term, but he also duplicates its semantic characteristics. As in the Septuagint, so in Luke-Acts, with a single exception in each, "filled" is an aorist passive. The single exception in both the Septuagint and Luke-Acts are the announcements that Jesse's descendant and John the Baptist will be filled with the Spirit—thus the explanation for the future rather than the aorist tense.

From this discussion we may conclude: 1) Luke is generally a debtor to the Greek Bible for his terminology by which he describes the activity of the Holy Spirit, and specifically, for his distinctive "filled with the Holy Spirit" terminology; 2) this Septuagintal terminology in Luke-Acts describes the same kind of experience for Luke as it did for the translators of the Septuagint; that is, it describes a charismatic activity of the Spirit. These conclusions will be confirmed later in this study.

---

[8]Ibid.

68 *Spirit, Scripture, and Theology: A Pentecostal Perspective*

"Filled with the Holy Spirit" Has the Same Meaning in Both the Gospel and the Acts

Ending several decades of scholarly skepticism concerning the literary unity of Luke-Acts, in his article, "Luke-Acts, A Storm Center in Contemporary Scholarship," W. C. van Unnik reports, "We speak of it [Luke-Acts] as a unit . . . It is generally accepted that both books have a common author; the possibility that the Gospel and Acts, contrary to Acts 1:1, do not belong together is not seriously discussed. By almost unanimous consent they are considered to be two volumes of a single work."[9]

While consenting with this scholarly consensus on the literary unity of Luke-Acts, many scholars paradoxically assume a theological discontinuity between Luke and Acts.

While it applies to many aspects of Lukan theology, this assumption of theological discontinuity certainly includes Luke's "filled with the Holy Spirit" terminology. The term is distributed between Luke-Acts on a ratio of 3/6. The following chart illustrates this distribution:

LUKE	ACTS
John the Baptist, 1:15	Disciples, 2:4
Elizabeth, 1:41	Peter, 4:8
Zacharias, 1:67	Disciples, 4:31
	Paul, 9:17
	Paul, 13:9
	Disciples, 13:52

In spite of the fact that the term is the same in both the Gospel and in the Acts, in his monograph, *The Holy Spirit in the Acts of the Apostles*, J. H. E. Hull asserts, "Elizabeth and Zacharias were, in Luke's view, momentarily filled with the Spirit. In other words, they could only be aware of His (seemingly) fleeting presence and His (seemingly) fitful and

---

[9]W. C. van Unnik, "Luke-Acts, A Storm Center in Contemporary Scholarship," in *Studies in Luke-Acts*, ed. by L. K. Keck and J. L. Martyn (London: S.P.C.K., 1967), 18.

necessarily limited activity. The disciples, on the other hand, were permanently filled with the Spirit."[10]

Similarly, Gerhard Delling, in his article on the words, *"pimplēmi/empimplēmi,"* in *Theological Dictionary of the New Testament,* writes,

> The Spirit of prophecy causes Elizabeth (1:41) and Zacharias (1:67) to magnify the fulfillment of God's promise of salvation in the sons of Mary and Elizabeth.... In Ac. *plesthenai* describes the work of the Holy Spirit in Christians. The primary reference here is not to the receiving of the Spirit of prophecy but to the fact that the filling with the Spirit conveys the power of preaching.[11]

In principle, since Luke-Acts is a literary unit, scholars should not assume a theological discontinuity between Luke-Acts unless the semantic and contextual evidence demands it. In general, however, the evidence compels the interpreter to recognize a strong continuity for such important Lukan themes as salvation, forgiveness, witness, and the Holy Spirit.[12]

Specifically, in spite of assertions to the contrary, the evidence compels us to recognize that the term, "filled with the Holy Spirit," has the same meaning in both the Gospel and the Acts. On the one hand, it means prophetic inspiration in both books, and not prophecy in the Gospel and preaching in the Acts. Luke, himself, makes this identification for Zacharias (1:67), and for the "other tongues" of the disciples on the day of Pentecost, where Luke not only describes the disciples as "filled," but where he also records Peter's interpretation of this as prophecy, such as Joel wrote about (Acts 2:4,16ff.). On the other hand, "filled" is not temporary in Luke and permanent in Acts. As the examples of Peter (Acts 2:4; 4:8, 31) and Paul (Acts 9:17; 13:9, 52) demonstrate, it is an occasional or repetitive experience for the

---

[10]J. H. E. Hull, *The Holy Spirit in the Acts of the Apostles* (London: Lutterworth Press, 1967), 68-69.
[11]Delling, *"pimplēmi, empimplēmi"* TDNT, VI, 130.
[12]Marshall, *Luke: Historian and Theologian,* 91; 93ff; 15ff; 190.

disciples.[13] We will demonstrate more fully that the term "filled with the Holy Spirit" is a potentially repetitive occasion of prophetic inspiration in both the Gospel and the Acts.

Summary

In order to adequately interpret the "filled with the Holy Spirit" terminology in Luke-Acts, the interpreter must integrate the following principles into his methodological program: 1) Luke's terminology is modelled after a similar term in the Septuagint, 2) this term has the same meaning in the Gospel as it does in the Acts. These points provide the interpreter with a methodological orientation and strategy which will enable him to best understand the Lukan data.

"Filled with the Holy Spirit": A Term Signifying Prophetic Inspiration

In general, for Luke the gift of the Holy Spirit is charismatic; that is, it is given to God's people to empower them for effective service in His kingdom. Specifically, Luke's most common charismatic terminology, "filled with the Holy Spirit," signifies the prophetic dimension of this charismatic pneumatology. The following table illustrates this charismatic and prophetic dimension of the term, "filled with the Holy Spirit."

TEXT	PERSON(S)	NO.	PHENOMENON
Luke 1:15	John	one	Messianic herald
1:41	Elizabeth	one	song of praise
1:67	Zacharias	one	prophecy
Acts 2:4	Disciples	group	other
4:8	Peter	one	witness

---

[13]In *The Acts of the Apostles: The Greek Text with Introduction and Commentary* (2nd ed; Grand Rapids: William B. Eerdmans, 1952), 120, F. F. Bruce comments, "The permanent in dwelling of the Holy Spirit in a believer must be contrasted with special moments of inspiration, such as the present (Acts 4:8), which was a fulfillment of our Lord's promise in Mk. xiii. 11 and parallel passages."

Chapter 4 "Filled with the Holy Spirit" Terminology in Luke-Acts 71

4:31	Disciples	group	witness
9:17	Paul	one	no record
13:9	Paul	one	judgement
13:52	Disciples	group	joy

On close examination these data yield several significant observations.

In the first place, the term, "filled with the Holy Spirit," describes a prophetic ministry in both Luke and Acts. This is explicit for Zacharias who, when he was filled with the Holy Spirit, broke forth with the *Benedictus,* which Luke identifies as prophetic speech (Luke 1:67). By analogy, Elizabeth's song of praise, sung when she also was filled with the Spirit, is prophetic speech. Similarly, John, the angel announces, "will be filled with the Holy Spirit, while yet in his mother's womb" (Luke 1:15). At the height of his popularity some three decades later, the people speculate that he might be the Messiah—the Christ (Luke 3:15). As Zacharias had prophesied, however, and as his ministry subsequently confirms, this herald is not the Messiah; rather he is, "the prophet of the Most High" (Luke 1:76, cf., 20:6). Thus, in each occurrence in the Gospel, the term, "filled with the Holy Spirit," describes either the prophetic vocation (John) or prophetic inspiration (Zacharias and Elizabeth).

What is true of the term, "filled with the Holy Spirit," in the Gospel is also true for the term in the Acts. For example, in his Pentecost narrative he makes the identification "to speak with other tongues = to prophesy." He makes this identification in two ways. First, Peter interprets the Pentecostal experience of the disciples according to the prophecy of Joel, who had announced the future restoration of the prophetic activity of the Spirit (Joel 2:28ff., Acts 2:16ff.). Second, Peter not only quotes from Joel, but he also qualifies his text by inserting the explanation, "And they shall prophesy," after the promise, "I will in those days pour forth of My Spirit" (Acts 2:18). This equation, "to speak with other tongues=to prophesy," is confirmed by Luke's subsequent description of the gift of the Holy Spirit to the disciples at Ephesus. He reports, "the Holy Spirit came on them, and they began speaking with tongues and prophesying" (Acts 19:6). Therefore, just as Zacharias was filled with the Spirit and prophesied when the Gospel era began, so the disciples are filled with the Holy Spirit and prophesy as the Apostolic era begins.

In Acts, to be filled with the Holy Spirit results in a variety of prophetic phenomenon more wide-ranging than the Pentecostal experience of speaking with other tongues. Thus, Jesus' earlier promise of the Spirit to the disciples is fulfilled, individually in Peter's defense before the Sanhedrin, and collectively in the bold witness of the disciples in Jerusalem (Luke 12:12; Acts 4:8ff., 31ff.). Significantly, both Peter and the disciples are "filled with the Holy Spirit" when they give their witness. Moreover, just as Peter, individually and as part of a group, had been filled with the Spirit three times (Acts 2:4; 4:8, 31), so Paul, individually and as part of a group, is also filled with the Holy Spirit three times (Acts 9:17; 13:9, 52). Similarly, just as "filled with the Holy Spirit" resulted in a prophetic ministry for Peter, so it subsequently resulted in a prophetic ministry for Paul; that is, having been "filled with the Holy Spirit," Paul is numbered among the prophets and teachers at Antioch (Acts 13:1). During his first missionary journey when Elymas, a Jewish false prophet, opposed Paul this true prophet, "filled with the Spirit," cursed this magician for his opposition to the Gospel (Acts 13:9). Finally, echoing an earlier experience of Jesus (Luke 10:21), Paul and his companions were "filled *(pleroo)* with joy and with the Holy Spirit" (Acts 13:52). This threefold parallelism between Peter, the leading Apostle to the Jews, and Paul not only authenticates Paul's experience of the Holy Spirit, but it also legitimizes him as a true prophet and Apostle to the Gentiles.

In summary, Luke uses the term, "filled with the Holy Spirit," in two different, yet complementary ways. First, he uses the term four times as a pointer to a general prophetic ministry, without necessarily specifying either the moment or duration of prophetic inspiration, or any phenomenon which might result from this gift of the Spirit (Luke 1:15, Acts 4:31, 9:17, 13:52). Second, he uses the term five times to describe a specific moment or episode of prophetic inspiration. When describing prophetic inspiration his narrative has two components: 1) the introductory formula, "filled with the Holy Spirit," and 2) the report of direct speech, which we may classify as a "Pneuma discourse." According to Luke's record, a Pneuma discourse may be either praise (Luke 1:41ff., 1:67ff., cf., 2:4ff.), witness (Acts 2:14ff., 4:8ff.), or an announcement of divine judgement (Acts 13:9). Thus, in the Acts, as well as in the Gospel, the term, "filled with the Holy Spirit," signifies both the prophetic vocation, in general, and specific moments of prophetic inspiration, in particular.

Luke's term, "filled with the Holy Spirit," is but one, albeit important, aspect of his overall emphasis on prophetic activity in the Messianic-Apostolicage. Luke uses the term "prophet(s)/prophetess(es)" for John the Baptist, Anna, Jesus, Agabus and companions, certain disciples at Antioch, Judas and Silas, and the four daughters of Philip (Luke 1:76, 2:36, 7:16; Acts 11:27-28, 13:1, 15:32, 21:9). Though they are not designated as such by Luke, many others must certainly be understood to be prophets. In addition to all those who are "filled with the Holy Spirit," Luke's technical term to describe the prophetic vocation/inspiration, includes those, such as Peter and Paul, who experience visions and dreams, which are the accredited mode of prophetic revelation (Num. 12:6, Joel 2:28ff., Acts 2:17ff.). These prophets engage in a variety of activities throughout Luke-Acts: exhortation (Luke 3:18), miracle working (Luke 7:14-16; Acts 2:43, 3:1ff., 5:15, 6:8, 8:13, etc.), prediction (Acts 11:28, 21:10ff.), judgement (Acts 8:20, 13:9), and worship (Luke 1:68ff.; Acts 2:11, 47, etc.). The large number of designated prophets and the relative frequency of prophecy in Luke-Acts is consistent with the universality of the prophethood of all believers in these "last days" of the Spirit (Acts 2:17, 39).

We have observed that for Luke, the Holy Spirit is the Spirit of prophecy in the Acts as well as in the Gospel. This is, moreover, but one dimension of his charismatic or vocational pneumatology. Luke is indebted to Jesus for his understanding of the vocational purpose of the gift of the Holy Spirit. In words which are programmatic for the subsequent mission of the disciples, Jesus informs them, "You shall receive power when the Holy Spirit has come upon you; and you shall be My witnesses both in Jerusalem, and in all Judea and Samaria, and even to the remotest part of the earth" (Acts 1:8). In this dominical saying Luke gives his readers the key to interpreting the purpose of the gift of the Spirit, not only to the disciples on the day of Pentecost but also throughout Luke-Acts.

If Luke's record accurately reflects the teaching of Jesus about the purpose of the gift of the Holy Spirit, then the result of receiving the Spirit will be consistent with that purpose. Where Luke records the result, we have observed this to be the case, not only for the gift of the Spirit throughout the Acts but also for the activity of the Spirit in the Gospel. Whether the Spirit is given to John as an unborn infant, to Jesus at the Jordan, to the disciples on the day of Pentecost, or to Saul in Damascus, the pattern is consistent: the gift of the Spirit always results in mission. Because Luke describes the gift of the Spirit to the Samaritans, the household of Cornelius, and the Ephesians in similar terms, the vocational result is implicit here as well. Though we may look to Luke in vain for directives for the so-called nonnative Christian experience, we do encounter an invariable pattern for the gift of the Spirit in the unfolding record of the inauguration and extension of the Gospel: the gift of the Spirit always precedes and effects mission or vocation.

"Filled with the Holy Spirit" and Other Terminology in Luke-Acts

Luke uses a variety of terms to describe the dynamic presence of the Holy Spirit. In addition to the verbal phrases which I have listed in the chart above, Luke uses several other terms; for example, the "promise," "the gift," and "full" of the Spirit (Luke 4:1; Acts 1:4; 2:33, 38; 6:3). The Pentecost narrative is a paradigm of his style: he gives a multiplex description of the Holy Spirit to describe a single outpouring. By way of promise, the Spirit will clothe, baptize, and empower the disciples (Luke 24:49, Acts 1:5, 8); by way of description, the Spirit "filled" the disciples (Acts 2:4); by way of interpretation, Jesus "poured forth" the Spirit upon the disciples (Acts 2:33); and finally, by way of application, the "promise" of this Pentecostal gift of the Spirit of prophecy is for all mankind (Acts 2:39). From Luke's Pentecost narrative it is evident that the term, "filled with the Holy Spirit" is intimately related to his other Spirit terminology. Due to the limitations of this chapter, we will compare: 1) the noun "full" (*pleres*) with the verbal phrase "filled" (*pimplēmi*) with the Holy Spirit, 2) the verbs "received" and "filled," and 3) the verbs "baptized" and "filled" with the Holy Spirit.

"Full" of the Holy Spirit

The noun *pleres* in the term, "full of the Holy Spirit," is derived from *pleroo* rather than from Luke's characteristic verb, *pimplēmi*. Luke uses the same term in both the Gospel and the Acts. He describes Jesus (Luke 4:1), the seven deacons (Acts 6:3), Stephen (Acts 6:5, 7:55), and Barnabas (Acts 11:24) as "full of the Holy Spirit." Power (Luke 4:1, Acts 6:8), wisdom (Acts 6:3), and faith (Acts 6:5, 11:24) are closely associated with being "full of the Holy Spirit." These latter terms describe the "content" of the Spirit's equipment for ministry. The distinction between "full of the Holy Spirit" and "filled with the Holy Spirit" is now apparent. The term "full of the Holy Spirit" describes the enabling of the Spirit for ministry, whereas the term "filled with the Holy Spirit" describes the prophetic office and inspiration.

"Received" the Holy Spirit

Luke describes the gift of the Holy Spirit in a variety of ways: 1) the Father "promised" the Spirit (Acts 1:5), Jesus "poured forth" the Spirit (Acts 2:33), the disciples were both "filled" with, and "received" the Spirit (Acts 2:4, 38). In Luke's narrative, contemporary and future converts will "receive" the gift of the Holy Spirit (Acts 2:38). In fulfillment of Peter's Pentecost promise, the believers in Samaria (Acts 8:15, 17), the assembled household of Cornelius (Acts 10:47), and the disciples at Ephesus (Acts 19:2ff.) received the Holy Spirit.

In contrast to "filled," which Luke consistently uses in the passive voice, Luke consistently uses "received" in the active or middle voice. In this context of the gift of the Spirit, God acts upon the believer and fills him with the Holy Spirit. In addition, however, the believer must respond in order to receive the Holy Spirit. On those occasions when the disciples are "filled with the Holy Spirit," Luke emphasizes the divine initiative; similarly, on those occasions when the disciples "receive the Holy Spirit," Luke emphasizes the complementary human response to that initiative. In using these complementary verbs, and in using the former in the active voice and the latter in the passive voice, Luke makes it clear that "received the Holy Spirit" is the necessary complement to being "filled with the Holy Spirit."

"Baptized" with the Holy Spirit

Luke uses the verbal phrase "baptized with the Holy Spirit" three times: 1) in contrast to himself, who baptizes with water, John announces that his successor "will baptize you in the Holy Spirit and fire" (Luke 3:16); 2) in conscious fulfillment of John's announcement, the risen Lord reiterates, "... you shall be baptized with the Holy Spirit not many days from now" (Acts 1:5); and 3) Peter subsequently compares the experience of the household of Cornelius and the disciples on the day of Pentecost, and identifies the former as a baptism of the Holy Spirit (Acts 11:16).

In an example of what James Barr classifies as "illegitimate identity transfer,"[14] scholars typically interpret these references to signify initiation-incorporation after the Pauline pattern of I Corinthians 12:13.[15] However, in the structure of Luke-Acts, the Pentecost narrative stands in the same relationship to Acts as the inauguration narrative does to the Gospel. Similarly, the anointing of Jesus is functionally equivalent to the Spirit-baptism of the disciples. Therefore, just as the gift of the Spirit to Jesus inaugurates and empowers his mission, then whatever meaning Spirit-baptism might have in non-Lukan contexts, in Acts it has the same primary charismatic meaning for the mission of the disciples as the anointing by the Spirit had for the charismatic mission of Jesus.

Different ecclesiastical and theological traditions interpret the relationship between "baptized" and "filled" with the Spirit in mutually contradictory and incompatible ways. The following chart summarizes these diverse interpretations.

TRADITION	BAPTIZED IN THE SPIRIT	FILLED WITH THE SPIRIT
Reformed	Incorporation into the body of Christ	Moral power
Wesleyan	Crisis experience of sanctification	Holiness

---

[14] James Barr, *The Semantics of Biblical Language* (London: Oxford University Press, 1961), 222.

[15] For a discussion of this methodological error see my *Charismatic Theology of St. Luke*, 9-11.

| Pentecostal | Initial enduement of power | Repetitive gift of power |

However, if you read Luke by himself, and listen to him, not only does a different meaning of the terms, "baptized," and "filled," with the Holy Spirit emerge from the data, but a different relationship between the two terms emerges as well. For Luke, "baptized in the Spirit," is the anointing or consecration of the disciples for (a prophetic) mission; "filled with the Holy Spirit," on the other hand, is the prophetic office and/or prophetic inspiration to which the disciples are anointed.

As Luke uses these two terms, then, because it is an anointing to ministry, "baptized in the Holy Spirit," is a once-for-all experience, whereas, "filled with the Holy Spirit," is both an office and, as the need arises, a (potentially) repetitive experience. Thus, the popular maxim, "One baptism, many fillings," is a surprisingly accurate summary of Luke's charismatic theology.

Conclusion

Having investigated Luke's "filled with the Holy Spirit" terminology, the challenge comes to us afresh to construct a biblical pneumatology for our generation—not only as to the meaning of this term, but also as to the emphasis which we give it in our overall theology. In the final analysis, John Calvin, John Wesley, Charles Parham, or any other leader, or the traditions which identify with them, cannot be allowed to shape our pneumatology. We must abandon our ecclesiastical prejudices and go where the biblical evidence clearly leads. In regard to the subject of this chapter we have found that Luke uses the term, "filled with the Holy Spirit," to describe neither moral behavior nor Christian service in general, but rather as a technical term to describe the office of the prophet, on the one hand, or to introduce prophetic speech (a pneuma discourse), on the other hand. We have also found that Luke gives pride of place to the term, "filled with the Holy Spirit," rather than to the term, "baptized with the Holy Spirit." Thus, "filled with the Holy Spirit," and not "baptized with the Holy Spirit," is to be the center of our own pneumatology. Our task, therefore, is not to make our pneumatology

Reformed, Wesleyan, or Pentecostal, *per se*, but, to make it biblical. In other words, rather than trying to conform Luke's pneumatology to ours, we must conform our pneumatology to his.

CHAPTER FIVE

SIGNS ON THE EARTH BENEATH

This chapter arises out of an observation that interpreters of Acts 2 all too often do not do full justice to the significance of Peter's quotation of Joel 2:28-32 (LXX) as the explanation of the pouring forth of the Holy Spirit on the day of Pentecost. Generally, this is because interpreters apply Joel's text to Acts 2:1-4 selectively rather than comprehensively.

In what follows I begin with a discussion of an appropriate hermeneutical program for interpreting Luke-Acts, and then give an exposition of Acts 2:1-21. In my exposition I hope to demonstrate that this post-resurrection Pentecost, this "day of the Lord," is a day of divine intervention for creating a community of charismatic prophets, attested by three signs, all of which fully and precisely fulfill Joel's ancient oracle about the pouring forth of the Spirit of God.

Hermeneutical Program

As I see it, hermeneutics has three elements. First, there is the range of presuppositions which every interpreter brings to the task of interpreting the text. Second, there are those principles which guide the interpreter in the task of exegesis. Third, there are those principles which guide the interpreter in applying the text to contemporary Christian living. In the discussion which follows, I will assume the hermeneutical model which generally characterizes an evangelical Protestant interpretation of the Bible. However, because I am interpreting a text which bears special significance for my experience as a Pentecostal, and, further, because the text is historical narrative, a genre over which there is much controversy concerning its didactic role, I will briefly summarize some points that are particularly relevant to my interpretation of the text.

Presuppositions

Every interpreter brings a variety of experiential, rational, and spiritual presuppositions to the interpretation of the Scriptures. In particular, Pentecostal interpreters, such as myself, bring their own experience of being filled with the Spirit as a presupposition to Luke's report that on the day of Pentecost the disciples "were filled with the Holy Spirit and began to speak with other tongues, as the Spirit was giving them utterance" (Acts 2:4), and believes that they are justified in understanding the experience of the disciples in the light of their own similar experience. Further presuppositions are pertinent to the study of Acts; namely, 1) that Luke's pneumatology is influenced by the charismatic pneumatology of the Old Testament as it is mediated to him through the LXX;[1] 2) that the two books, Luke and Acts, were written and published together as a literary unit, and, therefore, i) each book is the same genre, namely, historical narrative *(diegesis* Luke 1:1),[2] and ii) despite the historical particularity of each book they have a common, homogenous theological perspective.

Guidelines for Interpreting Luke-Acts

For the interpretation of Luke-Acts, three guidelines need to be noted. Those guidelines are: 1) Luke-Acts is selective history; 2) Luke-Acts must be set in the historical, political, social, and religious context

---

[1] Stronstad, "The Influence of the Old Testament on the Charismatic Theology of St. Luke," 17-20.
[2] Contra Gordon D. Fee, *How to Read the Bible for All Its Worth: A Guide to Understanding the Bible,* (Grand Rapids: Zondervan Publishing House, 1982), 90. He writes, ". . . Acts is the only one of its kind in the New Testament." This is an astonishing statement from a champion of "genre" hermeneutics. It is astonishing because Luke's term *diegesis*/Narrative (Luke 1:1) applies to his entire two-volume history. Thus, Luke is not one kind of genre and Acts a second kind of genre—the only one of its kind in the New Testament.

of the Greco-Roman World; and 3) Luke has a multiplex purpose in writing Luke-Acts.

1. Luke-Acts is Selective History

Like his predecessors and mentors, the editors and chroniclers of the sacred history of the Jews, Luke makes no attempt to give his patron, Theophilus (Luke 1:1-4, Acts 1:1-2), and all readers of his two books a complete history of either Jesus, the apostles and their fellow workers, or of the origin and spread of the Gospel. Rather, from out of his own participation in some of the events which he has recorded (note the "we" passages Acts 16:10ff., etc.), and also from out of the vast pool of information which he has gathered, he gives us a select history which reflects and supports the parallel structure of his two volumes, and, also, relates to the multiplex purpose which governs his writing. Undoubtedly, Luke knows much more than he writes. Conversely, in comparison to both the Gospels and the Epistles, he sometimes tells more than the others. Because Luke is the most prolific writer in the New Testament and the data is so immense, we must limit our illustrations of the selective character of Luke-Acts to a few select examples.

A comparison of Luke's "first book" with the Gospels written by Matthew, Mark, and John shows that Luke has included much distinctive material which the others have not. For example, Luke's infancy narrative (Luke 1:5-2:52) has few parallels with Matthew's infancy narrative (Matt. 1:18ff.) and has none with either Mark's or John's Gospels because both lack an infancy narrative. Further, Luke's so-called "travel narrative" (Luke 9:51ff.) contains much exclusive material, including the report of the mission of the seventy, (Luke 10:1-24) and a number of parables, such as the parable of the Good Samaritan (Luke 10:25-37). In addition, Luke's resurrection narrative is notoriously independent of the reports of the other Gospels containing, for example, the episode of Jesus' resurrection appearance to the two disciples on the road to Emmaus (Luke 24:13-35), and Jesus' promise of the divine empowering which awaited the disciples in Jerusalem (Luke 24:49).

Not only does Luke include much independent and exclusive data, Luke's selection is also evident by what he excludes from his narrative, whether or not this exclusion is a factor of the limited nature of his data, or whether it is a matter of his editorial strategy. For example, Luke's infancy narrative tells the reader little about the lives of Zacharias and Elizabeth, the now aged and soon to be parents of John the Baptist, or of Mary and Joseph, the soon to be parents of Jesus, the Son of God. Further, with the exception of Jesus' visit to Jerusalem with his parents at age 12 (Luke 2:41-51), Luke tells us nothing about his childhood or early adult life prior to his baptism. It is the tantalizing silence on these and other matters in Luke and the other Gospels which in the end proved to be such a powerful motivation in the creation of the apocryphal infancy Gospels of the second and third centuries.

What is true of Luke's selectivity in writing his "first book" is just as true for his writing of his sequel, the Acts of the Apostles. For example, of the 120 disciples, both men and women, who await the thrice promised gift of the Holy Spirit (Acts 1, 15), Luke tells us nothing further about Mary, the mother of Jesus, or about the conversion and Christian lives of Jesus' brothers. James is the only exception to this, and he appears in the narrative but twice (Acts 15:13ff, 21:17ff.). Further, of the Eleven (Acts 1:13), Luke tells us nothing except briefly for James and John, and more extensively for Peter. Moreover, he is silent on the history of Christianity in Galilee. In addition, of the spread of the Gospel to the three leading cities of the Empire, namely, Rome, Alexandria, and Antioch, Luke only tells his readers of the spread of the Gospel to Antioch. Alexandria never enters the focus of his interest, and Rome is the goal of Paul's ministry, which, when reached, brings his record to an end.

As limited as this brief survey is by space constraints, it clearly demonstrates the selectivity which Luke brought to the writing of his two volumes. Indeed, it is true that all historiography is necessarily selective and interpretive. And so, it was for Luke when he wrote his report of the origin and spread of Christianity, as well as it is for all historians, ancient and modern, sacred or secular. Both in what he includes in his narrative and what he excludes from his narrative, Luke reports only those sayings and events which conform to, advance, and illustrate his purposes.

2. Luke-Acts Must Be Set in the Context of the Greco-Roman World

Like the historians of Old Testament times who set the sacred history of Israel in the context of the political history of the nations of the Ancient Near East, Luke set his narrative of the origin and spread of Christianity in the political, cultural, and religious context of the Greco-Roman world. Since Jesus and his disciples were Jews in Galilee and ministered almost exclusively among the Jews in Galilee and Judea, this, at first, may seem to be a matter to be disputed. However, this observation is validated, in part at least, by the fact that Jesus was born in Bethlehem of Judea as a result of a decree from Caesar Augustus for a census which required Joseph to visit his ancestral home (Luke 2:1ff.), and Jesus was executed under the authorization of Pontius Pilate, the Roman governor of Judea (Luke 23:1ff.), and by the hands of Roman soldiers (Luke 23:23ff.).

In events less dramatic than the birth and death of Jesus under Roman influence, the fledgling church, as reported by Luke, put its roots down in the far flung, multinational soil of the Roman Empire. After the resurrection and ascension of Jesus, the disciples were initially restricted to Jerusalem and Judea, and were a sect within Judaism. Thus, the early church initially had little direct contact with the Greco-Roman world. As reported by Luke, this changed primarily, though not exclusively, through Paul's so-called missionary journeys. For example, in Cyprus, where Barnabas and Saul began their peripatetic witness, they were summoned to appear before the proconsul, Sergius Paulus (Acts 13:7), who believed, being amazed at the teaching of the Lord (13:12). Somewhat later in Philippi, Paul and Silas were accused by its citizens of "proclaiming customs which it is not lawful for us to accept, being Romans" (16:21, note 16:37). Shortly thereafter in Thessalonica, Paul and Silas were accused of acting "contrary to the decrees of Caesar" (17:7). Having travelled on from Thessalonica to Berea to Athens and then to Corinth, Paul met Aquila and Priscilla, who had been expelled from Rome (AD49) when, "Claudius had commanded all the Jews to leave Rome" (18:2). Also, while Paul was in Corinth, he was charged before the proconsul, Gallio, for persuading men to worship God contrary to the Law (18:12). Since Gallio was appointed proconsul of

Achaia in the summer of AD 51, the interpreter has a fixed date to synchronize New Testament history with Roman history.

From Paul's witness to the non-Jewish peoples of Lystra, Athens, and Ephesus (14:8-15, 17:16-34, 19:23-41), to his appeal to his Roman citizenship for protection and justice (16:37-40, 22:25-29, 25:10, etc.), and through to his arrest in Jerusalem and imprisonment and trials in Caesarea (21:27-26:32), and voyage to Rome (27-28) the interplay between Christianity and the Greco-Roman culture of the Mediterranean world increases. Theophilus, and most other readers of Luke-Acts in the first century, would have understood this with little difficulty because it was part of their native experience. In contrast, the interpreter who studies Luke-Acts in the twentieth century must develop a working knowledge of the history and culture of the Greco-Roman world in order to understand it as its author intended.

3. Luke-Acts Has a Multiplex Purpose

It is a commonplace among interpreters to affirm that authorial intentionality, that is, the author's purpose for writing his/her documents, is the essential criterion which governs the reader's understanding of the text.[3] But the question of authorial intentionality is complicated by a variety of factors. These include whether the purpose is explicit or implicit, whether it is simple or complex; that is, whether there is one primary purpose, or a combination of primary, secondary, and even tertiary purposes. Consequently, several dangers attend the search to determine authorial intentionality. One danger is the all-to-common tendency toward reductionism, putting forward the claims of one purpose to the exclusion of all others.

Another danger is to confuse the use to which the document, in whole or in part, might be put with the purpose of the document. The most insidious danger is to identify the interests and agenda of the interpreter to be those of the author.

Luke-Acts is the longest document in the New Testament. It is also a two-part document with two successive but complementary foci. On

---

[3]Fee, "Hermeneutics," 125ff.; *How to Read the Bible...*, 89.

the one hand, the first book focuses upon Jesus. Its setting is primarily the world of Judaism, and the subject is the origin of Christianity. On the other hand, the second book focuses on the disciples and their converts. Its setting progressively shifts from Judaism to the Greco-Roman world, and its subject is the spread of Christianity. Because of these factors, the question of Luke's purpose —as any survey of the relevant literature will show—is problematic![4]

Though the question of Luke's purpose has proven to be problematic it is not a matter for despair. The answer to the question of Luke's purpose lies in the recognition that it is multiplex. This multiplex purpose not only has a historical dimension, as the reader would expect from the genre of Luke-Acts, but it also has both a didactic dimension and a theological dimension. Luke, himself, identifies this multiplex purpose beginning with his prologue (Luke 1:1-4).

In the prologue to his two-volume work, Luke identifies the genre of his writing. It is a *diegesis* (account, Luke 1:1); it is also a *logos* (account, Acts 1:1). These terms identify Luke-Acts as historical narrative. In identifying his documents as historical narrative, Luke immediately alerts his readers to the historical purpose of what he writes. As he informs his readers, this historical purpose relates to "the things accomplished among us" (Luke 1:1). These things begin with the birth announcements of John (1:5ff.) and Jesus (1:26ff.), and continue through to the two-year imprisonment of Paul in Rome (Acts 28:30-31) —events in which Luke himself was a sometime participant. Not only does he identify his genre as historical narrative but he also identifies his credentials, that he has "followed everything (either mentally or as a participant) from the beginning" (Luke 1:3). Luke's historical purpose, then, is to narrate the events relating to the origin of Christianity and its spread in a sweep northwest to Rome.

Not only does Luke's multiplex purpose have a historical dimension, it also has a didactic dimension;[5] that is, he writes to instruct Theophilus

---

[4]C.f. Robert Maddox, The *Purpose of Luke-Acts,* Studies of the New Testament and Its World (Edinburgh: T. & T. Clark, 1982); W. W. Gasque, "A Fruitful Field: Recent Study of the Acts of the Apostles." Addendum to *A History of the Interpretation of the Acts of the Apostles* (Peabody: Hendrickson Publishers, 1980), 342-359; and I. Howard Marshall, "The Present State of Lucan Studies," *Themelios,* Vol. 14, No. 2 (1989): 52-57.

[5]Fee minimizes the didactic purpose of Luke's narrative. He writes, ". . . for a Biblical precedent to justify a present action, the principles of the action must be taught

and every other reader who will subsequently make up his audience. Specifically, he writes to bring Theophilus and others to a reliable/exact knowledge of the truth of the things which have already been taught. Thus, using the medium of historical narrative, Luke intends to supply Theophilus with a more reliable instruction than his earlier instruction *(katechethes)* had supplied him. If taken on his own terms, Luke makes a plain statement of his didactic intentionality. Clearly, as Luke practiced it, the writing of historical narrative was a medium and method of reliable instruction. Thus, as a historian Luke also saw himself as a teacher or instructor.

The didactic dimension of Luke's multiplex purpose is complemented by a theological dimension. His subject is, "all that Jesus began to do and teach" (Acts 1:1, cf. Luke 1:5-24:51), and, because he continues his narrative of the acts of Jesus with a narrative of the acts of the apostles, it is by implication the complementary subject of what the apostles, empowered by the same Spirit as their Messiah, also did and taught. Thus, the primary subject is theological; specifically, it is christological, soteriological and pneumatological. Therefore, in the same manner that Luke conceived the writing of historical narrative to be for the purpose of instruction, or teaching, so he also conceived the writing of historical narrative to be for the purpose of teaching theological truth. Through using this multiplex historical-didactic-theological purpose, Luke places himself in the historical tradition of the editors and chroniclers of the sacred history of Israel. This discussion of Luke's multiplex purpose commends itself for the following reasons: 1) it escapes the charge of reductionism; 2) it does not confuse the reader's real or imagined pastoral or apologetic use of Luke-Acts with Luke's purpose for writing his document; and 3) it does not identify the interests of subsequent interpreters with Luke's purpose.

Guidelines for Applying Luke-Acts

The study of Scripture is a twofold task, 1) interpretation, and 2) application. The two are not, however, always kept in complementary

---

elsewhere, where it is the primary intent so to teach. . . ." "Hermeneutics," 128-29; *How to Read the Bible. . .* ,101.

balance. Interpretation without application is like cooking a meal and then not eating it; application without interpretation is like eating the ingredients of the meal without cooking them. The issue of application is one of appropriateness and relevancy and contrary to the facile applications all too often given is, perhaps, the most challenging and difficult dimension of the study of Scripture. Therefore, just as there must be appropriate guidelines for interpreting Luke-Acts in order for the interpreter to understand the document as Luke intended it to be understood, so there must also be appropriate guidelines for applying the message of Luke-Acts in order that the Christian might do the things which Luke intended to be applicable for generations of Christians subsequent to that generation of his immediate audience.

Because Luke wrote in the genre of historical narrative the issue of the contemporary applicability of Luke-Acts generates contrasting views. On the one hand, some interpreters insist that because Luke wrote historical narrative, Luke-Acts has little to say to contemporary experience. John R. W. Stott, for example, writes, "The revelation of the purpose of God in Scripture should be sought in its *didactic*, rather than in its *historical* parts. More precisely, we should look for it in the teachings of Jesus, and in the sermons and writings of the apostles rather than in the purely narrative portions of the Acts."[6]

Similarly, Gordon Fee asserts: ". . . unless Scripture explicitly tells us we must do something, what is merely narrated or described can never function in a normative way."[7] On the other hand, other interpreters believe that Luke-Acts establishes patterns for normative Christian experience. Dr. L. T. Holdcroft writes, "The doctrines of the Holy Spirit that are popularly known as 'Pentecostal' are those that apply to

---

[6]Stott, *Baptism and Fullness*, 8-9. In response to my criticism of what he wrote here Stott has recently clarified and qualified his position in his recent commentary, *The Spirit, the Church, And the World* (Downers Grove: Inter-Varsity Press, 1990). He writes, "I am not denying that historical narratives have a didactic purpose, for of course Luke was both a historian and a theologian; I am rather affirming that a narrative's didactic purpose is not always apparent within itself and so often needs interpretive help from elsewhere in Scripture" (8). This statement represents a significant shift from what he actually wrote in his earlier work. *Baptism and Fullness*. Nevertheless, until Stott actually states how historical narrative functions in a didactic and theological way he has not really set aside the impression which he had left with his readers; namely, that historical narrative does not communicate the purpose of God for later readers of Scripture.

[7]Fee, *How to Read the Bible. . .* ,97.

contemporary experience that is the pattern of Acts chapter 2 and subsequent New Testament practice."[8]

These contrasting views on how historical narrative, (as in Luke-Acts) is to be applied to contemporary Christian experience means that the issue is neither a moot point nor merely academic or theological. It is at the heart of a great debate in the hermeneutics of Luke-Acts and a question whose resolution is a matter of urgency for the spiritual vitality of contemporary Christianity. The following guidelines address the question of how Luke-Acts as historical narrative, with particular focus on Acts, may be applied to contemporary Christian experience.

1. Identify Luke's Narrative Strategy and Structure

Interpreters who write of the "purely narrative portions of the Acts," or who write about what Luke has "merely narrated" have, I believe, a non-Lucan perspective on historical narrative. I have indicated earlier that Luke has a multiplex historical-didactic-theological purpose. Therefore, in light of this multiplex purpose, there are no "purely narrative portions," and, further, Luke has never "merely narrated" anything. Rather, Luke-Acts is a carefully structured two-part narrative with the second part (Acts) being patterned after the first (Luke). In general terms, both parts have 1) a "beginning" narrative, 2) an inauguration narrative, containing reports about the gift of the Holy Spirit and an inaugural sermon which explains that gift, 3) reports of ministry describing confirmatory miracles and the approval/disapproval response theme, 4) a travel narrative, and 5) a trials narrative. Out of his vast pool of data, Luke has selected, by inclusion as well as exclusion, information which fits his structure.

This structure reflects a complex narrative strategy. For example, in each case the inauguration narratives (Luke 3-4, Acts 2), with their reports of the gift of the Holy Spirit and the inaugural sermon which explains that gift, establishes the program of the subsequent ministries of Jesus and the disciples, respectively. Specifically, the inauguration narrative in Luke establishes Jesus as a charismatic prophet; similarly, the inauguration narrative in Acts establishes the disciples as a community

---

[8]Holdcroft, *The Holy Spirit: A Pentecostal Interpretation*, 90.

of charismatic prophets. In other words, everything subsequently reported about the ministries of Jesus and the disciples is to be understood as the work of charismatic prophets. Not only is Jesus' inauguration narrative programmatic for his ministry as a charismatic prophet, but also because the disciples will be baptized, empowered, filled with the Spirit, as Jesus Himself was, the inauguration narrative in Luke is also paradigmatic for the subsequent charismatic ministry of the disciples. Similarly, the programmatic inauguration narrative for the disciples (Acts 2) can function as a paradigm for the experience of subsequent generations of Christians.[9]

The narratives which follow the programmatic/paradigmatic inauguration narratives function to reinforce, illustrate, and develop what it means to be a charismatic prophet (Jesus), or a community of charismatic prophets (the disciples). Thus, each episode has a specific strategic function within the narrative. This means that the first matter to be decided in the question of how a narrative might be applied to contemporary Christian experience is to determine its place in the overall structure and narrative strategy of the author.

2. Recognize the Historical Particularity of Each Episode

Closely related to the issue of narrative structure and strategy on the problem of the applicability of historical narrative is the question of historical particularity. The stories of Jesus and the disciples are historically particular even when they have a programmatic/paradigmatic function. For example, both Jesus and the disciples are anointed/baptized with the Holy Spirit to inaugurate their ministries. Jesus, however, is at the Jordan when he is anointed by the Spirit; whereas

---

[9]Contra Fee, "Hermeneutics," 129. According to Fee the analogies of both Jesus' reception of the Spirit and subsequently that of the disciples is, "ruled out as irrelevant," for twentieth century Christian experience. Such a conclusion is purely gratuitous, having no basis in the exegesis of any text of Luke-Acts. If even Old Testament examples can be relevant for the experience of Christians (Rom. 4:23, 15:4; I Cor. 10:6, etc.) then Fee's position on the reception of the Spirit by Jesus and the disciples is an indefensible negation. In adopting his position Fee has missed the obvious Lukan perspective: that the Messianic age, which is also the era of the Spirit, began with the birth announcements of John and Jesus. Thus, Pentecost is not the "great line of demarcation" which Fee arbitrarily asserts it to be.

the disciples are in Jerusalem when they are baptized by the Spirit. Further, the voice from heaven and the descent of the Spirit in bodily form like a dove are the auditory and ocular signs which attest to Jesus' anointing; whereas, the sound of a violent wind from heaven and the tongues of fire are the auditory and ocular signs which attest to the disciples' Spirit- baptism. These differences of historical particularity do not mean that Jesus' inaugural reception of the Spirit differs in function from the disciples' inaugural reception of the Spirit.

What is true for the gift of the Holy Spirit first to Jesus (Luke 3-4), and subsequently to the disciples (Acts 1-2), is similarly true for subsequent gifts of the Spirit reported in Acts. Thus, the gift of the Spirit to the believers at Samaria (Acts 8), the household of Cornelius, the Roman centurion (Acts 10), or to the disciples at Ephesus (Acts 19) are reported according to the historical particularity of each event, rather than according to some theological formula. For example, the gift of the Spirit to the believers at Samaria follows their baptism by a significant time lapse and is administered by the laying on of hands; the gift of the Spirit to Cornelius and his household is on the same day as their conversion and is the sign which justifies their baptism in water; and the gift of the Spirit to the disciples at Ephesus follows their rebaptism and is administered by the laying on of hands. These episodes contrast with the gift of the Spirit to the disciples on the day of Pentecost, which was not administered by the laying on of hands, who had only received John's baptism, and were disciples of up to three years standing. Nevertheless, each subsequent episode, despite the differences of historical particularity, illustrates the extension of the same gift of the Spirit to Samaritans, Gentiles, and John's disciples as had been received by the disciples on the day of Pentecost. This conclusion is not debatable, for Peter explicitly identifies the experience of Cornelius and his household with that of the disciples on the day of Pentecost (Acts 11:17). Therefore, just as the gift signified charismatic empowering for Jesus and for the disciples on the day of Pentecost, so it must also signify charismatic empowering for Cornelius and his household, as well as for the earlier gift of the Spirit to the believers at Samaria and the later gift of the Spirit to the disciples at Ephesus.

From the above, it is clear that the historical particularity associated with these five receptions of the Holy Spirit defies all attempts to reducing the gift of the Spirit to some theological formula involving 1) the matter of prayer, 2) the relationship to John's baptism, 3) the chronological gap between belief and reception of the Spirit, 4) the administration of the gift by the laying on of hands. None of these factors are, therefore, to be applied to the contemporary reception of the Spirit. Rather, these episodes simply show that wherever the Gospel spreads, God's people can and should receive the charismatic empowering of the Spirit for their Christian service. This gift of the Spirit for charismatic empowering may be received as an individual experience or as part of a group experience; it may be in the context of prayer time or it may not; it may be administered by the laying on of hands or apart from any human agency; it may be nearly simultaneous with conversion or it may be later; and finally, it may precede water baptism or follow it. Clearly, the contemporary reception of the charismatic empowering of the Spirit will have its own contemporary particularity just as it had historical particularity for the early Christian community.

3. Distinguish Between Principle and Praxis

The need to distinguish between principle and praxis, that is, the practices of the early church which are reported in Acts, is a particular instance of the necessity of recognizing the historical particularity of each episode in Luke's narrative. This is especially important for the question of whether or not early church praxis can be applied to the contemporary church and, if so, how it is to be properly applied.

In Acts, Luke reports many practices, or customs, among the early Christians. This is not surprising because Christianity arose out of Judaism with its legacy of religious customs. As Christianity separated from Judaism and established its own identity, it, nevertheless, retained many of the essential features of the religious praxis of Judaism. Because they knew Jesus to be the once-for-all sacrifice for sins, the disciples dropped the sacrificial dimension of worship. However, they continued to perpetuate practices, or customs such as set hours of prayer, regular assembly for worship, baptism of converts, common meals, etc. These were recognized to be compatible with the expression of their new life in the Messianic age, and like the transformation of the Passover meal into the Lord's supper, were transformed and adapted to the new Christian reality. As reported in Acts, the practices of the early church included: 1) establishing appropriate leadership for the community, 2) water baptism, 3) common meals, 4) regular meetings, 5) laying on of hands, 6) prophecy as enacted parable, and, as some interpreters would add, 7) speaking in tongues.

The practice of the faith in the contemporary church relates to this early church practice in two ways. On the one hand, some practices are to be perpetuated in the contemporary church; that is, they are applicable transculturally and transtemporally. Specifically, these are the Lord's supper and water baptism. They are to be practiced by the contemporary church because they are established by the Lord. The mode, or manner, for the practice of the Lord's supper and water baptism may, however, vary in time and place. Evangelicals concede this *de facto* for the Lord's supper, which they do not celebrate as a common meal. Those in the Anabaptist or Believer's Church tradition are more reluctant to concede this for the mode of water baptism. Clearly, however, the essential thing is the meaning of the praxis rather than the mode.

On the other hand, many early church practices are not commanded by the Lord, and their continued practice in the contemporary church is as much a matter of indifference as is the mode by which they may be practiced. These include such things as set times for prayer, customary times for assembly, the method(s) of establishing leadership, etc. In other words, the contemporary church need not pray at the ninth hour (Acts 3, 1), nor choose its leaders by the drawing of lots (1:26), or establish leadership in units of twelve (1:16-26), or in units of seven (6:3), or hold property in common (2:44, 4:32-37). These are matters of the historical particularity of the early church and the contemporary church is under no Biblical/ hermeneutical compulsion to apply any of this early church praxis to its own situation.

Though the contemporary church is under no obligation to perpetuate these practices, they do, however, contain principles which are obligatory for contemporary Christians. For example, Acts does not obligate Christians to pray at a customary or set time, such as 3:00 p.m., but it teaches the principle that Christians ought to pray regularly. Similarly, though Acts does not obligate Christians to choose its leadership by any one method, such as casting lots, it does teach the principle that the church is to have a properly established leadership/organization. Further, though Acts does not obligate contemporary Christians to practice voluntary communism, it does teach the principle that the church, constituted of its individual members and collectively, is to minister to the needs of its poor and/or disenfranchised members. In conclusion, on the one hand, contemporary Christians are to apply the early church praxis of the Lord's supper and water baptism, though the mode of the practice may be a matter of indifference; on the other hand, for the non-obligatory customs, or practices, which were found in the early church contemporary Christians are to apply the principles inherent within the practice, rather than the practice itself.

Speaking in tongues, as reported by Luke, is sometimes included in the debate concerning the applicability of early church praxis to contemporary Christian experience.[10] It, therefore, requires special comment. To include speaking in tongues within the discussion on praxis is a confusion of categories. Speaking in tongues, as reported by Luke (Acts 2:4, 10:46, 19:6), is not a practice like church government, or even like the Lord's supper or water baptism when considered in terms of their mode. Speaking in tongues is an objective spiritual reality. It is a gift from God and not a human rite. Therefore, it is inappropriate to include it in a discussion about applying practices within the early church to contemporary Christian practice, as some do, often from an implicit or explicit motivation of discrediting Pentecostal theology.

To sum up, the hermeneutical question of the applicability of historical narrative (as in Acts) to contemporary Christian experience and praxis is found to be complex. Thus, that hermeneutical stance which reduces "the revelation of the purpose of God in Scripture . . . [to] its didactic, rather than its historical parts,"[11] or which asserts, "what is

---

[10]Fee, *How to Read the Bible. . .* , 88. He includes the "practice" of the baptism of the Holy Spirit accompanied by the speaking in tongues along with practices such as baptism, the Lord's supper and church polity, etc. Fee appears confused about the definition of "practice." In "Hermeneutics" he writes of "Christian experience or practice (what Christians do)," 126, of "Christian experience and practice," 127, and, "in matters of Christian experience, and even more so of Christian practice," 129. In the first two quotes the terms are synonymous; in the third quote they are properly separated and given their independent identity.

[11]John R. W. Stott, *The Baptism and Fullness of the Holy Spirit* (Downers Grove: Inter-Varsity Press, 1964), 8-9.

merely narrated or described can never function in a normative way,"[12] is seen to be a case of special pleading, and needs to be rejected for the arbitrary principle that it is. When the interpreter, having done his exegesis of the narrative in Acts, addresses the challenge of applying the message of that text to contemporary Christian living, he will be guided by several complementary and interdependent guidelines: 1) apply the lessons of a paradigmatic narrative, 2) apply the principle inherent in a relevant episode, rather than the details of historical particularity, and 3) apply the principle inherent in a particular practice, rather than the practice itself. When applied in the light of these guidelines, the narratives of Acts will spiritually enrich contemporary Christian living. However, where Acts remains shut out of contemporary relevance by a hermeneutic which is either hostile or antipathetic to the contemporary applicability of historical narrative, spiritual impoverishment will remain.

Pentecost: The Origin of the Charismatic Community (Acts 2:1-21)

Our analysis of Luke-Acts shows it to be a carefully crafted bipartite narrative. In the structure of Luke-Acts, the Pentecost narrative launches the public ministry of the disciples just as the inauguration narrative in Luke had earlier launched the public ministry of Jesus (Luke 3-4). In addition, in terms of Luke's narratival strategy the inauguration narrative (Luke 3-4) is programmatic for the ministry of Jesus as a charismatic prophet and, in turn, paradigmatic for the subsequent ministry of the disciples. Similarly, the Pentecost narrative is programmatic for the ministry of the disciples as a community of charismatic prophets[13] and, by extension, paradigmatic for the ministry of subsequent generations of

---

[12] Gordon Fee and Douglas Stuart, *How to Read the Bible for All Its Worth* (Grand Rapids: Zondervan, 1982), 97.

[13] Richard F. Zehnle, *Peter's Pentecost Address: Tradition and Lukan Reinterpretation in Peter's Speeches of Acts 2 and 3*, Society of Biblical Literature Monograph Series, Volume 15, (Nashville: Abingdon Press, 1971). Though his terminology differs from mine his observation is the same. He writes, "It will be maintained that the speech of Acts 2 is the 'Keynote address' of Acts, a summary statement of the theological viewpoint of the author from which the subsequent unfolding of the book is to be understood," 17. Further, "The outpouring of the Spirit signifies their prophetic consecration, just as the baptism of Jesus signified prophetic consecration for him," 117.

charismatic prophets. Clearly, in the structure of Acts the Pentecost narrative has pride-of-place and is the key to understanding the message of the entire book. Therefore, failure to understand Luke's narrative structure, and, especially, his narrative strategy, seriously jeopardizes the interpreter's ability to understand Luke's authorial intentionality.

While the Pentecost narrative, therefore, must be understood in the light of its place in the structure and function of Luke-Acts as a whole, it must also be understood in the light of its immediate context (1:1-26). This begins with the twofold promise of the Spirit (1:2-8), which, on the one hand, recapitulates John's earlier promise of Spirit baptism (1:2-5, Luke 3:16), and which, on the other hand, recapitulates Jesus' earlier promise of power (1:6-8, Luke 24:49). In this juxtaposition of the two promises of the Spirit, the second promise of the Spirit defines the first promise; that is, Spirit baptism is an empowering of the Spirit (not initiation). The ascension of Jesus is the next element in the immediate context of the Pentecostal narrative (1:9-11). It shows that the Spirit-baptized, Spirit-empowered witness of the disciples is to be carried out in Jesus' absence. The third element in the immediate context is the description of the community of disciples in unity and in prayer (1:12-14). The completion of the roster of apostles with the election of Matthias to succeed Judas the traitor (1:15-26) is the final element in the context leading up to the pouring forth of the Spirit on the day of Pentecost.

The Pentecost narrative itself (2:1-47) is complex. It consists of three main components: 1) the origin of the charismatic community (2:1-21); 2) Peter's proclamation of Jesus as Lord and Christ (2:22-42); and 3) a concluding summary of the life of the fledgling Christian community (2:43-47). That part of the Pentecost narrative which is the subject of this chapter, namely, the origin of the charismatic community (2:1-21), has three typical components: 1) sign (2:1-4), 2) wonder (2:5-13), and 3) explanation (2:14-21). This threefold structure is also to be found, for example, in the following narrative (3:1-26), where the sign is the healing of the lame man (3:1-8), the wonder is the crowd's amazement (3:9-11), followed by Peter's explanation of the source of the power by which this first example of witness by power, that is, miracle, was done (3:12-26).

Signs: The Disciples are Filled with the Holy Spirit (Acts 2:1-4)

Luke tells the story of Pentecost with simplicity and restraint, but the miracle of Pentecost would prove to be a dramatic, pivotal, life-changing experience for the disciples. On that day three signs—1) the noise like a violent rushing wind (2:2), 2) the tongues as of fire resting on each one (2:3), and 3) the speaking with other tongues (2:4) —give the experience of the disciples more drama even than the ocular and auditory signs which had attested to Jesus' prototypical reception of the Spirit (Luke 3:21-22). The dramatic dimension of these signs is entirely appropriate for the pivotal nature of the gift of the Spirit, for it signifies that the ancient promise of the gift of the Spirit of prophecy (Joel 2:28ff.), and that the more immediate dominical promises of the gift of the Spirit (Luke 11:13, 24:49; Acts 1:5, 8), have been fulfilled and, therefore, their role as heirs and successors to Jesus' ministry has been launched. Further, this pivotal event is also life changing for, from that time forward, the disciples have a relationship with the Spirit which parallels Jesus' fourfold relationship to the Spirit; that is, like Jesus they will be Spirit baptized, Spirit empowered, Spirit filled, and Spirit led (cf. Luke 3:22-4:1, 14, 18).

Acts 2:1. Having set the immediate context with a series of episodes which concludes with his report about the choosing of the twelfth apostle, namely, Matthias, Luke advances the scene to "when the day of Pentecost had come." Pentecost is the Greek name for the Feast of Weeks, which was an agricultural festival celebrated fifty days after the Passover. Like the feast of Passover and Atonement, Pentecost was a day of convocation. Thus, there was a crowd of thousands gathered on the Temple mount in Jerusalem on this day. Since the day of Pentecost had begun the previous evening, and the Holy Spirit is poured out at 9:00 a.m. (2:15), the day is being fulfilled; that is, closer to coming to an end than it was to dawning. Further, since Jesus had taught the disciples for forty days after the resurrection (1:3), itself the third day after the Passover, the disciples had spent seven to eight days in prayer prior to Pentecost.

Luke reports that on this day the disciples "were all together." This description emphasizes the unique unity which existed among the disciples until it was first broken by the complaint of the Hellenistic Jews concerning the distribution of food (6:1, cf. 1:14, 4:32, 5:12). In this unity of heart and soul (4:32) they had gathered together *"in one place."* This was either the Temple where they met to praise God (Luke 24:53) or else it was the upper room where they stayed (Acts 1:13). Along with a fact that they went to the Temple every day (2:46, 5:42), and that a crowd of many thousands gathered (2:6, 41; note: about three thousand of them were saved), it is almost certain that they were together on the Temple mount, perhaps in the vicinity of Solomon's portico (5:12).

Acts 2:2. Though reports of the miraculous pervade Luke's narrative from the angel Gabriel's appearance to Zacharias (Luke 1:8-23), through to Paul's survival of a viper bite on the island of Malta (Acts 28:1-6), he, Luke, is neither credulous nor a miracle monger. He describes the spectacular phenomena of Pentecost with both sobriety and austerity. As he reports the first sign, "suddenly there came from heaven a noise like a violent, rushing wind." The noise, then, came suddenly; that is, it came abruptly as, for example, the earthquake which would later shake the prison at Philippi (Acts 16:26). Not only did it come suddenly, or abruptly, but it also came from heaven. In other words, the noise came from the sky; that is, above. But in addition to this natural meaning, in Jewish usage heaven was a common reverential term, or circumlocution, for God. Thus, the noise which Luke reports came from God, just as earlier at Jesus' baptism, "a voice came out of heaven," that is, from God (Luke 3:22). Moreover, this noise was like the noise of a gale, but it was no more an actual windstorm than the Holy Spirit who descended upon Jesus at his baptism was a dove (Luke 3:22). Luke uses similes drawn from meteorology and ornithology to describe the forceful noise and the descending dove.

This abrupt, divine, forceful noise, Luke continues, "filled the whole house where they were sitting." In describing the place where the disciples had gathered (2:2) by the term house, Luke uses a typical Hebraic idiom to describe the Temple as the house of God (cf. Luke 19:46 [Isa. 56:7]; Acts 7:47, 49 [Isa. 66:1]). In other words, the whole Temple mount, thronged as it was with worshippers, both residents of Jerusalem and pilgrims, was filled with this noise from God.

Acts 2:3. Spectacular phenomenon follows spectacular phenomenon in Luke's report. Just as at Jesus' baptism the ocular sign is accompanied by the auditory sign, so in his report of the phenomena of

Pentecost the auditory sign is followed by an ocular sign, for "there appeared to them tongues as of fire distributing themselves." Though Luke's narrative will soon focus upon what the crowd witnesses (2:5-13), at this point he focuses upon what the disciples saw. Specifically, they saw tongues as of, or comparable to, fire. These tongues were distributed, "and they rested on each one of them." The tongues rested, or sat, upon each one in much the same way, for example, that Jesus sat down in the synagogue at Capernaum after reading the prophet Isaiah (Luke 4:20), or as Paul and Barnabas sat down after entering the synagogue at Antioch in Pisidia (Acts 13:14).

Acts 2:4. In describing the spectacular phenomena of Pentecost with metaphors of wind and fire, Luke has used typical language of theophany (for example 1 Kings 19:11-12). These theophanic phenomena are, in fact, the auditory and ocular symbols which announce the invisible presence of the Holy Spirit for "they were filled with the Holy Spirit." As early as the era of the Exodus, Bezalel and other servants of God had been filled with the Spirit of God in wisdom, understanding, knowledge and craftsmanship (Ex. 28:3, 31:3, etc.). This is the fourth time in his narrative to this point that Luke has used the Old Testament (LXX) term (cf. Luke 1:15, 41, 67). Its meaning here is determined by Luke's earlier use of the term. Earlier it described either a prophet (Luke 1:15), or introduced prophetic speech (Luke 1:41, 67), which we may, therefore, classify as a pneuma discourse. Subsequent usage of this term by Luke in Acts repeats this dual emphasis on prophetic ministry/prophetic speech (cf. Acts 4:8, 31; 9:17, 31).[14] In keeping with his invariable usage, Luke's use of the term

---

[14] Roger Stronstad, "'Filled with the Holy Spirit' Terminology in Luke-Acts," in *The Holy Spirit in the Scriptures and the Church: Essays Presented to Leslie Thomas Holdcraft on his Sixty-Fifth Birthday*, edited by Roger Stronstad and Laurence M. Van Kleek (Clayburn, B.C.: Western Pentecostal Bible College, 1977), 1-13. Because he is guilty of "illegitimate identity transfer" that is, defines what it means to be Spirit-filled by Pauline perspectives, Gordon D. Fee completely misses the prophetic significance of the term in Luke-Acts. In "Baptism in the Holy Spirit: The Issue of Separability and Subsequence," *Pneuma* 7.2 (1985) he writes: "... nowhere does the New Testament say, 'Get saved, and then be filled with the Spirit.' To them, getting saved... meant especially to be filled with the Spirit," 94. Actual exegesis of the nine Lukan passages (Luke 1:15, 41, 67; Acts 2:4, 4:8, etc.) shows that the term is related to prophecy and not to salvation. Of course, for Fee, Luke's pneumatology is to be pressed into the Pauline mold. Thus, concerning the experience of the Samaritans he writes,: "Although Luke *says* otherwise, we may assume the Samaritans and Paul to have become believers in the Pauline sense-- that without the Spirit they are none of his," 90. He concludes his discussion of the Samaritan case, writing, "In thus arguing, as a New Testament scholar, against some

to describe the disciples on the day of Pentecost describes inspired speech. Therefore, in the same way that a Bezalel or a Joshua of Old Testament times was filled with the Spirit and endowed with gifts appropriate for his task, and in the same way that John the Baptist was filled with the Spirit for his prophetic witness about the coming Messiah, so on the day of Pentecost the disciples who are to be witnesses (Luke 24:49, Acts 1:8) are endowed with a gift which is symbolic for their task; namely, "they began to speak with other tongues as the Spirit was giving them utterance." In other words, as the sign that they have received the power of the Spirit to witness "to the remotest part of the earth" (Acts 1:8), the disciples, filled with the Spirit, speak in the tongues or languages of the world (2:9-11), speak in languages other than their native language(s), speak in languages hitherto unlearned but now momentarily mediated to them by the Holy Spirit.

Observations

1. In Acts 2:2-3 Luke has described a dramatic theophany on the Temple mount, indeed, on the Mountain of God (2 Chron. 3:1, Micah 4:2). The first two manifestations of God's presence (the metaphorical wind and fire) are reminiscent of earlier theophanies at that other mountain of God; namely, Horeb/Sinai (Ex. 3:1, 19:16ff.; I Kings 19:11-13).
2. The metaphorical wind and fire (Acts 2:2-3), which accompany the outpouring of the Holy Spirit (2:4), are uniquely appropriate tokens of God's presence for several reasons: 1) As in Elijah's experience at the mountain of God they do symbolize a divine encounter or visitation from God; 2) these phenomena demonstrate objectively that the disciples' reception of the Spirit fulfills John's prophecy that the Messiah would baptize with the Holy Spirit and fire (Luke 3:16, Acts 1:5). In terms of this promise/fulfillment motif it is possible that for Luke the wind *(pnoes)* of Pentecost is cognate to the Spirit *(pneuma)* of John's promise, for *pneuma*, itself, often carries the meaning of wind; and 3) not only is wind an appropriate symbol for

---

Pentecostal interpretations. . . ," 91. It seems to be self-evident from what Fee writes that he believes that as a New Testament scholar it is legitimate for him to use Pauline perspectives to deny what Luke *says*.

a theophany, but fire is as well, on the one hand, symbolizing the divine presence (Ex. 3:6, 13:21, etc.), and, on the other hand, specifically symbolizing the Spirit of God, as for example, the Spirit of burning (Isa. 4:4).

3. Since Luke is likely aware of the rabbinic tradition that in the present, God only speaks to his people by the *bat kol,* the echo of his voice (Tos Sot 13:2), he may be portraying the two auditory phenomena of Pentecost: that is, the noise from heaven and the speaking in other tongues as the Christian equivalent of these two earlier modes of communication, the Old Testament and the Intertestamental, respectively. If this is so (and it is purely speculative) then the noise from heaven is equivalent to the *bat kol* of intertestamental Judaism, and the speaking in other tongues represents the renewal of the gift of prophecy among God's people.

4. The dual description, "filled with the Holy Spirit," and "began to speak with other tongues as the Spirit was giving them utterance," define one purpose of this dramatic theophany. It is to bestow the gift of prophecy to the disciples as heirs and successors to Jesus' ministry. In this context, there are a variety of typological correspondences. For example, the transfer of the Spirit from Jesus, who was the unique and absolute bearer of the Spirit during the years of his public ministry, to the disciples, attested by this outburst of prophecy, echoes the earlier transfer of the Spirit from Moses to the seventy elders, who also prophesy when the Spirit comes upon them (Num. 11:25-29). Further, it constitutes the disciples as a company of charismatic prophets, perhaps standing in relationship to Jesus as the Sons of the Prophets to an Elijah or an Elisha.

5. Finally, by his description, Luke intends to show that the baptism in the Holy Spirit which the disciples experienced on the day of Pentecost is functionally equivalent to the anointing of the Spirit which Jesus experienced at the Jordan (Luke 3:22, 4:18). Luke demonstrates this functional equivalency in a variety of ways: 1) in both cases the gift of the Holy Spirit is an empowering which launches or inaugurates their respective ministries (Luke 4:14, Acts 1:8); 2) in both cases the Spirit is given in the setting of prayer (Luke 3:21, Acts 1:13); 3) in both cases there are auditory and ocular signs;

and 4) in both cases these signs have their origin in heaven, that is, in God Himself.

Wonder: The People are Amazed by What They See and Hear
(Acts 2:5-13)

The outpouring of the Holy Spirit upon the disciples was not some hidden or private experience. It was public by divine design, and was witnessed by a large crowd of devout worshippers who had gathered on the Temple mount. In the unfolding structure of the Pentecost narrative, Luke's report of the response of the crowd to what they see and hear (2:5-13) complements his description of the signs (2:2-4). Thus, as the narrative advances, the focus shifts from the actual experience of the disciples to the observation and reaction of the crowd.

Luke describes the complex reaction of the crowd to the dramatic, totally unexpected phenomena of Pentecost by four terms: 1) to be bewildered (2:6), 2) to be amazed (2:7, 12), 3) to marvel (2:7), and 4) to be greatly perplexed (2:12). In the literature of the New Testament two terms, "to be bewildered" and "to be greatly perplexed," are exclusively Lucan. Of the other two terms, Luke uses "to be amazed" 11/17 New Testament occurrences and "to marvel" 18/42 New Testament occurrences. Among its range of meaning, "to be amazed" is a characteristic response of people to the miraculous, both in the Gospel (8:56) and in the Acts (8:13) and, where reported, also the invariable response to speaking in other tongues (2:7, 12; 10:45). Similarly, while "to marvel" is more characteristic as a response to the spoken word (Luke 2:18, 33; 4:22, etc.), like the term "to be amazed," it is also a typical response to the miraculous, both in the Gospel (9:43, 11:14), and in the Acts (3:12, 7:31). Luke uses this clustering of terms to describe the response of the crowd to the signs of Pentecost to alert his readers to the wonder and confusion which this theophany evoked among those who witnessed it.

Acts 2:5. Luke began his narrative by focusing upon the disciples, who had all gathered on the Temple mount for worship. Having just described their reception of the Holy Spirit as a theophany (2:2-4), he now shifts the focus of his narrative to the other devout Jews who were similarly gathered on the Temple mount that morning. There were "living in Jerusalem," Luke informs his readers, "devout men, from every nation under heaven." In other words, in addition to devout pilgrims who may have come up to Jerusalem from the countries of the Diaspora to celebrate Pentecost, there were living within Jerusalem Jews whose native homeland was from wherever Jews had been scattered by the march of Empires. Luke will catalogue these nations of the Diaspora in verses 9-11. In describing these Diaspora Jews as "devout men" Luke implies that their motivation for resettling in Jerusalem was religious. Joseph of Cyprus (4:36) and Saul of Tarsus (7:58) would be typical of these devout Jews who had moved to Jerusalem from the countries of the Diaspora. In stipulating that there were Jews from every nation under heaven who had gathered on the Temple mount, Luke implies that the whole world, in the persons of its representatives, witnessed this theophany.

Acts 2:6. Like the disciples, these devout Jews had come up to the Temple to worship, but suddenly their attention was arrested by the dramatic signs of the theophany. "When this sound occurred," Luke reports, "the multitude came together." Initially, "this sound" would have been the noise from heaven (2:2), but soon the "speaking with other tongues" by the disciples (2:4) would have superceded the noise from heaven in the attention of the crowd. The crowd, itself, is a multitude of indefinite size, but since 1) it is the Pentecost festival, and 2) about 3,000 were saved, it is likely to have numbered in the tens of thousands. As the crowd listened to this auditory miracle "they were bewildered," a not untypical response to the presence of the Gospel among the Jews and Gentiles (cf. 9:22; 19:32; 21:27, 31). They were bewildered "because," as Luke tells his readers, "they were each one hearing them speak in his own language." Thus, the "other tongues" which were spoken by the disciples are the foreign languages of the nations of the Diaspora (2:5, 9:11). As Galileans, the disciples would have spoken Aramaic as their native language. Aramaic was also widely spoken throughout the ancient near east but, by using the term "other" *(heterais)* to describe the languages spoken by the disciples, and by describing the bewilderment of these former residents of the Diaspora, Luke makes it absolutely clear that the multitude was not hearing the disciples speak in Aramaic, but in the languages native to their widely scattered homelands.

Acts 2:7. Not only were these devout Jews bewildered, but "they were amazed and marveled." Luke uses these two terms—to be amazed and to marvel—to describe the reaction of people to miracles in a variety of contexts, but only here does he use the two terms together. In this way he signifies that the signs of Pentecost are a greater wonder than any of the other miracles which he reports. The multitude was amazed and marveled, not because they simply heard a group of Jews speaking in the languages native to their homeland (that could be heard whenever devout pilgrims gathered at the Temple) but, as they were saying, "Why, are not all these who are speaking Galileans?" Thus, they were amazed because they recognized (both by dress and accent?) that the disciples, who were Galileans, and not men from every nation under heaven (2:5), as they themselves were, were speaking in the languages of their homelands.

Acts 2:8. Marveling that those who were speaking were Galileans, they also ask among themselves, "And how is it that we each hear them in our own language to which we were born?" Though the multitude still awaits Peter's answer to their question, namely, that God has poured forth the Spirit of prophecy (2:16ff.), Luke's readers already know the answer; namely, that the disciples were speaking these foreign languages "as the Spirit was giving them utterance."

Acts 2:9-11. The multitude, made up as it was "from every nation under heaven," included Jews born "Parthians and Medes and Elamites, and residents of Mesopotamia, Judea and Cappadocia, Pontus and Asia, Phrygia and Pamphylia, Egypt and the districts of Libya around Cyrene, and visitors from Rome, both Jews and proselytes, Cretans and Arabs." There are a variety of learned and ingenious explanations for the shape of this catalogue of nations including the theory that Luke is reflecting an astrological catalogue.[15] The inherent explanation, signified by the questions of verses 7 and 8, is that the multitude is in dialogue and they are comparing notes about their ancestry. Therefore, the catalogue of nations represents their actual origins, and is not a literary invention.

---

[15]For a thorough, judicious discussion of this thesis see Bruce M. Metzger, "Ancient Astrological Geography and Acts 2:9-11," in *Apostolic History and the Gospel: Biblical and Historical Essays presented to F. F. Bruce on his 60th Birthday,* edited by W. Ward Gasque and Ralph P. Martin (Grand Rapids: Wm. B. Eerdmans Publishing Company, 1970), 123-33.

Since 3,000 from among the multitude were saved, the disciples themselves, would have quickly discovered the cosmopolitan origins of their converts. In terms of the order of the catalogue the movement is generally from east to west, and from lands of the earliest scattering of Jews (Mesopotamia and Persia) to lands of the most recent scattering (Rome).

For the first time in his narrative, Luke identifies the content of what the disciples, inspired by the Spirit, were speaking in these foreign languages which they had never learned. He puts this identification on the lips of the multitude, who say, "we hear them in our own tongues speaking of the mighty deeds of God." Luke is tantalizingly ambiguous here. He does not tell us whether they were praising God for his mighty deeds or declaring his wonders to the nations. Perhaps Luke is deliberately ambiguous, for the inspiration of the Spirit may have resulted in both worship and proclamation. Luke's use of the identical term to describe the household of Cornelius speaking in tongues and "exalting God" (10:46), however, predisposes his readers to understand the content here to be worship rather than proclamation.

Acts 2:12. Though it takes but moments to read, the scene which Luke describes must have been lengthy; for, he writes, "they continued in amazement (cf. 2:7) and great perplexity." In the literature of the New Testament, Luke alone uses the term "to be perplexed." Earlier it had described Herod's state of mind, for example, upon hearing reports about the ministry of Jesus and the disciples (Luke 9:7; cf. Acts 5:24, 10:17). Clearly, the miracle of the Galileans speaking in the languages of the countries of the Diaspora defied any ordinary explanation, and they "continued . . . saying to one another, 'What does this mean?'" Their continued perplexity should caution interpreters against the too ready identification of Pentecost as a second Sinai, against the background of the intertestamental tradition that the nations heard the Law in their own languages; for, though there are echoes of the Sinai theophany at Pentecost, these devout Jews, themselves, did not make that explanation, though, if it is as early as New Testament times, it was available to them in their own tradition.

Acts 2:13. Not all Jews who made up the multitude were perplexed, however. In fact, some thought that they had the answer to the question. They *"were mocking and saying, 'They are full of sweet wine.'"* Not for them the confusion, amazement, marveling, and perplexity of their brethren, but rather mockery. And so, just as the work of God in Jesus had been mocked less than two months earlier (Luke 23:35-36), so now, also, the work of God, specifically, the inspiration of the Spirit was exposed to mockery. These mockers explain that the disciples, perhaps as one would expect of Galileans, are drunk.

Observations

The dramatic auditory and ocular signs of Pentecost (Acts 2:2-4) find their functional fulfillment in the complementary wonder of the crowd of devout worshippers (Acts 2:5-13). Just as the signs themselves are among the most dramatic reported in Luke-Acts and, indeed, in the New Testament, so, appropriately, the crowd's response of wonder is unequalled by any other response in Luke-Acts. Nowhere else in his two-volume narrative does Luke pile up such a concentration of terms to describe the response of the crowd. Thus, according to the narrative, no other event in the unfolding history of salvation in New Testament times, in a rich roster of many marvels, had such a dramatic impact as the theophanic pouring forth of the Spirit on the day of Pentecost.

This initial response of wonder to the theophanic visitation on the Temple Mount is programmatic for the subsequent gift of the Holy Spirit to Cornelius and his household (Acts 10:45), and also to the ongoing response to the signs and wonders which were performed by the disciples. The signs and wonders (Acts 2:42; 4:30; 5:12; 6:8; 8:6, 13, etc.) are after the pattern of Jesus' charismatic ministry (Acts 2:22). Therefore, just as his charismatic ministry characteristically evoked amazement (Luke 4:32, 36; 5:9, etc.) and astonishment (Luke 5:26), so the signs and wonders of the subsequent charismatic ministry of the disciples similarly evokes amazement (Acts 3:9, 11; 8:13, etc.).

Not only does Luke report the signs of Pentecost and their complementary response, but he also describes the first of two patterns in Acts for the advance of the Gospel. In Acts the spread of the Gospel has two movements: 1) centripetal, where representative peoples are drawn to Jerusalem as a center, and 2) centrifugal, where disciples fan out from Jerusalem.[16] As reported in the Pentecost narrative, the first movement is centripetal; that is, "devout men from every nation under heaven" (Acts 2:5) have gathered on the Temple Mount, the mountain of God. Here they also hear the disciples witness about Jesus (Acts 2:22ff.), who is Lord and Christ (Acts 2:36). They are pierced to the heart (Acts 2:37) and are saved (Acts 2:40) by the thousands (Acts 2:41). This centripetal gathering of the nations to Jerusalem (Acts 2:9-11), represented by devout Jews, is the initial fulfillment of a common prophetic picture about the last days. For example, as Isaiah declares:

> In the last days,
> The mountain of the house of the LORD
> Will be established as the chief of the mountains,
> And will be raised above the hills;
> And all the nations will stream to it.
> (Isa. 2:2)

This theme of the centripetal gathering of the nations in the last days to Jerusalem pervades the prophets, especially Isaiah (cf. 27:13, 56:7, 66:20; cf. Micah 4:1-3, etc.). Following this initial picture of centripetal missions to the nations in Jerusalem (Acts 2), a centrifugal pattern of missions develops, in which the disciples are thrust out of Jerusalem to bear witness about Jesus in Judea and Samaria and to the ends of the earth (Acts 1:8, cf. Isa. 49:6). This centrifugal action begins with the scattering of the disciples throughout the regions of Judea and Samaria following the martyrdom of Stephen (8:1) and concludes with Paul's witness in Rome for a period of two years (28:30-31).

Explanation: The Three Signs Fulfill Joel's Prophecy (Acts 2:14-21)

Neither in its immediate setting on the day of Pentecost, nor in its overall setting in the text of Acts, could the outpouring of the Spirit

---

[16]For this observation I am indebted to David W. Wead, "The Centripetal Philosophy of Mission," in *Scripture Tradition, and Interpretation: Essays Presented to Everett F. Harrison by his Students and Colleagues in Honor of His Seventy-Fifth Birthday,* edited by W. Ward Gasque and William Sanford LaSor (Grand Rapids: William B. Eerdmans Publishing Company, 1978), 176-86.

remain experienced and observed but unexplained. Apart from Peter's explanation, the Temple crowd would have remained bewildered (2:6), marvelling (2:7), amazed (2:7, 12), and perplexed (2:12), on the one hand, or mocking (2:13), on the other hand. Further, apart from Peter's explanation, the disciples themselves would not have understood their experience beyond the specific limits established by Jesus' promises of the Spirit (Luke 11:13, 24:49; Acts 1:5, 8).

Peter explains the pouring forth of the Spirit, which the disciples have just experienced, by appealing to an ancient oracle of the prophet Joel, of which he gives a pesher, or "this is that," interpretation. To Joel's ancient promise of the pouring forth of the Spirit, Peter, inspired by the Spirit (the verb *apophthengomai* is used in both Acts 2:4 and 2:14), makes three significant changes. First, he contemporizes the text replacing Joel's indefinite temporal reference, "after these things," with the definite reference, "in the last days" (2:17a). Second, he adds the phrase, "And they shall prophesy" (2:18b). Third, he inserts the word "signs" (2:19b) into the statement about the appearance of wonders in the sky above and on the earth beneath. In itself Joel's text adequately explains the meaning of the Pentecost theophany. Peter's three additions, however, both reinforce what Joel announces, and make the general announcement of the text much more precise. Indeed, when taken on its own terms, and in spite of the diverse and sometimes contradictory interpretations of the text in the contemporary church, Peter's explanation of Pentecost with special reference to Joel is capable of only one meaning.

Peter's explanation of the Pentecost theophany is, itself, only the first part of a two-part proclamation, the second part of which is a witness to the Temple crowd about Jesus of Nazareth (2:22-36). Though it appears as one unbroken speech in Luke's narrative, the distinct change of subject matter from explanation to witness, and from the Holy Spirit to Christ implies that these two parts are Luke's summaries of the opening and closing parts of a lengthy dialogue, with the bewildered and perplexed crowd on the one side and Peter and the disciples on the other side.

Peter's identification of the Pentecost phenomena as the pouring forth of the Spirit in the last days would have led to a dialogue along the following lines: "The last days only come with the appearance of the Messiah," someone would protest. "How is it that you are saying that they come with the Spirit? In fact, the Spirit isn't given apart from the Messiah."

"Men of Israel," Peter would respond, "how right you are. The gift of the Spirit today, which you have witnessed, proves that the Messiah has already come. Indeed, 'Jesus the Nazarene [is] a man attested to you by God [as Messiah] with miracles and wonders and signs which God performed through him in your midst'" (2:22).

Luke is silent about the kind of dialogue which necessarily underlies the transition in Peter's address from his explanation of the pouring forth of the Spirit to his witness about Jesus as Lord and Christ. As the carefully crafted narrative, which Luke-Acts is, the Pentecost narrative has close thematic and structural parallels with the inauguration narrative of the Gospel. In this comparison, Peter's explanation of the pouring forth of the Spirit with a pesher interpretation of an oracle from the prophet Joel parallels Jesus' earlier explanation of his reception of the Spirit with a pesher interpretation of an oracle from the prophet Isaiah (Isa. 61:1, Luke 4:18ff.).

Acts 2:14. As he had done many times before (Luke 9:20, Acts 1:15), Peter takes the initiative as the spokesman for the disciples. "Taking his stand with the eleven" he seizes the opportunity afforded to him by the charge of drunkenness, not only to rebut the charge (2:13), but also to witness about Jesus (2:22ff.). Because of the commotion and divided attention within this crowd of several thousands "he raised his voice" to be heard above the din. In reporting that with raised voice Peter "declared to them (*apopthengomai*)," Luke uses the same verb as when he had earlier reported that the tongues-speaking resulted when the Spirit "was giving them utterance (*apopthengomai*)." By this choice of verb in both texts in the same context, Luke compels his readers to understand Peter's speech to be also inspired by the Spirit, that is, to be a prophetic utterance. The crowd which had gathered together because of the signs and wonders which they had witnessed included "men of Judea, and all of you who live in Jerusalem" (cf. 2:5). Responding to the charge of drunkenness, Peter solemnly exhorts the crowd, "let this be known to you, and give heed to my words."

Acts 2:15. Rebutting the mocking charge of drunkenness, Peter affirms about the Eleven, "for these men are not drunk, as you suppose." As proof of their sobriety he reminds the crowd, "for it is only the third hour of the day," that is, nine in the morning. It is impossible for any reader of Luke's narrative to know Peter's tone of voice with certainty. On the one hand, he may simply have made a simple statement about the early hour of the day. On the other hand, he may have spoken with sarcasm, to the effect that even Galileans (2:7) don't get drunk as early as nine in the morning.

Acts 2:16. No, the disciples were not drunk, *but* continues Peter with a strong adversative, "this is what was spoken of through the prophet Joel." The devout Jews who made up his audience would have been familiar with four types of interpretation among their contemporary Jews: 1) literal, 2) midrash, 3) pesher, and 4) allegory.[17] At times all Jews would have interpreted the Scriptures in a literal way. In addition, the Jews of Alexandria interpreted the Scriptures allegorically; the Pharisees, who were the largest and most influential sect within contemporary Judaism, practiced mid rash interpretation, which moved from text to life setting; and the Essenes, the second largest sect within Judaism (with many of their members living at Qumran to the east of Jerusalem overlooking the northern shore of the Dead Sea), practiced pesher interpretation, which moved from life setting back to the text. In appealing to the text in Joel, Peter adopts the pesher principle known to us from the Biblical commentaries from Qumran; that is, this (life setting, namely, the gift of the Spirit) is that text (from Joel which announces an outburst of prophecy).

Acts 2:17. Through the prophet Joel, God had announced a future pouring forth of his Spirit, but as Peter himself, inspired by the Spirit (see 2:14 for comment on verb apopthengomai), declares the pouring forth "after these things" is *"in the last days."* Peter's language reflects the current Jewish historiography, which divided history in two ages: this age/age to come, or the former days/latter days. This age is the present; the age to come, or the latter days, is the age of the Messiah and his Spirit. Therefore, in contemporizing the message of Joel, Peter is affirming to the Temple crowd that the signs and wonders which they have just witnessed proves that the age of the Messiah, the last days, has already been inaugurated.

---

[17]See Richard N. Longenecker, *Biblical Exegesis in the Apostolic Period* (Grand Rapids: William B. Eerdmans Publishing Company, 1975), 28ff.

In the last days, God had promised, "I will pour forth of my Spirit on all mankind." In language which is reminiscent of the promise of the pouring down of the early and latter rains (Joel 2:23), Joel spoke of the "pouring forth of the Spirit." In other words, in contrast to the isolated and exclusive operation of the Spirit upon Israel's leaders in the former days, in the last days the Spirit would be poured forth as a deluge on "all mankind," literally, all flesh. This is the promise of a universal gift of the Spirit upon the nation of Israel, but as Peter made it clear later that day, it is upon all who repent (2:38). From the larger context of Acts, it is clear that the Gentiles are included in this promise (Acts 10, 19). When God pours forth his Spirit in the last days, Joel continued, "your sons and daughters shall prophesy." In other words, the text of Joel identifies the "speaking in other tongues as the Spirit was giving them utterance," which happened when the disciples were filled with the Spirit (2:4), to be the gift of prophecy. This universal gift of prophecy includes both sons and daughters; in addition, it was promised "your young men shall see visions, and your old men shall dream dreams." As God had announced as early as the time of Moses, both visions and dreams are the medium of prophecy (Num. 12:6). In this statement to Moses about how God reveals Himself to prophets, the terms "vision" and "dream" are in synonymous parallelism and, therefore, the terms identify one medium of revelation, rather than two. Because vision and dream are the medium of revelation, the earliest name for prophet was "seer" (I Sam. 9:9). Many of the prophets, including Isaiah (Isa. 1:1), Ezekiel (Ezek. 1:1), and Amos (Amos 1:1), reported a visionary state.

Acts 2:18. In the last days, God declares, he will pour forth his Spirit of prophecy, "even upon my bondslaves, both men and women." Though this promise through the prophet Joel is directly applicable to the experience of the disciples on the day of Pentecost, its fulfillment was anticipated one generation earlier. At that time when John and Jesus were born, prophecy was restored in Israel among bondslaves such as Simeon (Luke 2:29) and Mary (Luke 1:36-38); sons, such as John the Baptist (Luke 1:15); and the aging Zachariah (Luke 1:67), Elizabeth (Luke 1:41), and Anna (Luke 2:36). Thus, the last days, in contrast to Israel's earlier experience when only select leaders were endowed with the Spirit, are characterized by a universal pouring forth of the Spirit of prophecy which crosses all age, gender, and economic barriers. In other words, beginning with the infancy narrative (Luke 1:5-2:52) and given fresh impetus on the day of Pentecost, young men and women, old men and women, the free man and the bondslave had the Spirit poured forth upon them to create a community of charismatic prophets. Peter's addition of the phrase, "and they shall prophesy," to Joel's announcement forces Luke's subsequent audience to understand both the formula, ". . . filled with the Holy Spirit," and the report "[they] began to speak with other tongues" (2:4) to describe prophecy.

Acts 2:19. God's announcement through Joel about the pouring forth of the Holy Spirit continued, "And I will grant wonders in the sky above," literally, in the heaven *en to(i) ourano(i))*. In the context of the Pentecostal narrative, the wonder in the sky above/heaven can be nothing more nor less than the noise like a violent, rushing wind which suddenly came from heaven *(ek tou ouranou)* (2:2). In announcing the wonders in the sky above/heaven, Joel's text contains one-half of the common formula: "wonders and signs" (cf. 2:22, 43 et al.). As he quoted Joel's prophecy, Peter inserted the other half of the formula into the text, contemporizing it to the reality of Pentecost. Thus, in addition to wonders in the heaven, God would also grant "signs on the earth beneath" when he poured forth his Spirit. In the context of Pentecost, the signs on the earth beneath are both: 1) the tongues of fire (2:3), and 2) the other tongues which the disciples spoke (2:4). The amazing appropriateness of Joel's prophecy to explain the phenomena of Pentecost extends even to the qualifying phrase, "blood, and fire, and vapor of smoke." Joel's language is conventional apocalyptic terminology, but all three terms, not just the term "fire" fittingly describes the blood red, smoking tongues of fire which divided and rested upon each of the disciples.

Acts 2:20. The apocalyptic language continues with the description, "the sun shall be turned into darkness and the moon into blood." This language further describes the theophanic fire, specifically the vapor of smoke, which appeared on the Temple mount and which not only darkened the light of day, but which also caused the moon to appear blood red. There is no justification for wresting this apocalyptic language out of context and applying it either to the events surrounding Jesus' crucifixion, or to the end of the age.[18] Neither Peter nor Luke gave us this option. These apocalyptic wonders and signs have appeared "before the great and glorious day of the Lord shall come." The "day of the Lord" is a common formula in the Old Testament which describes the day of divine visitation, for the purpose of either cursing or blessing. In the Hebrew text of Joel, this day of the Lord is a day of judgement, for it is awesome or fearful. In the Septuagint translation, however, it is a day of blessing, for it is a glorious day rather than a fearful day. In the context of Peter's Pentecost application, it is a day of divine blessing; specifically, a day of forgiveness and the gift of the Holy Spirit (2:38). Therefore, it is a great and glorious day.

Acts 2:21. This day of the Lord is a great and glorious day for, ". . . it shall be, that everyone who calls on the name of the Lord shall be saved." What Joel announced is initially fulfilled later that day, when in response to Peter's twofold command: 1) "Repent" (2:38), and 2) "Be saved from this perverse generation" (2:40) ". . . there were added about three thousand souls" (2:41), assuredly a great and glorious divine visitation for blessing.

Observations

To an amazing degree Joel's text, which Peter quotes in response to the perplexity and mockery of the people (2:12-13), is an exact description of the pouring forth of God's Spirit upon the disciples on the day of Pentecost.[19] From first to last the text from Joel is fully and

---

[18]Walter C. Kaiser, Jr., "The Promise of God and the Outpouring of the Holy Spirit: Joel 2:28-32 and Acts 2:16-21," in *The Living and Active Word of God: Essays in Honor of Samuel J. Schultz*, edited by Morris Inch and Ronald Youngblood (Winona Lake: Eisenbrauns, 1983), 109-22. While correctly rejecting attempts to show that the wonders announced by Joel were fulfilled in Jesus' first advent (i.e., his crucifixion) Kaiser wrongly relegates them to Jesus' second advent (121). In fact, Luke's description of the phenomena of Pentecost (Acts 2:1-4), and Peter's appeal to Joel to explain the same (2:17-21), makes it clear that the wonders which Joel announced were fulfilled on the day of Pentecost, and not at either Christ's first or second advents.

[19]Contra Richard D. Israel, "Joel 2:28-32 (3:1-5 Mf): Prism of Pentecost," in *Charismatic Experiences in History*, edited by Cecil M. Robeck, Jr. (Peabody: Hendrickson Publishers, Inc., 1985), 2-14. He writes, "One must say that the text of the Joel passage does not really accord well with the phenomena described in Acts 2:1-4. The only real point of contact is the reception of the Spirit, though even at this point, the word 'filled with the Spirit' does not really tally with the effusion referred to by the Hebrew word for 'pouring out.' Note also that the accompanying phenomena of wind, tongues of

precisely fulfilled in the experience of the disciples. Specifically, according to Joel's prophecy, the pouring forth of the Spirit is: 1) prophetic, 2) universal, and 3) attested by wonders. In other words, just as Luke's formula, "filled with the Holy Spirit," and his complementary report of inspired speech (2:4) means that this theophany on the mountain of the Lord culminates in an outburst of prophecy, so Joel's text announces an outburst of prophecy (2:17). Further, just as Luke reports that on the day of Pentecost the disciples become a community of prophets (the antecedent of "they" [2:1] is the gathering of about 120 persons, which includes both men and women, some younger, such as Jesus' brothers, and some older, such as Jesus' mother [1:14]), so Joel's text announces a community of prophets, sons and daughters, young and old men, and bondslaves, both men and women (2:17-18b). Finally, just as Luke reports that wonders, such as the noise like a violent, rushing wind, came suddenly from heaven (2:3), so Joel's text announces that the pouring forth of the Spirit would be attested by wonders in the heaven (2:19).

In addition to these exact descriptions of the theophany of Pentecost which are to be found in the text of Joel, Peter's quotation of the text contains three major alterations and/or additions which emphasize the applicability of the text to their experience and reinforce the meaning of the theophany. On the one hand, Peter transforms the indefinite time indicated in Joel's text to the more definite time, the last days (2:17). Thus, in Peter's perspective the pouring forth of the Spirit is an eschatological reality. Further, to Joel's statement that your sons and daughters, young men and old, and male and female bondslaves shall prophesy (2:17-18b), Peter adds the statement, "And they shall prophesy" (2:18c). Thus, in Peter's perspective this eschatological pouring forth of the Spirit results in the universal gift of prophecy. Finally, the theophanic phenomena of Pentecost not only include wonders in the heaven but, according to Peter's last adaptation of Joel's

---

fire, and speaking in tongues are not explained by the quotation of the Joel passage," and further, "...of this disparity between the events of Joel 3:1-5" (11). The above exposition of 2:17-21 is the answer to Israel's failure to observe the many, comprehensive and detailed points of contact between Acts 2:1-4 and Joel 2:28-32. Further, the points of contact between the two texts are far closer than between any other Old Testament prophecy of the giving of the Spirit and Luke's description of the phenomena described in Acts 2:1-4.

text, "signs" on the earth beneath, specifically the tongues of fire and the speaking with other tongues (2:3-4). Thus, in Peter's perspective, speaking with other tongues, which Joel identifies as a form of prophecy, is a divinely ordained sign. Luke, himself, reports this sign on two subsequent occasions: 1) the gift of the Holy Spirit to the household of Cornelius (10:44-48), where its sign function is explicit, and 2) the gift of the Holy Spirit to about twelve disciples at Ephesus (19:1-7), where, as in Acts two, it is explicitly identified as prophecy.

One important implication of Peter's peshering of Joel 2:28-32 to explain the pouring forth of the Holy Spirit upon the disciples on the day of Pentecost is that the Pentecostal's "evidential" pneumatology is a truer reflection of Luke's "signs and wonders" pneumatology than that of their critics and opponents. But this is a subject which must be discussed on another occasion.

CHAPTER SIX

THE HOLY SPIRIT IN LUKE-ACTS

Whether we are considering either hermeneutics or theology, this series of essays is about the Holy Spirit in Pentecostalism and in Luke-Acts. In studying the subject of the Holy Spirit in isolation from its full and proper context, we are, of course, susceptible to the danger of falsifying the subject by a distortion of proportion. That is, though our focus is on the Holy Spirit, the Holy Spirit is not Luke's primary focus (though I would insist that it is far more important for Luke than most scholars allow). To guard against this inherent danger of a distortion of proportion, therefore, I will begin by relating the subject of the Holy Spirit to Luke's primary subject, which is, obviously, Christology. In comparison to the other Gospels, and more so in comparison to Matthew and Mark than to John, Luke's Christology is radically distinctive. It is a Christology, for example, which reflects the resurrection-ascension-exaltation perspective of Acts. It is, moreover, a Christology which is complemented by a pervasive pneumatology. Thus, in a way that Matthew and Mark ignore, Luke portrays Jesus as a man of the Spirit, a charismatic leader who is anointed, led, and empowered by the Holy Spirit. For Luke, in a way which is unique in the New Testament, Jesus is the charismatic Christ.

It is this Christological context which gives Luke's pneumatology its proper context and proportion. In what follows I will first give a synopsis of Luke's Christology as the foundation for my discussion of Luke's pneumatology. This approach not only safeguards Luke's proportion between Christology and pneumatology, but it will also demonstrate that the portrait which Luke paints of Jesus as the charismatic Christ in the Gospel is paralleled in his subsequent portrait of the disciples in Acts. In other words, according to Luke, not only was Jesus the founder of Christianity, anointed, led, empowered by the Spirit, but the disciples, his followers, are also baptized, led, and empowered by the Spirit. This is not surprising, for their mission is to continue to do and teach those things which Jesus had begun to do and teach. Thus, while Luke's first volume of his two-volume history of the origin and spread of Christianity narrates the story of the charismatic Christ going about and doing good, his second volume narrates the story of the charismatic community of disciples going about and doing good, for the Spirit of Christ was with them.

Synopsis of Lucan Christology

Each of the Gospels portrays a common subject: the saving ministry of Jesus of Nazareth. Though what they have in common is vastly more important than their differences, each evangelist has a distinct Christology. John, of course, differs radically in his portrait of Christ in comparison to the so-called synoptic evangelists, Matthew, Mark, and Luke. Nevertheless, in terms of content, emphasis, and style, even these evangelists have a distinct Christology. The Evangelist Mark, for example, portrays Jesus as a man of vigorous action. In successive and increasingly significant portraits he shows Jesus, first in the role of teacher (1:16-4:41); then as prophet, first to Israel (5:1-7:23) and, secondly, to the Gentiles (7:24-37); next, as the Messiah (8:1-9:50); and finally, as the King of the Jews (10:1-16:20). Matthew, on the other hand, emphasizes that Jesus is the King of the Jews—a royal Messiah—from the beginning of his Gospel (note the genealogy, 1:1-17, and especially the visit of the Magi, 2:1-12), and a Moses-like figure in his ministry to Israel (for example, the Sermon on the Mount, 5:1-7:29, and the five blocks of discourse/teaching). Of the Synoptic evangelists, Luke has the most fully developed Christology, in that it is an Old Testament Christology, incarnational, and the most fully Trinitarian.

Luke's Christology Is Rooted in the Old Testament

Luke's Christology is an Old Testament Christology. This is a perspective which Luke naturally shares with the other three evangelists. Nevertheless, one of the most immediate and dominant impressions of Luke's Christology is that it is massively rooted in the Old Testament. This impression is just as true of Acts as it is for the Gospel. From the Infancy Narrative (1:5ff.), which launches the Gospel narrative, to the concluding report that Paul testified to the Jews in Rome, "trying to persuade them concerning Jesus, from both the Law of Moses and from the Prophets" (Acts 28:23), Luke presents Jesus of Nazareth to his readers in terms of Old Testament language and themes. Since Luke-Acts accounts for twenty-five percent of the bulk of the New Testament, and also because the primary subject of this essay is Luke's pneumatology, it is impossible to do justice to this pervasive indebtedness to the Old Testament. Briefly, we note the following: Jesus will inherit the throne of his father David (Luke 1:32); He is born in Bethlehem, the city of David (2:5); and He is a light to the Gentiles (2:32). He is, furthermore, the Servant (Acts 3:13), the Holy and Righteous One (Acts 3:14), and the stone which the builders rejected (Acts 4:11).

In addition to this general, all pervasive Old Testament background to Luke's Christology, there is also, more specifically Luke's proof-from-prophecy presentation of his Christology. This proof-from-prophecy is typified in his "it is written" formula which appears in Luke-Acts over a dozen times (as in Luke 2:23, 3:4 et al.). Often Luke simply uses this formula independently as, for example, when Jesus announces to the twelve, "Behold we are going up to Jerusalem, and all things which are written through the prophets about the Son of Man will be accomplished" (Luke 18:31). The three "fulfillment" verbs which Luke uses, *pimplēmi* (Luke 21:22 et al.), *pleroo* (Luke 4:21 et al.), and *teleo* (Luke 22:37), complement the "it is written" formula. Jesus' post resurrection explanation to his disciples is the most comprehensive statement of this "it is written", "fulfilled" relationship: "These are My words which I spoke to you while I was still with you," Jesus reminded them, continuing, "that all things which are written about Me in the Law of Moses and the Prophets and the Psalms must be fulfilled" (Luke 24:44). From this brief survey it is clear that the sacred history and literature of the Old Testament both anticipates, and is fulfilled, in the person and redemptive mission of Jesus.

Luke's Christology is Incarnational

Not only is Luke's Christology an Old Testament Christology, it is also incarnational. This is an emphasis which he shares with Matthew, though even here each evangelist has his individual perspectives. Because Mark lacks an infancy narrative, this emphasis is not shared with him. To the Virgin Mary the angel Gabriel announces: ". . . behold, you will conceive in your womb, and bear a son, and you shall name him Jesus. He will be great, and will be called the Son of the Most High; and the Lord God will give Him the throne of His father David . . . and His Kingdom will have no end" (1:32-33).

Perplexed by this portentous announcement, Mary asks, "How can this be?" Gabriel answers, "The Holy Spirit will come upon you, and the power of the Most High will overshadow you; and for that reason the holy offspring shall be called the Son of God" (Luke 1:35). Because it is incarnational, Luke's Christology is also ontological: Mary's baby Jesus will be "the Son of the Most High" and "the Son of God."

Jesus is early and uniquely conscious of this ontological reality. Thus, at age twelve, when his parents find their delinquent son in the Temple after the Passover he asks them, "Why is it that you were looking for Me? Did you not know that I had to be in My Father's *house?*" (2:49). God is his Father; He is God's Son. It is this reality which gives immediate significance to the voice from heaven at His baptism and, subsequently, at His transfiguration, "Thou art My beloved Son" (3:22, 9:35). While David's son may enjoy a father-son relationship with God by adoption, "I will be a father to him and he will be a son to Me" (2 Sam. 7:14), Jesus is God's Son through the miracle and sacred mystery of the incarnation. Luke emphasizes this incarnational-ontological Christology by concluding Jesus' genealogy: ". . . the *son* of Adam, the *son* of God" (3:38). In other words, just as Adam was uniquely created by God, so Jesus, the second Adam, was also uniquely created by God.

Luke's Christology is Trinitarian

Luke's Gospel is Christology, but it is a Christology which is more robustly Trinitarian than that which is to be found in either Matthew or Mark. Luke's Christology is both theological (related to God as Father) and pneumatological (related to God as Spirit). Many of the same texts which report the incarnational dimension of Luke's Christology also encode one (theology) or the other (pneumatology), or both complementary dimensions of his Trinitarian Christology. On the one hand, Luke's "sonship" language ("Son of the Most High," "Son of God," "Thou art My beloved Son") implies the fatherhood of God toward Jesus in a way which is distinctly different from the fatherhood of God toward mankind in creation (Matt. 5:45), toward Israel in election (Ex. 4:22), or toward the Davidic King by adoption (2 Sam. 7:14, Psalm 2:7). Since he is God's Son, He calls God his Father as a boy of twelve (Luke 2:49), at Gethsemane (22:42), in death (23:46), and resurrection (Acts 1:4,7), a claim which is blasphemous on any lips other than His own.

Luke's Christology not only has a theological emphasis, it also has a pneumatological emphasis which is both unexpected and startling in comparison to the pneumatology of Matthew and Mark. Luke, as does Matthew, reports that it is by the overshadowing power of the Holy Spirit that the miracle of the incarnation is effected. All four evangelists report the announcement of John the Baptist that his successor, in contrast to himself who baptizes only in water, will baptize in the Holy Spirit (Matt. 3:11, Mark 1:8, Luke 3:16, John 1:33). All four evangelists, moreover, also report the descent of the Holy Spirit upon Jesus after He had been baptized by John (Matt. 3:16, Mark 1:9, Luke 3:22, John 1:32). The synoptic evangelists, finally, report that after His baptism, Jesus was led by the Spirit into the wilderness to be tempted by the devil (Matt. 4:1, Mark 1:12, Luke 4:1). This is the relationship between Jesus and the Holy Spirit which Luke holds in common with one or more of the other evangelists. That relationship between Jesus and the Holy Spirit, which is unique to Luke-Acts, makes Luke the historian-theologian of the Spirit and Jesus the charismatic Christ.

For example, Luke, and Luke alone, reports that the descent of the Holy Spirit means that Jesus has been anointed by the Spirit (4:18ff./Isa. 61:1, cf.; Acts 4:27, 10:38). It is this anointing by the Spirit which constitutes Jesus as the Messiah or Christ, indeed, the pneumatic or charismatic Christ. Moreover, Luke alone reports that, as the Anointed One, Jesus was full of the Holy Spirit when He returned from the Jordan (4:1), and that following His temptation by the devil, He "returned to Galilee in the power of the Spirit" (4:14). Having been anointed by the Spirit at the beginning of His ministry, He becomes the baptizer in the Spirit when His ministry is transferred to the disciples. In Peter's words to the crowd on the day of Pentecost, "Therefore having been exalted to the right hand of God, and having received from the Father the promise of the Holy Spirit, He has poured forth this which you both see and hear" (Acts 2:33).

This exclusively Lucan data on the relationship between Jesus and the Spirit, coming as it does at the beginning and conclusion of his earthly ministry, brackets that entire ministry. By bracketing Jesus' ministry by these references to the Spirit, Luke informs his readers that from first to last Jesus ministers as a charismatic: He is full of the Holy Spirit, He is led by the Spirit, He is empowered by the Spirit. Lest his readers miss this obvious fact Luke inserts several incidental reports to remind them that Jesus is the charismatic Christ in experience. For example, when the seventy disciples return from their mission and report its success, Luke reports, "At that very time He [Jesus] rejoiced greatly in the Holy Spirit" (10:21). Moreover, when Luke introduces book two of his two-volume history of the origin and spread of Christianity, he reminds Theophilus "about all that Jesus began to do and teach, until the day He was taken up, after He had by the Holy Spirit given orders to the apostles whom He had chosen" (Acts 1:2). Finally, Luke reports Peter's witness to Cornelius and his assembled household, *"You know of* Jesus of Nazareth, how God anointed Him with the Holy Spirit and with power, and *how* He went about doing good, and healing all who were oppressed by the devil; for God was with Him" (Acts 10:38). From Luke's data the reader discovers, almost incidentally, that Jesus rejoiced in the Spirit, gave unrecorded orders to the apostles by the Holy Spirit, and in general terms went about doing good in the power of the Spirit. Thus, Luke, and no other evangelist, compels us to conclude that the entire ministry of Jesus, all that He said and did, was directed, inspired, and empowered by the Holy Spirit.

To sum up, Luke-Acts presents a Trinitarian Christology, that is, a Christology which is shaped, qualified, and conditioned by both theology (proper) and a unique pneumatology. Of the two, Luke's pneumatology is more dramatically prominent. Therefore, Luke's pneumatology is a dominant aspect of his Christology.

Luke's Christology is Vocational

In addition to being incarnational and Trinitarian, Luke's Christology is also vocational or functional. In other words, Jesus, the Son of God had a mission to perform. As in the Gospel of Mark so in the Gospel of Luke, Jesus performs four successive though overlapping, vocational roles: 1) rabbi or teacher (Luke 4:15, 31; 5:3, 17; 6:6); 2) prophet, particularly after the pattern of the charismatic prophets, Elijah and Elisha (Luke 7:16, 39; 9:7-9, 19; 24:19); 3) Messiah, that is, Christ (Luke 4:18, 9:20); and 4) King of the Jews (Luke 19:38, 23:2-3, 37-39). As Jesus adopts each successive role, He advances to a new stage of His self-revelation and the offering of Himself to Israel. In addition to passing on this traditional fourfold portrait of Jesus' self-revelation, Luke also has his distinctive vocational Christological emphasis. For example, though Jesus is identified as a prophet in all four Gospels (Matt. 21:11, Mark 6:15, Luke 7:16, John 6:14), Luke develops the portrait of Jesus as prophet most fully.[1] Moreover, in addition to his unique portrait of Jesus as prophet, Luke also portrays Jesus as Savior, a portrait which is absent, or at most, incipient in the other Gospels.

The verb "to save" (*sozo*), is found in all four Gospels, most commonly to describe Jesus' healing ministry (eg. Matt. 9:21, Mark 5:23, Luke 8:48, John 11:12), and also to describe deliverance from danger (Matt. 8:25, John 12:27), and most importantly to describe salvation from sin (Matt. 1:21, Luke 19:10, John 3:17). With two exceptions (John 4:22, 42), the nouns "savior, deliverer, preserver" (*soter*)[2], "deliverance, preservation, salvation" *(soteria),* and the substantive, "saving,

---

[1] For a fuller discussion of Luke's portrait of Jesus as prophet see Stronstad, *The Charismatic Theology of St. Luke*, 42-45.

[2] Walter Bauer, *A Greek-English Lexicon of the New Testament and Other Early Christian Literature,* translated by W.F. Arndt, F.W. Gingrich and F.W. Danker from the 5th German ed. (Chicago: University of Chicago Press, 1979), 800.

delivering, preserving, bringing salvation" *(soterios)* are exclusive to Luke among the Gospel writers. As Luke uses these savior-salvation-saving words, God is our Savior (Luke 1:47) and is the source of salvation (Luke 1:69, 2:30, 3:6; Acts 28:28), a salvation which is mediated through the successive ministries of Jesus (Luke 19:10), and the disciples (Acts 13:26, 47; 16:17). Not only is God Savior but His Son, Jesus, is Savior as well (Luke 2:11, Acts 5:31), coming "to seek and save that which was lost" (Luke 19:10). Indeed, as Peter bears witness to the Sanhedrin, "there is salvation in no one else; for there is no other name under heaven that has been given among men, by which we must be saved" (Acts 4:12).

In reporting the identity of Jesus as Savior, something which the other Gospel writers do not do, Luke uses a title of rulership, on the one hand, and of deity, on the other hand. Applied to Jesus the title "Savior" *(soter)* puts Him in continuity with the leaders of Israel such as the Judges (Jud. 3:9, 15), and gives Him a titular status equal to Hellenistic Kings, such as the Ptolemies, or Roman emperors, such as Julius Caesar, Nero or Vespasian.[3] The title also ranks Jesus with the God of Israel (Deut. 32:15, Luke 1:47) and the gods of the Greco-Roman world such as Zeus, Apollo, and Hermes.[4] Apart from the title "Lord" *(kurios)*, no other title elevates Luke's vocational Christology so highly.

Luke continues to develop his multiplex vocational Christology more fully in Acts, where, for example, Jesus is proclaimed as the Christ (Acts 2:36 et al.), the Servant (3:13 et al.), the Prophet like Moses (3:22, 7:37), the Prince (5:31), and most especially, in comparison to the Gospel account, as Lord (2:36 et al.). Curiously, it is Peter, who first proclaimed Jesus to be the Messiah, or Christ, who, on the day of Pentecost, first announces that "God has made Him (this Jesus whom the Jews crucified) both Lord and Christ" (2:36). Throughout Acts, as it is never done in the Gospel except on the lips of angels (Luke 2:11), Jesus is commonly identified as Lord. In Jerusalem, "the apostles," Luke reports, "were giving witness to the resurrection of the Lord Jesus" (4:33). Those who are saved when the Gospel is preached are "believers in the Lord" (5:14; cf., 9:35, 42; 13:12 et al.). Stephen, the first Christian martyr prayed,

---

[3] James Hope Moulton and George Milligan, The *Vocabulary of the Greek Testament Illustrated from the Papyri and Other Non-Literary Sources* (Grand Rapids: Wm. B. Eerdmans, 1963), 621.
[4] Liddell and Scott, *A Greek-English Lexicon,* 1751.

"Lord Jesus, receive my spirit" (7:59), and Barnabas and Paul risked their lives for the name of the Lord Jesus Christ (15:26, cf., 21:13). Ananias is sent to Saul in Damascus by the Lord Jesus (9:17); Apollos was "instructed in the way of the Lord... teaching accurately the things concerning Jesus" (18:25). Whereas the title Christ, or Anointed One, identifies Jesus in His roles as Prophet and King, the title Lord identifies Jesus both with the God of Israel, and as a rival to the Roman Lord, or Caesar. Ironically, in ancient Rome, the imperial seat of the Roman Lord, for two years Paul taught about his rival; namely, "the Lord Jesus Christ with all openness, unhindered" (28:31). To sum up, as the many traditional titles (teacher, prophet, Messiah, and King) and the titles with a uniquely Lucan emphasis (prophet, Savior, and Lord) indicate, in the same way that Luke's incarnational Christology is ontological, so his vocational Christology is functional.

A Synthesis of Luke's Pneumatology

Luke brings the same attitude, understanding, and procedure to his portrait of the Holy Spirit as he did to writing his narrative history (genre) and his portrait of Jesus (Christology). In other words, just as Luke's historiography is modelled after Old Testament historiography (chapter two), and his Christology is rooted in the Old Testament (above), so his pneumatology, in terms of language and motifs, is rooted in the Old Testament. Moreover, just as Luke's Christology is incarnational and, therefore, both ontological and Trinitarian, so Luke's pneumatology has both ontological and Trinitarian dimensions. Finally, in the same way that Luke's Christology is vocational, or functional, so his pneumatology, not only in its relationship to Jesus, but also in its relationship to the disciples, is, in explicitly prophetic terms, vocational or functional.

Luke's Pneumatology is an Old Testament Pneumatology

If no other evidence existed, Luke's two inauguration narratives (Luke 3:1ff., Acts 2:1ff.) alone would compel the reader to understand the activity of the Spirit which he records in terms of the Old Testament. In these narratives we have the proof-from-prophecy for the activity of the Spirit. For his synagogue homily at Nazareth based on the text from Isaiah, Jesus declared, "Today this Scripture has been fulfilled in your hearing" (Luke 4:21). Similarly, Peter claims that the reception of the Spirit by the disciples fulfills an oracle from Joel, announcing, "but this is what was spoken of through the prophet Joel" (Acts 2:16). There is, however, other evidence for the Old Testament roots of Luke's portrait of the Spirit, evidence, as pervasive, in fact, as for the Old Testament roots of his Christology.

The terminology by which Luke describes the present activity of the Spirit is almost totally derived from the Septuagint. An observation by Nigel Turner is germane to this. He writes, "He [Luke] conceived the Christian revelation as the fulfillment of the old Dispensation, and would in consequence tend by his language to emphasize the links between Old and New."[5]

As to terminology which describes the activity of the Spirit of God in the Scriptures of Israel, the translators of the Septuagint used twenty-three different verbs.[6] Of the nine verbs which Luke employed to show the activity of the Spirit, eight of them are derived from the Septuagint.[7] These are: "to fill" (Luke 1:15 et al.), "to come upon" (Luke 1:35 et al.), "to lead" (Luke 4:1), "to give" (Luke 11:13 et al.), "to clothe" (power = H.S., Luke 24:49), "to speak" (Acts 1:16 et al.), "to fall upon" (Acts 10:44 et al.), and "to witness" (Acts 15:8). Only the verb "baptized" in the Holy Spirit is not Septuagintal. Lest Luke's indebtedness to the Old Testament/Septuagint to describe the activity of the Holy Spirit seem either natural or inevitable, simply observe that both John and Paul use an almost entirely different set of terms to describe a similar activity of the Spirit.

In addition to this Septuagintal terminology, there is a complex of complementary Old Testament motifs which are echoed in Luke-Acts; primarily, 1) transfer, 2) the sign, and 3) the vocation motifs. At strategic points in the advance of Israel's history, when there is a transfer of responsibility from a leader (or leaders) to others, there is also a complementary transfer of the Spirit. For example, when Moses begins

---

[5]Turner, *A Grammar of New Testament Greek*, 62.
[6]Stronstad, "The Influence of the Old Testament on the Charismatic Theology of St. Luke," 38.
[7]Ibid., 44-45.

to share his leadership responsibilities with the seventy elders, the Lord "took of the Spirit who was upon him and placed Him upon the seventy elders" (Num. 11:25). There are similar transfers of the Spirit from Moses to Joshua (Num. 27:18-20, Deut. 34:9), from Saul to David (I Sam. 16:13-14), and from Elijah to Elisha (2 Kings 2:9-15). While the transfer of the Spirit from Moses to the elders, which is a transfer from an individual to a group, most closely approximates the transfer of the Holy Spirit from Jesus to the company of disciples on the day of Pentecost, each of these transfers anticipates the day of Pentecost.

The sign motif closely complements the transfer motif. The purpose of the sign is twofold: 1) to authenticate to the recipient of the Spirit that his call to leadership is divine in origin, and 2) to witness to others that this man is God's chosen. The sign is often, though not invariably, an outburst of prophecy. Thus, for example, when the Spirit rested upon the elders, they prophesied (Num. 11:25). The sign function of this prophesying is confirmed by the report which immediately follows: "they did not do it again." Furthermore, paralleling the experience of Saul, when Samuel anointed David to be King over Israel, "the Spirit of the LORD came mightily upon David from that day forward" (1 Sam. 16:13). Later David will claim prophetic inspiration, declaring, "The Spirit of the LORD spoke by me, and His word was on my tongue" (2 Sam. 23:2). Later still, Peter can declare, "the Scripture had to be fulfilled, which the Holy Spirit foretold by the mouth of David" (Acts 1:16). For both Joshua and Elisha, the most immediate, though not only, sign of their succession seems to have been the ability to part the Jordan River (Josh. 3:7, 4:14; 2 Kings 2:14-15).

The vocational motif complements the transfer and sign motifs. The call to leadership is not so much a call to authority as it is a call to service, and those whom God calls to service are equipped and/or empowered by the Spirit for that service. These enabling gifts of the Spirit, or *charismata*, in Old Testament times differ from our catalogues of gifts (as in 1 Cor. 12). For example, for Bezalel and others, it is manual skill or craftsmanship (Ex. 28:3, 31:3, 35:31; LXX). Moreover, for Joshua it is wisdom (Deut. 34:9), and for the Judges it is military prowess (Jud. 3:10 et al.), as it is also for Israel's two charismatic Kings, Saul and David (2 Sam. 1:10, 11:6ff., 16:3). Furthermore, for Elijah and Elisha it is raising the dead (1 Kings 17:17ff., 2 Kings 4:34ff.), multiplying a little food into much food (1 Kings 17:9ff.; 2 Kings 4:3ff., 42ff.), and other miraculous powers. Finally, for the forthcoming scion of David, it is the sixfold plenitude of gifts: the spirit of wisdom, understanding, counsel, strength, knowledge, and the fear of the Lord (Isa. 11:2). These enabling gifts of the Spirit (craftsmanship, military prowess, wisdom, etc.) are appropriate to the vocation, the kind of service which God's people in Old Testament times were called upon to render.

In Luke-Acts there are strong echoes of this same complex of complementary gift-of-the-Spirit motifs. Thus, the transfer of the Holy Spirit from Jesus to the disciples on the day of Pentecost echoes the earlier transfer of the Spirit from Moses to the elders (Acts 2:1ff., Num. 11:25). Moreover, just as prophesying is the sign, par excellence, of the transfer of the Spirit in Old Testament times, so on the day of Pentecost speaking in other tongues/prophesying (Acts 2:4,17) is the sign that the Spirit has been transferred to the disciples. As in Old Testament times, so in Luke-Acts, there are other signs as well (dramatic signs such as the descent of the Spirit in bodily form like a dove, and the tongues of fire and the sound of a violent wind) which, and this is Luke's emphasis, others could see and hear (Acts 2:33, 8:18, 10:46). In addition, whether Luke is writing about Jesus or the disciples, as in Old Testament times, the Spirit which is given to them empowers their service. In the power of the Spirit, Jesus, like Elijah and Elisha before him, raises the dead (Luke 7:14ff.), multiplies a little food into much food (Luke 9:12ff.), heals the sick (Luke 4:40), and performs other acts of good. Similarly, the disciples serve their Lord in the power of the Spirit, witnessing in both word, as in Peter's Pentecost sermon (Acts 2:14ff.), and in deeds, signs and wonders such as the healing of the cripple who daily begged at the gate of the Temple which is called Beautiful (Acts 3:1ff.).

Certainly, there are differences in detail between the gift-of-the-Spirit motifs in Old Testament times and Luke-Acts, but these are differences of historical particularity rather than differences of fundamental orientation. Clearly, both in terminology and motifs, Luke's pneumatology echoes the Old Testament pneumatology. This is not surprising. Indeed, it is exactly what the interpreter of Luke-Acts ought to expect since, as we have observed, both Luke's historiography and his Christology are heavily indebted to the Old Testament. Every interpretation of the Holy Spirit in Luke-Acts, therefore, which does not give full weight to this Old Testament heritage must inevitably prove to be a distortion of Lucan pneumatology.

Luke's Pneumatology Is Ontological-Trinitarian

In Old Testament times, the Spirit of God is not, to use a term of Christian theology, a person. Having canvassed the relevant data, one scholar writes, "The final conclusion is overwhelmingly negative: there is no personalization of the Spirit within the limits of the Old Testament."[8] Most scholars concur with this conclusion. Rather than acting as a person, the Spirit of God functions as the "power, anger, will, mind, presence" of God manifested throughout Israel's history. Similarly, it might appear that the Holy Spirit in Luke-Acts is not a person but a power or substance. Obviously, Luke uses impersonal language to describe much of the Spirit's activity. For example, Jesus is anointed by the Holy Spirit (Luke 3:22, 4:18), but this language echoes the oil poured by Samuel over the heads of Saul and David to anoint them as King over Israel (1 Sam. 10:1, 16:13). The followers of the Anointed One, John and Jesus announce, will be baptized *in* the Holy Spirit (Luke 3:16, Acts 1:5), but this parallels being baptized *in* water. In addition, the Holy Spirit is "poured forth" (Acts 2:33), "fills" people (Luke 1:15 et al.), and is the "power from on high" (Luke 24:49). Though Luke frequently uses this impersonal language to describe the activity of the Holy Spirit, it would not only be superficial, but it would also be incorrect to conclude that the Spirit in Luke-Acts is impersonal.

Complementing this impersonal language in Luke-Acts, Luke frequently describes the activity of the Holy Spirit in personal, or ontological terms. The Holy Spirit, for example, witnesses, perhaps through the signs and wonders which filled Jerusalem after the outpouring of the Holy Spirit on the day of Pentecost (Acts 5:32; cf., 2:22, 43; 4:30), or through a prophet, "saying that bonds and afflictions" await Paul (Acts 20:23; cf. 21:4, 11). Less ambiguous than the witnessing of the Holy Spirit, the Spirit also speaks. At times his speaking is indirect and mediated. His voice is the words of Scripture (Acts 1:16), or the voice of

---

[8]Lloyd Neve, *The Spirit of God in the Old Testament* (Tokyo: Seibunsha, 1972), 129.

anonymous prophets at Antioch and Tyre (Acts 13:2, 21:4), or the prophecy of Agabus at Caesarea (Acts 21:11). At other times, such as when the Spirit spoke to Philip and Peter (Acts 8:29, 10:19, 11:12), his voice is direct and unmediated, though we do not know, in these cases, if the voice of the Spirit is an audible voice, or the voice of inner consciousness. In addition to speaking, the Holy Spirit can be spoken to, that is, lied to (Acts 5:3), forbids (Acts 16:6), and prohibits (Acts 16:7). The Holy Spirit can also be tested (Acts 5:9), resisted (Acts 7:51), and makes elders to be overseers of the church (Acts 20:28). Individually, some of this evidence is more ambiguous than we would like. Inanimate objects as well as persons, for example, can be witnesses (Josh. 24:26-27). Cumulatively, however, the evidence is overwhelmingly conclusive: there is a personalization of the Spirit in Luke-Acts.

The personalization of the Holy Spirit finds its fullest significance in the Trinitarian dimension of Luke's theology. Our discussion of Luke's pneumatology necessarily leads to the doctrine of the Trinity. Luke identifies the Holy Spirit as God. The Spirit is, variously, the Spirit of the Lord = Father = Jesus (Acts 5:9, 8:39), and the Spirit of Jesus (Acts 16:7). To lie to the Holy Spirit is the same as lying to God (Acts 5:3-4), and men not only test God but they also test the Holy Spirit (Acts 15:10, 5:9). In Luke-Acts there are also several Trinitarianisms, both unconscious and conscious. There is, for example, the formula, "in the fear of the Lord and the comfort of the Holy Spirit" (Acts 9:31). The angelic announcement to Mary that she will conceive and bear a son is Trinitarian. "The Holy Spirit will come upon you, and the power of the Most High will overshadow you; and for that reason, the holy offspring shall be called the Son of God" (Luke 1:35). At Jesus' baptism, the Father's voice from heaven publicly declares His approval of His Son, while the Holy Spirit descends upon the Son, in bodily form like a dove, anointing Him for service (Luke 3:22). Clearly, Luke's Trinitarian theology if repertorial rather than speculative, is incipient and embryonic rather than fully developed. Though Luke's Trinitarian theology is not as fully formulated as it will become in later Church Councils, in Luke-Acts the Holy Spirit appears as God the Spirit, just as Jesus appears as God the Son, and God in heaven is the Father.

Luke's Pneumatology is Vocational

Not only is Luke's pneumatology both rooted in the Old Testament and ontological, but it is also vocational or functional. Therefore, just as there was a vocational dimension to the activity of the Spirit of God in Old Testament times, and just as Luke's Christology was vocational or functional, so Luke's pneumatology has a dominant vocational dimension. This vocational dimension, we will discover, is just as significant for the mission of the disciples as it was for the earlier mission of Jesus. In other words, in Luke's pneumatology, just as Jesus is necessarily the charismatic Christ, so the disciples, his successors in mission, must necessarily become a charismatic community, for only when they have received the empowering of the Spirit will they do, and teach in the absence of their Lord, those things which He had earlier begun to do and teach.

Luke inaugurates the missions, first, of Jesus, and, subsequently, of the disciples with two statements which give programmatic shape to their respective vocations. Explaining the significance of His reception of the Holy Spirit at his baptism Jesus reads from the prophet Isaiah, "The Spirit of the Lord is upon Me because He anointed me to preach the gospel to the poor. He has sent Me to proclaim release to the captives, and recovery of sight to the blind, to set free those who are downtrodden, to proclaim the favorable year of the Lord" (Luke 4:18, 19). For Jesus His Messianic mission, or program, is to preach the Gospel: the good news of God's favor to the poor, the needy, and the disenfranchised. After his resurrection, however, Jesus transfers this mission to his disciples. For their mission, now about to be deprived of his earthly presence, he assures them, "but you shall receive power when the Holy Spirit has come upon you; and you shall be My witnesses both in Jerusalem, and in all Judea and Samaria, even to the remotest part of the earth" (Acts 1:3). This dominical promise of the Holy Spirit proves to be programmatic for their mission, a witness about Jesus in word and deed, as it unfolds, beginning in Jerusalem and culminating in Rome, the ends of the earth.

It is commonplace among many scholars to interpret the gift of the Holy Spirit to the disciples on the day of Pentecost primarily in initiation-incorporation terms and only secondarily in vocational terms.⁹ This initiation-incorporation depends upon a restrictive definition of baptism arbitrarily imported from the Pauline Literature. Luke, however, gives a different meaning to Spirit baptism than does Paul. In the structure of Luke-Acts, the Pentecost narrative stands in the same relation to the mission of the disciples as the inauguration narrative does to the mission of Jesus.¹⁰ Moreover, the experience of both Jesus at His anointing and of the disciples on the day of Pentecost in prayer, etc., is parallel.¹¹ Furthermore, the explicit dominical promise of the empowering of the Spirit for witness (Acts 1:8) is the context by which we must interpret the purpose of baptism in the Holy Spirit (Acts 1:5). Finally, Peter's "poured forth" language to describe the gift of the Spirit is reminiscent of the anointing oil poured upon the head of Saul (1 Sam. 10:1). Therefore, though Luke uses two different terms (Spirit anointing and Spirit baptism), the experience of the disciples on the day of Pentecost is functionally equivalent to the experience of Jesus at the Jordan. In other words, the miracle of Pentecost is primarily the anointing, or consecration, of the disciples for mission after the pattern of Jesus' experience. To interpret it in primarily initiation-incorporation terms does great violence to the complementary inauguration texts in Luke-Acts.

Having been anointed by the Holy Spirit for mission, the Spirit first leads Jesus, now full of the Spirit, into the Wilderness to be tested in preparation for that mission (Luke 4:1). Just as Jesus experiences this leading of the Spirit, so his followers will similarly experience the leading of the Spirit in their service to God. The Spirit, for example, instructs Philip to join the chariot of the Ethiopian (Acts 8:29) and instructs Peter to go to the household of Cornelius (Acts 10:19). During a prayer meeting at Antioch, the Spirit, through a prophetic word, sends Barnabas and Saul out upon their missionary careers, beginning at Cyprus (Acts 13:1-4). Paul's missionary enterprise is guided by the Spirit, forbidding him, for example, to speak the word in Asia, and not permitting him to enter Bithynia (Acts 16:6-7). Finally, as his ministry approaches its

---

⁹Dunn, *Baptism in the Holy Spirit*, 54.
¹⁰Stronstad, *Charismatic Theology*, 34.
¹¹Charles H. Talbert, *Literary Patterns, Theological Themes, and the Genre of Luke-Acts*. Society of Biblical Literature Monograph Series, 20 (Missoula: Scholars Press, 1974), 16.

conclusion, Paul inexorably sets his face to Jerusalem, and the bonds and afflictions which await him there, bound in spirit (Acts 20:22- 23). Thus, it is the Holy Spirit who leads God's people in mission, launching the missionary enterprise, initiating personal contact with those prepared to receive the message which leads to salvation, and directing the footsteps of these intrepid evangelists who carried the Gospel along the highways of the Empire.

In addition to being led by the Holy Spirit, Jesus also ministered in the power of the Holy Spirit (Luke 4:14). Similarly, His successors, the disciples, will subsequently minister in the power of the Spirit. On the day of Pentecost, the transfer of the Spirit from Jesus to the disciples is also a transfer of the power of the Spirit from Him to them. This transfer of power fulfills two dominical promises: "[you will be] clothed with power from on high," and "you shall receive power when the Holy Spirit has come upon you" (Luke 24:49, Acts 1:8). The purpose of this gift of the power of the Spirit is that the disciples might be witnesses to Jesus. Complementing the inspiration of the Spirit to witness in word, signified by Luke's "filled with the Holy Spirit" terminology, this power is the power of the Spirit to witness in deed. In other words, the power of the Spirit is miracle-working power, not only in the ministry of Jesus, but also for the disciples. Thus, having received the power of the Spirit on the day of Pentecost, the disciples heal the sick (Acts 3:1ff., 9:32ff.), raise the dead (Acts 9:36ff.), and do many other signs and wonders (Acts 2:43, 4:33 et al.). Indeed, just as God had earlier anointed Jesus with the Holy Spirit and power, with the result that he went about doing good and healing all who were oppressed by the devil, so God baptized the disciples with the Holy Spirit and power, so that they also went about doing good and healing all who were oppressed by the devil, for the Spirit of God was with them.

The Holy Spirit, having descended upon Jesus makes him the Anointed prophet, priest, and king in Israel, combining all three offices in His one person. In a simplification of an admittedly complex interrelationship, Jesus fulfilled the royal office in His ascension to heaven where He reigns as Lord, the sacerdotal office in His self-sacrifice at Calvary, and He fulfilled the prophetic office during His three years of public ministry. Beginning with the birth announcements of John and Jesus, the gift of prophecy was restored to Israel after four centuries of silence.[12] It is renewed, for example, in the inspired praise of Elizabeth and Zacharias (Luke 1:41ff., 1:67ff.), and also in the adult ministries of John and Jesus (Luke 20:6, 7:16). So unprecedented and dramatic was this restoration of prophecy that the people speculated that John might be the Christ, or Anointed One (Luke 3:15). He denied the speculation, but Jesus, his successor to whom he pointed, proved to be the anointed prophet, full of the Holy Spirit and ministering with the leading and empowering of the Spirit (Luke 3:22; 4:1, 14, 18).

As the unique bearer of the Spirit, Jesus has a complex and comprehensive prophetic ministry. Rooted in the Old Testament, it is patterned after three prophetic traditions. First, in terms of His anointing and His agenda for ministering to the disenfranchised, Jesus' prophetic ministry is patterned after the prophet Isaiah (Luke 4:18ff., cf., Isa. 61:1). Second, in terms of His miracle working power, raising the dead (Luke 7:16ff.), for example, or multiplying food (Luke 9:12ff.), His prophetic ministry is patterned after the charismatic ministries of Elijah and Elisha (1 Kings 17:16ff., 2 Kings 4:3ff.). Third, in terms of Jesus as the leader of God's people He is heir and successor to Moses, and is identified by His followers as the prophet like Moses (Acts 3:22, 7:37, cf.; Deut. 18:15ff.).

Though the rejection motif is common to all four Gospels, in Luke it is not only the most fully developed, but is also most directly related to the theme of the rejection of the prophets. Luke introduces the rejection motif in his report of Jesus' inaugural sermon at Nazareth (Luke 4:16-30). There, at the beginning of His ministry, Jesus identifies Himself as a rejected prophet after the pattern of Elijah and Elisha, who were rejected in Israel and subsequently ministered to Gentiles (Luke 4:24-27). Enraged by this identification, the synagogue crowd attempts to kill Him by throwing Him over a cliff (Luke 4:28- 30). From the beginning, then, in Luke's record Jesus, the anointed prophet, is under the cloud of imminent rejection and death. In addition, in the context where Peter reports Jesus' reputation to be that of a prophet such as John the Baptist, Elijah or one of the other prophets (Luke 9:19) Jesus first announces His own death, saying, "The Son of Man must suffer many things, and be rejected by the elders and chief priests and scribes, and be killed, and be raised on the third day" (Luke 9:22). Moreover, Jesus indicts His future

---

[12]Stronstad, *Charismatic Theology*, 38.

murderers as those who, "... build the tombs of the prophets, and it was your fathers who killed them" (Luke 11:47). Consequently, the generation of Jesus' day would kill some of the prophets and apostles whom God is sending to them, "in order that the blood of all the prophets... may be charged against this generation" (Luke 11:50). Later, when Jesus is warned by some Pharisees that Herod wants to kill Him, He solemnly affirms: "... I must journey on today and tomorrow and the next day; for it cannot be that a prophet should perish outside of Jerusalem. O Jerusalem, Jerusalem, *the city* that kills the prophets and stones those sent to her!" (Luke 13:33-34a).

Clearly, from the time of his inauguration sermon onwards, Jesus is conscious that He will die in Jerusalem as a prophet who is rejected by His own people, just as the prophets of old were rejected and killed by Israel. Thus, as Luke emphasizes it, Jesus dies, not merely as the King of the Jews (Luke 19:11-27, 21:1-3, 36-38), but also as the anointed Prophet.

As Luke describes it in Acts, the disciples fill a wide variety of offices and functions: apostles (Acts 1:2), deacons (6:1ff.), elders (14:23), bishops (20:28), and evangelists (21:11). However, just as the public ministry, which Jesus performed was primarily that of a prophet, so the successors to His ministry in Acts primarily fill the office and perform as prophets. Twice Luke mentions groups of prophets (11:27, 13:2). He names as prophets: Agabus (11:28), Barnabas, Simeon, Lucius, Manaean and Saul (13:1), Judas and Silas (15:32), and daughters of Philip (21:9). In addition, he reports several episodes of prophesying, particularly in regard to Paul's final journey to Jerusalem (20:23, 21:4). Moreover, groups such as the disciples on the day of Pentecost (2:4, 17ff.), the household of Cornelius (10:46, exalting God = prophesying, compare 2:11/17, and the disciples of Ephesus (19:6) speak in tongues and prophesy when the Holy Spirit comes upon them. Visions and dreams, such as those given to Peter and Paul (10:9ff., 16:9), are to be understood as prophetic, for these are the accredited mode of prophetic inspiration (2:17, cf., Num. 12:6, Joel 2:28). As announced by Joel, in the last days the gift of prophesy would be universal, that is, free from all age, sex, and economic barriers (Joel 2:28-29). As reported by Luke in Acts, prophecy is a pervasive phenomenon among the disciples, whom, in fact, constitute a prophethood of all believers.

This observation is reinforced by Luke's most prominent term to describe the activity of the Holy Spirit; namely, "filled with the Holy Spirit."[13] This term is distributed between Luke and Acts on a ratio of 3/6 (Luke 1:15, 41, 67; Acts 2:4; 4:8, 31; 9:17; 13:9, 52) and invariably signifies the prophetic dimension of Luke's vocational pneumatology. Luke uses the term "filled with the Holy Spirit" in two different, yet complementary ways. On the one hand, he uses the term as a pointer to describe a general prophetic ministry, without necessarily specifying either the moment or duration of prophetic inspiration, or any phenomena which might result from this gift of the Spirit (Luke 1:15; Acts 4:31, 9:17, 13:52). On the other hand, he uses the term five times to describe a specific moment or episode of prophetic inspiration (Luke 1:41, 67; Acts 2:4, 4:8, 13:9). When describing prophetic inspiration his narrative has two components: 1) the introductory formula, "filled with the Holy Spirit," and 2) the report of direct speech, which we may classify as a "pneuma discourse." According to Luke's record, a pneuma discourse may be either praise (Luke 1:41ff., 1:67ff.; Acts 2:4ff.), witness (Acts 2:14ff., 4:8ff.) or an announcement of divine judgment (Acts 13:9ff.). Thus, in the Acts, as well as in the Gospel, the term "filled with the Holy Spirit," signifies both the prophetic vocation, in general, and specific moments of prophetic inspiration, in particular.

Luke's data on the successive ministries of Jesus and the disciples, which we have briefly surveyed, is more than just a report of isolated charismatic/prophetic activity. Rather, Luke intends his readers to understand that everything that Jesus said and did from His baptism onwards, when He was anointed by the Holy Spirit, is the ministry of a charismatic prophet. Similarly, Luke also intends his readers to understand that everything that the disciples (and later, their converts) said and did from the Day of Pentecost onwards, when they were all baptized with the Holy Spirit, is the ministry of a community of charismatic prophets.

To sum up, Luke's pneumatology serves and complements his Christology. We have demonstrated that Jesus' experience of the Holy Spirit from his Jordan experience onwards is a paradigm for the disciples' experience of the Holy Spirit from Pentecost onwards. This is entirely

---

[13] Stronstad, "'Filled with the Holy Spirit' Terminology in Luke-Acts," 9.

appropriate, for the disciples are heirs and successors to his prophetic ministry. Jesus is the pneumatic Christ, the charismatic prophet. The disciples are a charismatic community of prophets. This picture of Luke's complementary Christology-pneumatology, of the parallels between the Gospel and Acts, and between the charismatic experience of Jesus and that of the disciples is neither incidental nor peripheral to Luke's purpose; it belongs to the warp and woof of the canvas of the history of salvation, and similarly to the warp and woof of Luke's record of that history.

There are clear implications from Luke's charismatic theology for the contemporary church. If the gift of the Spirit was charismatic or vocational for Jesus and the early church, so it ought to have a vocational dimension in the experience of God's people today. In other words, if they needed the anointing-baptism of the Spirit, the leading of the Spirit, and the empowering of the Spirit to render their ministries effective, we do as well. If their vocation was prophetic, so ours is to be prophetic. If Jesus was the charismatic Christ, and the disciples were a charismatic community, so the church in our generation is also charismatic, whether or not it functions at the level of our charismatic potential. Luke-Acts challenges the church in our generation, both individually and collectively, to function up to the level of its charismatic heritage which it derives from Jesus and the disciples. Only then will the contemporary church be a prophethood of believers in reality as well as in promise.

CHAPTER SEVEN

UNITY AND DIVERSITY: LUCAN, JOHANNINE, AND PAULINE PERSPECTIVES ON THE HOLY SPIRIT

The Scriptures, both of Israel and the Church, are characterized by unity and diversity, that is, a unity in diversity. Concerning the Scriptures of Israel, this unity and diversity was recognized in early Christianity. Thus, the writer of the epistle to the Hebrews begins his "word of exhortation" (Heb. 13:22) with a statement about revelation, "God, after He spoke long ago to the fathers in the prophets in many portions and in many ways, in these last days has spoken to us in His Son." (Heb. 1:1-2a). As described by this early Christian writer the unity of all revelation is rooted in the God who has spoken. But this unity is expressed in a diversity of speaking. This diversity which is not only within the Scriptures of Israel itself ("He spoke to the fathers in the prophets in many portions and in many ways"), but it is also between the words of God spoken in the past and spoken in the present— "in these last days [He] has spoken to us in His Son." This unity and diversity which the writer of the epistle to the Hebrews observed about the Old Testament, and also about the difference between the former and the latter revelation, has also been observed about the revelation of God in the New Testament. Indeed, one could similarly write concerning the New Testament, "God spoke to the Church in the apostles in many portions and in many ways." To state the obvious, God spoke in Luke through his two-volume narrative history, Luke-Acts. God also spoke in

John through his Gospel, his epistles and his apocalypse. Furthermore, God spoke in Paul through his thirteen epistles to the churches.

In spite of this self-evident diversity of divine revelation, however, on the principle of the analogy of faith in the history of the Protestant interpretation of Scripture there has always been a tendency to emphasize the unity of the message at the expense of diversity. Thus, whether we are speaking of the entire canon of Scripture, or of either the Old Testament or the New Testament, the unity and diversity is often reduced to mere uniformity. This uniformity is often the expression of some "pet" center, a canon within a canon, such as the Deuteronomic history for the Old Testament or the Pauline Epistles for the New Testament. This problem is particularly acute for the would-be interpreter of Luke-Acts. Wherever he turns in the literature on the subject, he encounters a hermeneutical strategy which presses Luke into the Pauline mold.

This prevailing pressure to conform Luke's pneumatology to Paul's pneumatology can be illustrated from any number of books and articles, both popular and scholarly, which fall to hand. For example, concerning the hermeneutics of historical narrative, as in Acts, Fee asserts, ". . . for a biblical precedent to justify a present action, the principle must be taught elsewhere, where it is the primary intent so to teach."[1] Similarly, though Luke writes of the "baptism in the Holy Spirit" three times (Luke 3:16; Acts 1:5, 11:16) and Paul but once (1 Cor. 12:13), John R. W. Stott arbitrarily presses all six non-Pauline references (Luke 3:16 and parallels) into the Pauline mold. He writes, "The Greek expression is precisely the same in all its seven occurrences and, therefore, *a priori*, as a sound principle of interpretation, it should refer to the same baptism in each verse,"[2] that is, "the means of entry into the body of Christ." In addition, James D. G. Dunn conforms Luke's report of the gift of the Spirit to the Samaritans, with its reported temporal gap between faith and the reception of the Spirit (Acts 8:1-24), to Paul's doctrine. He writes,

---

[1] Fee, "Hermeneutics and Historical Precedent - A Major Problem in Pentecostal Hermeneutics," 128-29; "Acts - the Problem of Historical Precedent," in *How to Read the Bible*, 101.

[2] Stott, *The Baptism and Fullness of the Holy Spirit*, 23.

The problem is that in the context of the rest of the New Testament these facts appear to be mutually exclusive and wholly irreconcilable. If they believed in the name of the Lord Jesus (v. 16) they must be called Christians. But if they did not receive the Holy Spirit till later they cannot be called Christians (most explicitly Rom. 8:5).³

These examples are merely the tip of the iceberg, but they graphically illustrate the ongoing reluctance to concede that there is a very real diversity in the doctrine of the Spirit among all three of the major New Testament witnesses to the Spirit.

The interpreter who accords to Luke a status independent of Paul as I have done in my monograph, *The Charismatic Theology of St. Luke*, is liable to misunderstanding and opposition. For example, in his book *Showing the Spirit: A Theological Exposition of 1 Corinthians 12-14*, D. A. Carson reacts in the following way to my thesis that characteristic Lucan terminology such as "baptized in the Holy Spirit," and "filled with the Holy Spirit," must be interpreted independently of Paul's use of similar terminology.⁴ He writes, "[Stronstad] adopts a charismatic exegesis of numerous passages in Acts, and argues that his interpretations are most natural *provided* [italics Carson's] one does not read Paul into Luke."⁵ Falsely implying that I argued that Luke and Paul develop contradictory rather than complementary theologies, Carson finds my methodology to be unacceptable. The price of interpreting Luke independently of Paul is too high for Carson, for, as he writes,

> One can no longer speak of canonical theology in any holistic sense. Worse, mutually contradictory theologies cannot both be true, and one cannot even speak of the canon establishing the allowable range of theologies, since one or more must be false. Stronstad's thesis generates more problems than it solves.⁶

---

³Dunn, *Baptism in the Holy Spirit*, 55.
⁴Stronstad, *The Charismatic Theology of St. Luke*, 9-12.
⁵D. A. Carson, *Showing the Spirit: A Theological Exposition of 1 Corinthians 12-14* (Grand Rapids, MI: Baker Book House, 1987), 151.
⁶Ibid.

Carson's criticism of my thesis is irrelevant, for I do not advocate the position which he attributes to me. It is Carson's apparent unwillingness to let Luke be Luke, his apparent readiness to read Luke as though he were Paul, which generates more hermeneutical problems than it solves. It leads to a canon within a canon. In fact, only that methodology which interprets Luke independently of Paul (that is, the methodology which recognizes unity in diversity among the New Testament) can alone be truly canonical in any holistic sense.

It is my thesis that when we survey the relevant Lucan, Johannine, and Pauline data, we will observe that there is both unity and diversity in their perspectives on the Holy Spirit. The unity in their perspectives on the Holy Spirit arises primarily out of the Christ event which gave rise to New Testament faith. This Christ event, which gave a fundamental unity to their theologies, however, is sifted through the grid of the diverse theological heritage of each author. Thus, in terms of their diverse perspectives on the Holy Spirit, Luke's characteristic terminology and charismatic motifs derive from the Septuagint, John's characteristic terminology and emphasis parallel non-conformist or sectarian Judaism of which the Dead Sea Scrolls are presently our only written exemplars, and Paul's characteristic terminology and themes reflect the outlook of pharisaic or rabbinic Judaism.

Unity in New Testament Pneumatology

Through all the differences of authorship, theological expertise, temperament, genre, and historical circumstances in the literature of the New Testament, there is a manifest unity in the message of the New Testament. On the one hand, it is God, who has intervened in human affairs, who gives unity to this diverse literature. On the other hand, since God is most fully revealed in his Son, Jesus of Nazareth, it is he who ultimately is the unifying factor in the New Testament literature. The ministry of the Spirit, moreover, complements that of the Son in a variety of ways. Luke, John, and Paul, the major authors in the New Testament, alike unite in presenting a pneumatology which is both Christological and charismatic.

The Holy Spirit is Christological

Though it may be somewhat of a simplification, it is fair to say that the Spirit is an anonymous presence in the New Testament: he does not speak of himself, but of Jesus. More than this, however, the Holy Spirit is an essential complement to the Christology of Luke, John, and Paul. With varying emphases, these writers portray the Spirit as the agent in the incarnation, the Anointer of Jesus, given by Jesus, and for the disciples, the *alter ego* of Jesus.

In chapter five, "The Holy Spirit in Luke-Acts," we canvassed Luke's data on the relationship between Jesus and the Spirit. Therefore, it will suffice to briefly recapitulate it here. Along with Matthew, Luke alone describes the dynamics of the incarnation by which the Son of God became the Son of Mary. In the words of the angelic annunciation to Mary: "The Holy Spirit will come upon you, and the power of the Most High will overshadow you; and for that reason, the holy offspring shall be called the Son of God" (Luke 1:35). Not only was Mary's Son conceived by the overshadowing power of the Spirit, but His public ministry is inaugurated by the descent of the Holy Spirit upon Him, anointing Him for service (Luke 3:22, 4:18). Having been anointed by the Spirit, the Christ is a charismatic prophet, full of the Spirit, led by the Spirit, and empowered by the Spirit (Luke 4:1, 14; Acts 10:38). Because He is the Christ, from His anointing to His ascension, the Spirit is concentrated exclusively upon Him. When His earthly ministry comes to its climax and conclusion, however, Jesus pours out, or transfers, His Spirit from Himself to His disciples (Acts 2:33), whom He has appointed heirs and successors to His ministry. The Spirit now becomes the *alter ego* of Jesus, for the things which He began to do and teach, they will continue to do and teach. Clearly, in Luke's pneumatology, the Holy Spirit is the Spirit of the Lord (Jesus) —the Spirit of Jesus (Acts 8:39, 16:7).

Apart from the fact that John, in contrast to Luke, lacks any direct reference to the birth of Jesus, the Holy Spirit is as much the Spirit of Christ in John's perspectives as it is in Luke's. In one of the few periscopes which John shares with Matthew, Mark, and Luke, John reports that the public ministry of Jesus, the eternal Word, who became flesh and dwelt among men, is inaugurated by the descent of the Spirit upon Him at His baptism by John (John 1:32). Though it is clearly implied by Luke, and to a lesser extent by Mark and Matthew, John explicitly tells us that the Spirit, "remained upon Him." Jesus' abiding, indeed, exclusive, possession of the Spirit is emphasized throughout the Gospel. John states that the Spirit was given to Him, "without measure," (3:34), and reports that the Spirit was not yet given to the disciples (7:39), and that if Jesus did not go away the Helper, that is, the Spirit, would not come to them (16:7).

In addition to being the exclusive possession of Jesus, the Holy Spirit is also a witness to Jesus. On the one hand, the Spirit is a witness to John the Baptist, who reports, "And I did not recognize Him, but He who sent me to baptize in water said to me, 'He upon whom you see the Spirit descending and remaining upon Him, this is the one who baptizes in the Holy Spirit'" (1:33). On the other hand, the Spirit will also witness to the disciples. Thus, Jesus announces, "When the Helper comes . . . He will bear witness of Me" (15:26). Later, in opposition to false teachers (antichrists), John declares that Jesus is the Son of God, affirming, "And it is the Spirit who bears witness, because the Spirit is the truth. For there are three that bear witness, the Spirit and the water and the blood; and the three are in agreement" (1 John 5:7-8). Finally, John writes, ". . . for the testimony of Jesus is the spirit of prophecy" (Rev. 19:10).

Not only is His ministry inaugurated and witnessed to by the descent of the Holy Spirit upon Him, but Jesus is also the giver of the Spirit. Specifically, having received the Spirit at His baptism, He gives the Spirit after His resurrection. "It is to your advantage that I go away," Jesus assures His disciples, "for if I do not go away, the Helper shall not come to you" (16:7). The Spirit will be "given" by the Father, and "sent" by the Father (14:16, 26), but is given at the request of Jesus (14:16) and is sent in His name (14:26). Because Jesus and the Father are one (17:21-22), Jesus, Himself, will send the Helper from the Father (15:26), that is, when He has gone away, He will send Him to the disciples (16:7). For His immediate disciples this promise is fulfilled after the resurrection when Jesus breathed upon them, and said, "Receive the Holy Spirit" (20:22). Concerning the gift of the Spirit to the disciples more generally, John writes, "But you have an anointing from the Holy One. . . . And as for you, the anointing which you received from Him abides in you" (1 John 2:20, 27).

Perhaps because Paul writes circumstantial letters, rather than writing history, as does Luke, or a Gospel, as does John, his pneumatology has a different Christological focus than does theirs. Whereas in Luke's history the Spirit relates to Jesus beginning with the incarnation, and in John's Gospel the Spirit first relates to Jesus at His baptism, in Paul's epistles the Spirit first relates to the Jesus of history in His resurrection— "[he] was declared the Son of God with power by the resurrection from the dead, according to the Spirit of holiness" (Rom. 1:4). Nevertheless, the relationship between Christ and Spirit in Paul's pneumatology is not inconsequential. Paul commonly refers to the Holy Spirit simply as "the Spirit." But "the Spirit" is "the Spirit of Christ" (Rom. 8:9), and "the Spirit of Jesus Christ" (Phil. 1:19).

In a text fraught with exegetical pitfalls (which, for our purposes, we can safely ignore) Paul writes that "the Lord [Jesus] is the Spirit, and where the Spirit of the Lord is, *there* is liberty. But we all . . . are being transformed into the same image from glory to glory, just as from the Lord, the Spirit" (2 Cor. 3:17-18). At the least this text claims that Christ and Spirit have the same function, specifically, to liberate from the Law (2 Cor. 3: 1 ff.). In addition, the Spirit is the Spirit of the Lord who transforms God's people into the image of His Son. Not only is the Spirit operative in transforming God's people into Christlikeness, but also the Spirit, and only the Spirit, enables God's people to confess that Jesus is Lord (1Cor. 12:3).

The Holy Spirit is Ontological-Trinitarian

In contrast to the Old Testament, where there is no hypostatization of the Spirit, in the Lucan, Johannine, and Pauline pneumatologies, the Holy Spirit is fully personal. As we have already observed in chapter five, Luke describes the Spirit in personal terms. Specifically, the Spirit speaks (Acts 8:29, 10:19, 11:12), forbids (Acts 16:6), prohibits (Acts 16:7), and makes overseers of elders (Acts 20:28). In addition, the Spirit can be lied to (Acts 5:3), tested (Acts 5:9), and resisted (Acts 7:51). Moreover, the Spirit is the *alter ego* of Jesus; that is, the Spirit does in Acts what Jesus did in the Gospel. For example, just as Jesus commissioned the disciples to go and preach the Kingdom of God, so does the Spirit (Luke 9:1-2, Acts 13:2-4); just as Jesus invested the disciples with power, so does the

Spirit (Luke 9:1, Acts 1:8); just as Jesus directed the itinerary of the disciples, so does the Spirit (Luke 10:1; Acts 8:29, 10:19-20, 10:16-19); and just as Jesus gave the laws of the Kingdom, so does the Spirit (Luke 6:27-39, Acts 15:28).

For John, as well as for Luke, the Holy Spirit is fully personal. On the one hand, though the Greek noun *pneuma* is neuter in gender, John, violating the rules of grammar, frequently uses masculine pronouns in combination with the neuter noun (14:26, 15:26, 16:13). That this is ontological or a hypostatization of the Spirit, rather than a mere metaphorical personalization, is confirmed by another line of evidence—this coming from Jesus Himself. "I will ask the Father," Jesus assured his disciples, "and He will give you another Helper, that He may be with you forever" (John 14:16). Thus, as Jesus announced it, the Spirit is the Paraclete—a function which, by definition, can only be personal. Moreover, the Spirit is another *(allos)* Paraclete, that is, another of the same kind of Helper as Jesus Himself is (cf. 1 John 2:1). Because the Spirit is the *alter ego* of Jesus, both teach (John 7:14, 14:26), witness (8:14, 15:25), convince the world of sin (3:18-20, 16:8-11), do not speak of themselves (14:10, 16:13), are "in" the disciples (16:3, 14:17), are sent by the Father (14:24, 26), and go forth from the Father (16:27, 15:26).[7] For Paul, as well, the Spirit is fully personal. For example, in his great chapter in Romans on life in the Spirit (Rom. 8), the Spirit functions as a person. Specifically, the Spirit dwells (8:9), leads (8:14), bears witness (8:16), and helps and intercedes (8:26). Moreover, as person, the Spirit has mind (8:27) and teaches (1 Cor. 2:13). Furthermore, for Paul, as also for Luke and John, the Spirit is the *alter ego* of Jesus. For example, just as the believer is "in Christ" (8:1), the believer is also "in the Spirit" (8:9). Similarly, Christ and Spirit are each in the believer (8:8-10). In addition, both Jesus and the Spirit are the source of the life of the believer (1 Cor. 15:35, Rom. 8:11), intercede for the believer (8:34, 26), and are the source of the believers' righteousness, joy, and peace (Rom. 5:1ff., 14:17). Though there is much more evidence that might be marshalled, this mustering of data, brief as it is, amply illustrates that in Pauline

---

[7]E. Schweizer, *"Pneuma,"* in *Theological Dictionary of the New Testament*, VI, edited by Gerhard Friedrich, translated by Geoffrey W. Bromiley (Grand Rapids: Wm. B. Eerdmans, 1970), 442-43.

pneumatology, as well as in Lucan and Johannine pneumatology, the Spirit is fully a person.

Though it may be often incidental, and sometimes unconscious, the data about the Holy Spirit in the writings of Luke, John, and Paul which we have canvassed is, to use the terminology of the Church Fathers, Trinitarian. Being revealed to them in personal categories, and having experienced the Spirit as the *alter ego* of Jesus, it could not be otherwise. These Trinitarian intimations begin with the angelic annunciation to Mary about the Son she will conceive and give birth to (Luke 1:35), reappear at the baptism of Jesus (Luke 3:21-22, John 1:32), carry through to the resurrection of Jesus (Rom. 1:3-4), and the subsequent gift of the Spirit to the disciples (Acts 2:33, John 15:26). In addition to these Trinitarian episodes there are several other Trinitarianisms, including, for example, the "same Spirit . . . same Lord . . . same God" formula for the *charismata* (1 Cor. 12:4-6), the benediction invoking, "the grace of the Lord Jesus Christ, and the love of God, and the fellowship of the Spirit" (2 Cor. 13:14), and the epistolary greeting, "from Him who is and who was and who is to come; and from the seven Spirits who are before His throne; and from Jesus Christ" (Rev. 1:4-5). The significance of these and other Trinitarianisms is that they come from men who, in the case of John and Paul, at least, were lifelong monotheists. Yet all three witnesses, Luke, John, and Paul, not only knew that Jesus was divine, but also that the Holy Spirit was both fully personal and divine.

The Gift of the Holy Spirit is Vocational

Not only do Luke, John, and Paul portray the Holy Spirit as Christological, personal, and, therefore, as a corollary, Trinitarian, but, in their own way, they also portray the gift of the Spirit as vocational. In other words, for all three, the Holy Spirit is given to God's people to equip them for service. We have already seen that in Luke's Christology Jesus is a pneumatic. That is, from His conception by the Spirit (Luke 1:35), to the transfer of the Spirit from Himself, the risen Lord and Christ, to the disciples, Jesus is uniquely and exclusively a Man of the Spirit. As a pneumatic, a Man of the Spirit, He is also a charismatic. In other words, He is anointed by the Spirit for ministry (Luke 3:22, 4:18), and empowered by the Spirit to make that ministry effective (Luke 4:14). As a pneumatic Jesus' vocation is that of a charismatic prophet. In Luke's pneumatology, with the exception that the conception of Jesus is supernatural, while that of the disciples is natural, the experience of the disciples parallels, and is functionally equivalent to that of Jesus. From Pentecost onwards they are also pneumatics, or men and women of the Spirit. In other words, just as the ministry of Jesus was inaugurated by the anointing by the Spirit, so the ministry of the disciples is inaugurated by the baptism in the Holy Spirit. Similarly, just as Jesus was empowered by the Spirit, so the disciples launch their ministry only when they too have been empowered by the Spirit. Clearly, just as Jesus was a charismatic prophet, so, from Pentecost onwards, the disciples are a company of charismatic prophets. Therefore, for the disciples, as for Jesus earlier, the gift of the Spirit is vocational.

In spite of the obvious differences in genre and content between John and the historian Luke, John's pneumatology is amazingly similar to Luke's. In John, as well as in Luke, Jesus is a pneumatic, a man of the Spirit. As John reports it, from Jesus' baptism to the post-resurrection transfer of the Spirit to the disciples, Jesus is uniquely and exclusively the bearer of the Spirit. Though, like Luke, John portrays Jesus as a pneumatic, in contrast to Luke, John does not portray Jesus as a charismatic. That is, he does not portray Jesus as a charismatic prophet, after the pattern of the charismatic prophets Elijah and Elisha, performing miracles in the power of the Spirit. In John, as in Luke, Jesus is prophet, rather "the prophet" (John 6:15), but not a charismatic. Significantly, in John, as well as in Luke, the disciples are pneumatic, or men of the Spirit. They became pneumatic when, after the resurrection, Jesus appeared among them, breathed on them, and said, "Receive the Holy Spirit" (John 20:22). Like Jesus Himself, they are given the Spirit for mission: "as the Father has sent Me, I also send you" (John 20:21). Not only are they pneumatic but the disciples are also charismatic. As in Acts, having been commissioned and having received the Spirit, their mission or vocation is to bear witness to Jesus (John 15:27). In John, however, this charismatic mission is merely announced, and not reported, because John has nothing equivalent to Luke's second book, his Acts of the (charismatic) Apostles. In a real sense, Acts is as much a sequel to John's Gospel as it is to Luke's first book, which is his report of the charismatic Christ. Because he has nothing equivalent to Luke's "Acts," the nearest that John comes to reporting any charismatic experience of the disciples is his oft-repeated autobiographical claim, "I was in the Spirit" (Rev. 1:10, cf. 4:2, 17:3, 21:10).

Because Paul does not write the story of the Jesus of history, as do both Luke and John, he lacks their pneuma-Christology. Nevertheless, he parallels their vocational pneumatology, both in his own experience, and that of his converts. According to Luke's report, Paul was filled with the Holy Spirit when the disciple Ananias visited the convert of just three days in Damascus (Acts 9:17). Having been filled with the Holy Spirit Paul is numbered among the prophets and teachers at Antioch (Acts 13:1). Being subsequently sent into mission by the Spirit (Acts 13:4) Paul, the true prophet, opposes the false prophet, Bar-Jesus, at Paphos (Acts 13:9), is led by the Spirit (Acts 16:6-7; cf. 20:22-23; 21:4, 11), and is the agent by whom the disciples at Ephesus receive the Holy Spirit (Acts 19:6). As Luke reports it, Paul's charismatic experience closely parallels that of Peter. In other words, just as Peter is filled with the Holy Spirit three times (Acts 2:4; 4:8, 31), so is Paul (Acts 9:17; 13:9, 52). Moreover, just as Peter is led by the Spirit (Acts 10:19-20), so is Paul (Acts 13:1-2, et al.). Finally, just as Peter is the agent for the Samaritans to receive the Holy Spirit (Acts 8:15- 17), so Paul is the agent for the Ephesians to receive the Spirit (Acts 19:6). From these parallels, Luke intends his readers to understand that Paul's charismatic experience and vocation is fully equal to that of Peter, the prophet of Pentecost.

As Luke portrays it in Acts, then, Paul's experience of the Holy Spirit is vocational-charismatic. Incidental autobiographical information in his epistles both confirms and supplements Luke's portrait. For example, whereas Luke only reports that Paul was filled with the Holy Spirit (Acts 9:17, et al.), Paul tells us that, like the disciples on the day of Pentecost, he spoke in tongues. He writes to the Corinthians, "I thank God I speak in tongues more than you all" (1 Cor. 14:18). Writing later to the same church he boasts, "The signs of a true apostle were performed among you with all perseverance, by signs and wonders and miracles" (2 Cor. 12:12). These signs and wonders attested to his ministry, not only at Corinth, but everywhere Paul preached the Gospel, "from Jerusalem and round about as far as Illyricum" (Rom. 15:19b). This preaching of the Gospel "in the power of signs and wonders," moreover, is preaching "in the power of the Spirit" (Rom. 15:19a). It seems to be an inescapable conclusion that for Paul the only authentic apostolic ministry was one empowered by the Spirit.

Not only is Paul's experience and vocation charismatic, but that of his converts is also. Though neither Luke, in Acts, nor Paul, in his epistles, gives any details, the Galatians had "begun by the Spirit," that is, God had provided them with the Spirit and worked miracles among them (Gal. 3:5). Similarly, as Paul reminds the Thessalonians, "for our gospel did not come to you in word only, but also in power and the Holy Spirit" (1 Thess. l:5a). The Thessalonians, in common with Christians at Corinth, lacked no gift (1 Cor. 1:8), including the more spectacular gifts of the Spirit, such as the word of wisdom, the word of knowledge, faith, the gift of healing, the effecting of miracles, prophecy, the distinguishing of spirits, various kinds of tongues, and the interpretation of tongues (1 Cor. 12:8-10). The Christians in Rome, as well, Paul reminds them, have a variety of gifts, including the ubiquitous gift of prophecy (Rom. 12:6ff.). Because, with the possible exception of his epistles to the churches at Rome and Ephesus, Paul's letters are circumstantial, our knowledge of the charismatic experience of his converts is as incidental as it is of Paul's own charismatic experience. In particular, we know so much about the experience of the Corinthians because of their misunderstanding of the gifts of the Spirit and their undisciplined excesses in the exercise of those gifts. Significantly, then, wherever the evidence is explicit, the churches which Paul founded are charismatic in reality, as well as in theory. And this is exactly what we would expect from reading about the ministry of this charismatic apostle to the Gentiles in the Acts.

Diversity in New Testament Pneumatology

The evidence which we have canvassed in the writings of Luke, John, and Paul demonstrates a primary and fundamental unity in New Testament pneumatology. First and foremost, for Luke, John, and Paul the Holy Spirit has a Christological focus. Each of these writers also understands the Holy Spirit in personal terms. Consequently, each has an incipient Trinitarian theology. Complementing this Christological focus, the Holy Spirit is given for vocation—Jesus is the charismatic Christ and the disciples and their converts are a charismatic community in mission. In addition to this fundamental and pervasive unity of perspective on the Holy Spirit, there is also a diversity of perspectives on the Holy Spirit among these leading witnesses to New Testament pneumatology. This diversity of perspectives relates more to each author's terminology and to the range of activity which each author assigns to the Holy Spirit in Christian experience than it does to their fundamental theology. The Christ event is the decisive factor in their unity of perspective on the Holy Spirit. In contrast, the diverse religious heritage of each author best explains the diversity of perspectives. Luke has a Septuagintal heritage. John reflects Non-conformist Judaism, and Paul was a converted Pharisee.

Diversity of Religious Background

As we have already seen, Luke's history of the origin and spread of Christianity reflects a distinctively Septuagintal heritage. This Septuagintal influence includes genre. Luke-Acts is historical narrative, and, in regards to genre, is closer to the histories of Israel, both sacred and secular (for example 2 Maccabees) than to the literature of the New Testament. Both Luke's Christology and his pneumatology have a pervasive Old Testament heritage. In particular, his charismatic motifs and his characteristic terminology echo the charismatic pneumatology of the Septuagint. Of course, there are significant differences between the pneumatology of the Septuagint and Luke-Acts. In the main, in Luke's pneumatology the charismatic activity of the Holy Spirit is potentially universal, rather than limited to leaders, and is hypostatized—the Holy Spirit is fully personal. But these differences are developments, rather than contradictions to, or new directions of, Septuagintal Pneumatology. Therefore, Luke's pneumatology reflects a Septuagintal heritage in a way which the pneumatology of John and Paul, in spite of their own indebtedness to the Old Testament, does not.

Whereas the conceptual world of Luke is Septuagintal, the conceptual world of John is Non-conformist Judaism (the Judaism which doesn't conform to Pharisaism). Of the four sects of Judaism which Josephus writes about, only Pharisaism survived the Jewish Revolt of AD 66-73 and became normative Judaism by default. The Sadducees, the Essenes and the Zealots (the political, the pietistic and the revolutionary sects, respectively), all disappeared when the Romans reconquered the land and destroyed its institutions. John the Baptist, the Essenes and other pietistic groups constituted what is best called Non-conformist Judaism. The discovery of the Dead Sea Scrolls beginning in 1947, and their subsequent publication, reveals another community of Non-conformists, probably of the Essene type. The Johannine literature has many affinities with this recently discovered library of the Qumran sectaries.

In his monograph, *John—Evangelist and Interpreter*, Stephen Smalley summarizes the numerous links between the Scrolls and John's Gospel. He writes,

> There are, to begin with, obvious literary parallels. These are particularly evident in the *Manual of Discipline* (or *Community Rule)*, the best manuscript of which was discovered in cave 1; although they also exist in other documents from Qumran. The opening column of the *Rule*, for example, refers to "practicing truth", and loving the "sons of light" while rejecting the "sons of darkness", in a way that is reminiscent of the Fourth Gospel. Again, the concept of knowledge in association with the existence and activity of God, and man's relationship to him, is present in both the *Rule* and John. Similarly, the Scrolls and the Fourth Gospel both contain references to the wisdom of God, and his enlightenment of the worshipper (and initiant) in answer to (covenant) faith. Even the title of the *War* Scroll (IQM), *The War of the Sons of Light and the Sons of Darkness* (in Vermes, *The War Rule)*, has a Johannine ring about it; although its apocalyptic content approximates more closely to the ethos of the Revelation than the Gospel of John.[8]

Of particular interest for our subject is the similarity of the "two-spirit" theology between Non-conformist Judaism and John. We read of this as early as the Testament of the Twelve Patriarchs. According to the Testament, Judah admonished his children, "Know, therefore, my children, that two spirits wait upon man—the spirit of truth and the spirit

---

[8] Stephen S. Smalley, *John: Evangelist and Interpreter* (Greenwood, S.C.: The Attic Press, Inc., 1978), 31.

of error" (Judah 20:1) Furthermore, "And the spirit of truth testifieth all things, and accuseth all; and the sinner is burnt up by his own heart and cannot raise his face to the judge" (Judah 20:5). All of this sounds very Johannine. Jesus promised the disciples:

> And I will ask the Father, and He will give you another Helper, that He may be with you forever; *that is,* the Spirit of truth (John 14:16-17a). When the Helper comes, whom I will send to you from the Father, *that is* the Spirit of truth, who proceeds from the Father, He will bear witness of Me (John 15:26). And He, when He comes, will convict the world concerning sin, and righteousness, and judgement . . . But when He, the Spirit of truth, comes, He will guide you into all truth (John 16:8, 13).

To those who have received the "anointing" but who are, nevertheless, in danger from "antichrists" or "false prophets", John himself warns, "We are from God; he who knows God listens to us; he who is not from, God does not listen to us. By this we know the spirit of truth and the spirit of error" (1 John 4:6).

Clearly, the Spirit-Paraclete in the Johannine literature echoes the "two-spirit" language in the literature of Non-conformist Judaism. This language is at the center, rather than the periphery, of Johannine pneumatology, in the same way that, "filled with the Holy Spirit" and other terminology is at the center of Lucan pneumatology. Just as the latter is clearly Septuagintal, so the former belongs to the world of Non-conformist Judaism in general. Specifically:

> . . . John was familiar with Qumranic patterns of thought. . . . It is otherwise difficult to account for the proximity of John's Gospel to the Scrolls, and for the fact that certain features in both afford a closer parallel than that which exists in any other Jewish or Greek non-Christian literature of the time or earlier. John's relation to sectarian Judaism as exemplified by Qumran, then, helps to fill in the picture so far as the Jewish influence on his background is concerned.[9]

---

[9] Ibid., 66.

This is not to suggest that the Johannine Spirit-Paraclete is *derived* from Qumran. It is merely to suggest that John shares a common background with this Non-conformist Judaism. Furthermore, we must not forget that, whether John had any personal contacts with Qumran, or not, and as striking as the parallels between the two are, the chief influence of Johannine pneumatology is Christian and not Qumranian.

Paul's religious heritage is radically different from Luke's Septuagintal background and John's Jewish Non-conformist heritage. In contrast to Luke and John, Paul was a converted Pharisee. For example, he reminds the Galatians, "For you have heard of my former manner of life in Judaism, how I used to persecute the church of God beyond measure, and I tried to destroy it; and I was advancing in Judaism beyond many of my contemporaries among my countrymen, being more extremely zealous for my ancestral traditions" (Gal. 1:13-14). Similarly, he boasts about his former advantages in Judaism, which he now discounted in the light of Christ, when writing to the Philippians, "...circumcised the eighth day, of the nation of Israel, of the tribe of Benjamin, a Hebrew of Hebrews; as to the Law, a Pharisee" (Phil. 3:5). While there are many differences among scholars about the impact of Paul's rabbinic background upon his theology, few would be so brash as to deny that Paul, the apostle to the Gentiles, was formerly a fanatical Pharisee.

The subject of Paul and Pharisaic Judaism is massive and fully deserving of the magisterial treatment it receives, for example, in *Paul and Rabbinic Judaism* by Davies, and *Paul and Palestinian Judaism* by E. P. Sanders. For our purposes it must suffice to observe that just as Luke's pneumatology echoes a Jewish Non-conformist heritage, so Paul's pneumatology echoes his Rabbinic heritage. According to Davies, for the Rabbis on the one hand, "the experience of the Holy Spirit demanded membership in a certain kind of community," and, on the other hand, "the Spirit could only be experienced in a fitting 'age.'"[10] Similarly, on the one hand, the most characteristic aspect of Paul's pneumatology, "is his

---

[10] W.D. Davies, *Paul and Rabbinic Judaism: Some Rabbinic Elements in Pauline Theology*. Revised Edition (New York: Harper and Row, Publishers, Inc., 1967), 208.

emphasis on the Spirit as the source of Christian fellowship and unity."[11] The evidence for this is both obvious and ample. For example:

> ... for Paul the Spirit is not only the life of the new man but of the New Israel, the Church. The latter is the Body of Christ and is animated by the Spirit (1 Cor. 12:13); the solidarity of all Christians with one another and with their Lord, through the one Spirit, is such that Christians as a Body no less than individuals constitute a temple of the Holy Spirit (1 Cor. 3:16). It is wholly consonant with this that gifts of the Spirit are bestowed not for individual self-gratification but for the upbuilding or edification of the whole society of Christians (1 Cor. 12:14ff.).[12]

Having surveyed the relevant Rabbinic and Biblical data, Davies concludes, "[Paul's] insistence on the essentially social nature of the Spirit's activity falls into line with Rabbinic thought."[13] Furthermore, on the other hand, Paul is, "a Pharisee who believed that the Messiah had come."[14] We have seen earlier that for Paul the Holy Spirit is the Spirit of Christ and will not repeat this data. To conclude, "The Pauline doctrine of the Spirit, then, is only fully comprehensible in the light of Rabbinic expectations of the Age to Come as an Age of Spirit and of the community of the Spirit."[15]

To sum up, the pneumatology of Luke, John, and Paul is shaped by the Christ-event and their own subsequent and complementary experience of the Spirit. Moreover, the pneumatology of all three is rooted in the Old Testament revelation of the Spirit of God (though, due to the constraints of time, we have not discussed this in relationship to the pneumatology of John or Paul). Though the pneumatology of all three is shaped by Christ and rooted in the Old Testament revelation, it is mediated through the particular religious heritage of each author: the Septuagint for Luke, Non-conformist Judaism for John, and Pharisaic

---

[11]Ibid., 201.
[12]Ibid.
[13]Ibid., 207.
[14]Ibid., 216.
[15]Ibid., 217.

Judaism for Paul. Herein, then, is the explanation for the unity and diversity in New Testament pneumatology. The unity derives from the common Christian experience of each author; the diversity lies in the way each author expressed this common Christian experience according to the canons and idioms of his particular theological heritage.

Diversity of the Holy Spirit's Roles

In addition to the diversity of religious background which impacted upon their respective pneumatologies, Luke, John, and Paul also assign a variety of roles to the ministry of the Holy Spirit. This diversity of role is loosely related to a combination of factors such as: 1) their diversity of religious heritage, 2) the experience of each author, and 3) the authorial intent of each for his writings. The three primary roles for the Spirit are in the areas of service, salvation, and sanctification. We have already discovered that not only for Luke, but also for John and Paul, the gift of the Holy Spirit to God's people is vocational in purpose and result. That is, it is charismatic, gifting them for service and empowering that service to make it effective. In respect to Christian vocation, the charismatic experience of God's people parallels that of Christ. For John and Paul, as well as for Luke, therefore, God's people are a charismatic community. This dimension of the Spirit's activity is the only one which is common to the pneumatology of all three.

While Luke describes the role of the Holy Spirit exclusively in terms of charismatic vocation, or service, John describes it in terms of service, as we have seen, and also in terms of salvation. Thus, not only will the Spirit-Paraclete teach and succor the disciples, but the Spirit is also part of the salvation process. In this regard, the Spirit-Paraclete, "He, when He comes," Jesus announces to his disciples, "will convict the world concerning sin, and righteousness, and judgment; concerning sin, because they do not believe in Me" (John 16:8-9). Thus, the Spirit of Truth, who will come as Jesus' *alter ego*, will give succor to the disciples, and will bring conviction of sin to the world. Moreover, the Spirit is the agent by which the sinner is transformed into a disciple, or believer. To the Pharisee Nicodemus, Jesus announces, "unless one is born again, he cannot see the Kingdom of God" (John 3:3). Further, for one to enter the Kingdom of God, he must be, "born of water and the Spirit" (3:5), because, "that which is born of flesh is flesh, and that which is born of the Spirit is spirit" (3:6). Nicodemus is not to marvel that Jesus had said, "You must be born again" (3:7), for, "the wind blows where it wishes and you hear the sound of it but do not know where it comes from and where it is going; so is everyone who is born of the Spirit" (3:8). In salvation, then, the Spirit both convicts of sin, and causes the sinner to be "born again," or born of the Spirit. In contrast to Luke's pneumatology, then, in John's pneumatology the Spirit has two roles: service and salvation.

Whereas Luke has but one dimension of the activity of the Spirit in his pneumatology, namely, service, and John has two, service and salvation, Paul has three dimensions: service, which he shares with both Luke and John; salvation, which he shares with John alone; and sanctification, which is his exclusive emphasis. In regards to the role of the Spirit and salvation, the Spirit initiates the salvation process; that is, it is through the agency of the Spirit that the individual is brought into the community of believers, the body of Christ (1 Cor. 12:13). As Paul points out to the Romans, if anyone does not possess the Spirit, he actually does not belong to Christ, regardless of what he professes (Rom. 8:9). Moreover, the Spirit's actions in the salvation process include washing, sanctification, and justification (1 Cor. 6:11). In writing to Titus, Paul insists that salvation did not come on the basis of righteous acts which man performed, but by the "washing of regeneration and renewing by the Holy Spirit" (Titus 3:5). The Spirit's presence in the believer's life is also the pledge or guarantee (*arrabon*) that the salvation process which began in regeneration, renewal and incorporation, will be brought to completion (2 Cor. 1:22, 5:5; Eph. 1:14). With this hope, the Spirit is also the firstfruits (*aparche*) of final salvation (Rom. 8:23), and the Christian is one who is sealed (*sphragizo*) until the time of God's redemption (2 Cor. 1:22, Eph. 1:13-14).

For Paul, the Spirit's role is also to be seen in the sanctification of the believer. Sanctification speaks of dedication to God, and entails a process by which a believer moves on to a life of holiness in his walk with God. In 2 Thess. 2:13, Paul writes that salvation comes through a belief in the truth and the sanctification of the Spirit. In this process of sanctification, the fruit of the Spirit—the very character of Christ—is reproduced in the lives of the believers (Gal. 5:22-23). This sanctification which the Holy Spirit brings has an ethical dimension. For example, Paul contrasts it with sexual immorality (1 Thess. 4:1-8), and with the works of the flesh, such as immorality, impurity, sensuality, idolatry, sorcery, and many other sins, both social and religious (Gal. 5:19-21). Thus, those who have been made "saints" in salvation by the washing of the Spirit, are to live saintly lives through the fruit of the Spirit.

To sum up, Luke, John, and Paul each has his own perspective on the roles of the Spirit. For all three, the Spirit is brought into relation to service. For John and Paul, the Spirit is brought into relation to salvation, and for Paul, the Spirit is brought into relation to sanctification. In other words, in Luke's pneumatology the Spirit has one role, service; in John's pneumatology the Spirit has two roles, service and salvation; and in Paul's pneumatology the Spirit has three roles, service, salvation and sanctification. Clearly, Luke, John, and Paul each has his own distinctive and yet complementary perspective on the Holy Spirit. For each one, his pneumatology is rooted in the Old Testament, is mediated by his religious heritage, is shaped by the Christ-event and his own experience of the Spirit and is expressed through the role(s) which he attributes to the Spirit. The following chart illustrates this complex chain of interrelationships, influences and emphasis.

Septuagint →	Christ →	Luke →	Service
OT Non-conformist →	Christ →	John →	Service Salvation
OT Rabbinic Judaism →	Christ →	Paul →	Service Salvation Sanctification

Thus, there is unity and diversity in the pneumatology of Luke, John, and Paul. Every interpretation which ignores the unity and/or denies the diversity will distort the New Testament doctrine of the Holy Spirit.

The observation that there is unity and diversity in the Lucan, Johannine, and Pauline perspectives on the Holy Spirit has far-reaching implications for the doctrine of the Holy Spirit, furthermore, for the suspicion, hostility, misunderstanding, and acrimony which deplorably divides the main Protestant traditions from each other. In fact, the New Testament reality of unity and diversity is the key to breaking the impasse which characterizes much Protestant theologizing on the Holy Spirit. The key is to recognize that the Reformed, Wesleyan and Pentecostal traditions, with their soteriological, holiness and charismatic emphases, respectively, are each legitimate expressions of the diversity of the New Testament witness to the Holy Spirit. The challenge which then comes to each tradition is to recognize that the emphasis in the pneumatology of the other traditions is not contradictory to its own emphasis, but is complementary. Consequently, each tradition then faces the Biblical mandate to embrace the full unity of New Testament pneumatology and to produce a doctrine of the Holy Spirit which is fully canonical, neither denying nor despising any dimension of the role of the Spirit in salvation, sanctification and service.

CHAPTER EIGHT

THE REBIRTH OF PROPHECY:
TRAJECTORIES FROM MOSES TO JESUS AND HIS FOLLOWERS

I begin with an observation. This is that many biblical scholars and theologians, alike, explain Jesus, either primarily or exclusively in titular terms i.e., Son of God, the Son of Man, Christ and *Kurios*.[1] But these emphases are inadequate, if not actually misleading. According to the witness of Luke, John, and Paul, Jesus ministers publicly as the eschatological anointed prophet—an often-ignored scholarly emphasis.[2] My thesis, therefore, is that the prophethood of Jesus, and subsequently that of his followers, is the rebirth of the prophet's ministry which was born in the leadership of Moses and his associates.

---

[1] For example, see "Four well-known descriptions of Jesus," in C.F.D. Moule, *The Origin of Christology* (Cambridge: Cambridge University Press, 1977), 11-46.

[2] Numerous scholars write about the Christology of, for example, Luke, John, and Paul, either ignoring or minimizing the explicit, interrelated themes of prophet, prophecy, to prophesy. These include: Joel B. Green, *Theology of the Gospel of Luke* (Cambridge: Cambridge University Press, 1995); Andreas J. Kostenberger, *A Theology of John's Gospel and Letters* (Grand Rapids, MI: Zondervan, 2009); Herman Ridderbos, *Paul: An Outline of His Theology* (ET, John Richard De Witt, Grand Rapids, MI: Wm. B. Eerdmans, 1975) et al.

Moses and the Birth of Prophecy

Prophecy is as early as, and as extensive as, Israel's history.[3] Abraham is the first person to be identified as a prophet (Genesis 20:7, Psalm 105:15) and, chronologically, Malachi is the last of the writing prophets. But the prophetic *movement* in Israel did not begin with Abraham nor did it end with Malachi. Rather, the prophetic *movement* is born with Moses' prophethood (Deuteronomy 18:15-19) and that prophethood which was transferred to Moses' associates (Numbers 11:24-29).

Moses Prophesies About His Successor (Deuteronomy 18:14-22)

Moses functions as God's prophet before he is ever identified as one. For example, the book of Numbers repeatedly reports that "God/the LORD spoke to Moses" (1:1; 2:1; 3:1, 11; 4:1; 5:1, 5, 11, etc.). This speaking is a "face to face" encounter between God and Moses (Number 12:6-8). As such, Moses is the prophet of prophets. Indeed, he is the greatest of prophets within a brotherhood of prophets, which in his generation include his siblings Miriam and Aaron.

At the end of his life the Lord will affirm that Moses is the greatest prophet. He, in fact, will be the standard by which future prophetic leaders will be assessed. At the time when Israel is finally about to enter Canaan, the promised land, Moses informed the assembled nation, "The LORD your God will raise up for you a prophet like me, from your countrymen, you shall listen to him" (Deuteronomy 18:15).[4]

In due time Joshua, Moses' servant, will succeed him as the leader of Israel.

Undoubtedly, it appeared to many Israelites that Joshua is the promised successor, for he "was filled with the spirit of wisdom, for

---

[3]Helpful surveys of the origins and development of the prophetic movement in Israel include the following: Gerhard von Rad, *Old Testament Theology, Volume II The Theology of Israel's Prophetic Traditions* (New York: Harper & Row, Publishers, 1965); Wilf Hildebrandt, *An Old Testament Theology of the Spirit of God* (Peabody, MA: Hendrickson Publishers, 1995); Robin Routledge, *Old Testament Theology: A Thematic Approach* (Downers Grove, IL: InterVaristy Press, 2008), 209-15.

[4]For a helpful discussion of this text see Patrick D. Miller *Deuteronomy* (Interpretation: A Bible Commentary for Teaching and Preaching, Louisville, KY: John Knox Press, 1990), 151-56.

Moses had laid his hands on him; and the sons of Israel listened to him" (Deuteronomy 34:9). Nevertheless, whereas Joshua proved to be *a* prophet like Moses he did not prove to be *the* prophet like Moses—because he lacked the "face to face" relationship with the Lord which Moses had experienced (Deuteronomy 34:10-12). In this way the prophet like Moses theme becomes an unfulfilled trajectory down through the generations.

Moses Earnestly Desires the Prophethood of All Israel
(Numbers 11:29)

In his own time, though Moses is the unique, incomparable prophet, he is not the only prophet of his generation. At the appropriate time the LORD will support Moses in his leadership duties by transferring some of the Spirit of prophecy from Moses to the seventy elders of Israel (Numbers 11:25). When this happens Moses, perhaps wistfully, exclaims, "Would that all the LORD's people were prophets, that the LORD would put His Spirit upon them!" (Numbers 11:29). Earlier God had covenanted that his people would function as a nation of priests (Exodus 19:6). Now, to this Moses adds the desire that God's people might function as a nation of prophets.

As Israel's history advances, four or five secondary trajectories develop the theme of prophethood within the nation. For example: David functions as a royal prophet, who is empowered and inspired by the Spirit (1 Samuel 16:13, 2 Samuel 32:1); the prophet Isaiah prophesies about a future servant prophet (Isaiah 11:2, 42:1, 61:1); Elijah and Elisha minister as charismatic prophets who multiply food, raise the dead, etc. (1 Kings 17-2 Kings 9); and many often-anonymous prophets suffer rejection (2 Kings 17:13, 2 Chronicles 36:16). In addition, prophets like Isaiah and Ezekiel prophecy about a time of inward renewal for the nation (Isaiah 4:4, 44:1; Ezekiel 36:25-27), and Joel prophesies about a time when the nation's renewal is followed by an outpouring of the Spirit of prophecy on the nation (Joel 2:28-32).[5]

---

[5] A more extensive discussion of the birth and growth of prophecy within Israel can be found in Walter Eichrodt, *Theology of the Old Testament*, Volume I (ET J.A. Baker, Philadelphia: Westminster Press, 1961), 289-391; Wilfred Hildebrandt, *The Cessation of Prophecy in the Old Testament*, unpublished thesis, (University of South Africa, 2004).

Summary

Within Israel, Moses is the fountainhead of prophecy. The first trajectory, the prophet like Moses motif, promises to be fulfilled in Joshua, his companion and successor, and perhaps later in Elijah and Elisha. But in the end, the early assessment holds true—no prophet like Moses arises to fulfill Moses' prophecy. Complementing his prophecy about his successor being a prophet like himself, Moses also expresses the earnest desire that the LORD would raise up a nation of prophets. This trajectory becomes a swelling stream as first one freshet and then another swells the onflowing waters. In the end, both trajectories of prophecy come to an end, unfulfilled. They will remain unfulfilled until the births of the two most remarkable prophets in the history of God's people—John, known as the Baptist, and Jesus of Nazareth.

Jesus and the Rebirth of Prophecy

The births of these two remarkable prophets, John and Jesus, herald the rebirth of prophecy within Israel. Ultimately, Jesus proves Himself to be the prophet like Moses, and his companions fulfill the nation of prophets stream extended from Moses through the prophet Joel to the first post-Easter Day of Pentecost. Each of the major writers of the books of the New Testament, namely, Luke, John, and Paul, individually and diversely report about this rebirth of prophecy in their own day. The following exposition surveys these important witnesses to the restoration of prophecy in New Testament times according to their place in the canon of New Testament writings.

The Witness of Luke[6]

Luke reports about the restoration of prophecy in his two-volume history about the origin and spread of the Gospel. His first volume, which

---

[6]Essential bibliographical surveys include: Francois Bovon, *Luke the Theologian* (Second Revised Edition, Waco, TX: Baylor University Press, 2006) and Martin William Mittelstadt, *Reading Luke-Acts in the Pentecostal Tradition* (Cleveland, TN: CPT Press, 2010).

is traditionally identified as The Gospel of Luke, is primarily about Jesus, the prophet like Moses. Volume two, traditionally identified as the Acts of the Apostles, is primarily about Jesus' companions and successors who serve as the prophethood of all believers. Together, these two volumes, Luke-Acts, report the initial fulfillment and unprecedented extension of Moses' prophecies about a successor prophet who is the leader of a growing nation of prophets.

Jesus is the Prophet like Moses (Luke 1-24)

After Moses' death Joshua succeeded him as the leader of Israel. Contrary to all expectations, however, Joshua did not fulfill Moses' prophecy that his successor will be a prophet like himself, one to whom the Lord speaks face to face (Deuteronomy 34:10).

Nevertheless, across the generations a later Joshua (Jesus in Greek) will arise to be the eschatological prophet like Moses.

The Restoration of Prophecy: The births of John and Jesus (Luke 1:5-2:52)

It is an observable fact that in Israel's history canonical prophecy ceased in the time of Malachi. This is reflected in a famous rabbinic tradition, which reports that when Haggai, Zechariah, and Malachi died prophecy ceased within Israel (Tosefta Sotah 8.2).[7] The vacuum, which the cessation of prophecy created was, in time, filled by the Jewish apocalyptic movement. Furthermore, about 400 years after Malachi God restored prophecy among His people. This restoration of prophecy began to happen with the events which were associated with the births of two cousins, namely, John and Jesus. Luke reports about this restoration of prophecy in his so-called, "Infancy Narrative" (Luke 1:5-2.52).

The restoration of prophecy about which Luke reports in his Infancy Narrative is both sudden and unexpected. It begins with an

---

[7]Quoted from George Foot Moore, *Judaism in the First Centuries of the Christian Era: The Age of Tannaim* (Volume 1, New York: Schocken Books, 1971 repr.), 421. For a more nuanced interpretation of the data from the Second Temple period see Max Turner, *Power from on High: The Spirit in Israel's Restoration and Witness in Luke-Acts* (JPT Sup. 9, Sheffield: Sheffield Academic Press, 1996).

announcement to an aged priest, Zacharias, that his barren wife, Elizabeth, will in due time give birth to a son (Luke 1:5-25). In this setting, the son, the mother, and the father are all filled with the Holy Spirit and prophesy (1:15-17, 76; 1:41, 67). In addition, Mary, the mother-to-be of Jesus, and an aged worshipper, Simeon, also prophesy (1:58, 2:25ff). Finally, Luke concludes by reporting about a prophetess, Anna (2:36, 38). Luke, I suggest, expects that his readership will recognize that this restoration of prophecy is an initial, incipient fulfillment of Joel's prophecy—of which the outpouring of the Spirit on Jesus' disciples on the Day of Pentecost is a second, greater fulfillment.

In addition to reporting about the restoration of prophecy in the persons of John, Elizabeth, Mary, Zacharias, Simeon, and Anna, Luke also clearly establishes the identity of Mary's son, Jesus. Mary's son, by a miracle of the Holy Spirit is "the Son of God," a.k.a., "The Son of the Most High" (Luke 1:32, 35). In subsequent narratives Luke confirms this identity. For example, Luke's genealogy of Jesus identifies him, "supposedly [to be] *the* son of Joseph," but in actuality, "the [human] *son* of Adam, the [divine] *Son* of God" (3:23-38). Also, Luke reports that when Jesus was twelve years old he was conscious of the fact that the Temple in Jerusalem is his "Father's *house*" (2:49). Further, when he was about the age of thirty, the Father, in the setting of Jesus' baptism by John, speaks from heaven, publicly identifying Jesus to be His son (Luke 3:21, 22). Even the devil understands who Jesus is, tempting him on the basis that he is, "the Son of God" (Luke 4:3). Therefore, in his narrative, the Son of God theme is not only the first thing which Luke proves about Jesus, but it is, unarguably, the most important fact about Jesus which he will teach.

Jesus ministers throughout Galilee (Luke 3:1-9:50)

Luke divides the prophetic ministry of Jesus into two phases. The first phase is his ministry in Galilee (3:1-9:50) and the second phase is his ministry "On the Road" from Mt. Transfiguration in Galilee to Mt. Ascension outside of Jerusalem (Luke 9:51- Acts 1:11).

Luke brackets or book-ends (the principle of *inclusio*[8]) these two phases by Jesus' experience of theophany. Thus, Luke introduces Jesus' public ministry in Galilee by reporting the theophany when he was baptized by John (A) and he concluded his report about Jesus' ministry in Galilee by reporting his experience of theophany on the so-called Mount of Transfiguration (A1). Luke's report of the theophany on Mt. Transfiguration, in turn, also introduces Jesus' "On the Road" ministry (B), which is not concluded until the theophany which is associated with his ascension (B1).

(A) Theophany: The Lord commissions Jesus (Luke 3:1-4:30)

Luke's primary purpose in his narrative about Jesus is to demonstrate that the Son of God, once he has been anointed by God, functioned or ministered as the eschatological anointed prophet. This anointing happened when Jesus was baptized by John the Baptist (Luke 3:21, 22). This baptismal experience turns into a dramatic theophany—the tangible appearance of God. The two signs of this theophany—the voice from heaven, and the descent of the Spirit—echo those of Isaiah 42:1. These signs are appropriate for the setting, which is his commissioning for ministry. On the one hand, it is his anointing; on the other hand, he will henceforth minister as the Servant Prophet (Luke 4:16-21, Isaiah 61:1, 2). But, his ministry as prophet will also include many of the charismatic elements which were typical of the prophetic ministries of Elijah and Elisha (Luke 4:14-17). And before the day is out Jesus experiences that rejection which typified the prophets of earlier generations (Luke 4:18-30; 2 Kings 17:14,15). This theophany, then, anoints or commissions the Son of God to be the prophet of God for a complex prophetic ministry throughout Galilee.[9]

---

[8]For a brief discussion of *inclusio* see David E. Aune, *The Westminster Dictionary of New Testament & Early Christian Literature & Rhetoric* (Louisville, KY.: Westminster John Knox Press, 2003), 229.

[9]Contra Joseph Verheyden, "Calling Jesus a Prophet" in *Prophets and Prophecy in Jewish and Early Christian Literature*, edited by Joseph Verheyden, et al. Wissenschaftliche Untersuchungen zum Neuen Testamet 2. Reihe 286. (Tubingen: Mohr Siebeck, 2010), 177-210. Having examined select Lukan texts Verheyden concludes, "Luke does not want Jesus to be called a prophet or to be presented like one" (204). But his methodology is truncated. The *full range* of Jesus' prophetic acts (signs and wonders),

(B) Jesus establishes his prophethood throughout Galilee (Luke 4:31-9:30)

Luke's readership is "omniscient" i.e., privy to everything which Luke has chosen to report. But no one in any of Jesus' immediate and various audiences would have understood the prophetic character of Jesus' words and deeds either clearly or fully. In his inaugural ministry activity Jesus had identified Himself to be a prophet—a claim which his town's people had violently rejected. But having been commissioned to be a prophet, and having identified Himself as a prophet he must next confirm that he is a prophet. In other words, he must "put up or shut up." Luke reports this very thing in his narrative which reports Jesus' Galilean ministry.

In his narrative about Jesus' ministry Luke records some of the questions which people ask about Jesus in their struggle to understand who he is. Initially, Jesus sparks the question, "What is this message? For with authority and power He commands the unclean spirits, and they come out" (Luke 4:36). Then there are the questions, "Why do you eat and drink with tax-gatherers and sinners?" (5:30); "Why do you do what is not lawful on the Sabbath?" (6:2). But the most significant question which Jesus' ministry evokes is the "who" question. For example, when Jesus forgives the sins of the paralytic some scribes and the Pharisees ask, "Who is this *man* who speaks blasphemies?" (5:21). Later, John the Baptist asks, "Are You the One who is coming, or do we look for someone else?" (7:19). A Pharisee muses, "If this man were a prophet (as he is reputed to be, e.g., 7:16) he would know who and what sort of person this woman is" (7:39). Even that old fox, Herod, asked, "Who is this man about whom I hear such things?" So, scribes, Pharisees, and kings ask about Jesus' identity but, ironically, the "multitudes" do not. Based on Jesus' words and works they correctly, but not precisely, understand that Jesus must be either John the Baptist, or Elijah, or one of the prophets of old (who has arisen again [9:18]). And before Jesus moves on from Galilee to Judea, God, once again, reveals that Jesus is his prophet (9:35).

---

such as multiplying food, raising the dead, etc are not integrated into his discussion. For a corrective perspective see Luke Timothy Johnson, *Prophetic Jesus, Prophetic Church* (Grand Rapids: Wm. B. Eerdmans, 2011).

Leading up to the theophany on the Mount of Transfiguration the uncertainty about who Jesus is becomes increasingly clear to those who have eyes to see and ears to hear.

For example, Jesus has healed a leper, reminiscent of Elisha healing Naaman the leper (Luke 5:12-16). Also, Jesus gives to God's people the blessings and the cursings (6:20-26) just as Moses had laid out the blessings and the cursings before Israel. In addition, he teaches in parables (6:39-45), reminiscent of Isaiah and the other prophets. Further, he raises the dead (7:11-17) a miracle which was uniquely associated with Elijah and Elisha. Finally, he multiplies a little food into much food, echoing similar miracles by Moses, Elijah, and Elisha. Either witnessing one or more of these prophetic activities for themselves, or else having heard reports about them from others, the multitudes rightly conclude that Jesus is a prophet (9:19). At this point in Jesus' ministry God makes explicit to Jesus' inner circle of disciples (Peter, James, and John) what Jesus' unprecedented prophetic ministry is all about. His Spirit-empowered words and works—from healing lepers to feeding the five thousand—must mean that Jesus is the long-awaited prophet like Moses.

(A_1) Theophany: Jesus concludes his ministry in Galilee (Luke 9:28-50)

Jesus' lengthy and extensive ministry in Galilee concludes with a theophany whereby God, Himself, confirms that Jesus is the prophet like Moses (Luke 9:28-36). This confirmation, by words and works and then by theophany, is the double witness required in the Law to confirm a truth (Deuteronomy 19:15). And so, there on the so-called Mount of Transfiguration Jesus' metamorphosis (a.k.a., transfiguration) matches Moses' earlier glorification on Mount Sinai; his impending departure (i.e., ἔξοδος) matches Israel's earlier Exodus from Egypt; the theophanic cloud of God's presence, which envelopes Jesus and his companions, matches the cloud of God's presence which earlier had enveped Mount Sinai. Finally, God's command to "listen to Him" fulfills Moses' command to Israel that they must listen to the prophet like himself whom God will raise up to be his successor.

Therefore, the theophany at the Jordan River when John baptized Jesus commissioned him to be that long-awaited prophet like Moses and the theophany on the Mount of Transfiguration has recommissioned

Jesus as the prophet like Moses. This is a timely recommissioning and confirmation for Jesus' ministry now begins to move into its final, decisive phase.

Jesus ministers "On the Road" from Mt. Transfiguration to Mt. Ascension (Luke 9:51- Acts 1:11)

(B) Theophany: Jesus departs from Mt. Transfiguration (Luke 9:28-51)

The theophany on the Mount of Transfiguration is not only the defining moment in Jesus' prophetic ministry in Galilee, it is also the pivot point in his ministry. As Luke reports it, "And it came about, when the days were approaching for His ascension, that He resolutely set His face to go to Jerusalem" (Luke 9:51). For Jesus this will be a journey from popular acclaim to ultimate rejection; from triumph to tragedy. In Jerusalem he will die both as the rejected prophet and the rejected king.

(C) Jesus extends his ministry "On the Road" (Luke 9:51-24:49)

As Jesus journeys along the way toward Judea and Jerusalem he, of course, ministers as the recommissioned prophet like Moses. First, he sends out the seventy to minister on his behalf (Luke 10:1-25). This is reminiscent of the seventy elders who earlier extended Moses' ministry among God's people (Numbers 11:16-29).[10] He next reaffirms the twofold love command—love God and love one's neighbor—as the basis for life (Luke 10:25-28). Further, as he travels toward Jerusalem he is conscious that his present popularity is transient and that he will die in Jerusalem as the rejected prophet (11:45-52, 13:31-35). When he approaches Jericho, just a day's journey from Jerusalem, a blind beggar implores, "Jesus, Son of David, have mercy on me!" (18:37, 38). Jerusalem, of course, is not only the city that kills the prophets (13:31-

---

[10]For a recent discussion of the relationship between Luke's narrative and Numbers 11.24-30 see Robert P. Menzies, "The Sending of the Seventy and Luke's Purpose," in *Trajectories in the Book of Acts*, ed. by Paul Alexander, et al. (Eugene, OR: Wipf & Stock, 2010), 87-113. Other interpreters, relate the 70 to the table of nations in Genesis 10, and interpret the sending of the 70 (72) to prefigure/anticipate the later mission to the Gentiles. Octavian D. Baban, *On the Road Encounters in Luke-Acts: Hellenistic Mimesis and Luke's Theology of the Way*. (Milton Keynes: Paternoster, 2006).

35), but it is also the city of David, where his sons are crowned king. Therefore, from this point forward Luke's narrative begins to meld into one theme the two earlier trajectories in Jesus' life—*born* to be king but *commissioned* to be prophet. From now on, i.e., from Jericho to Golgotha, Jesus will minister as both prophet and king; indeed, as the rejected royal prophet.

Jesus is the Prophet-Maker. Just as the Lord had raised up a small community of prophets to assist Moses, so he will also raise up a larger, ever multiplying community of disciples to extend Jesus' prophetic ministry. In regard to their future prophethood Jesus promised his disciples: 1) that God would give his Spirit to those who asked him (Luke 11:13); 2) that the Spirit would inspire words of defense for when the disciples suffered persecution (Luke 12:12; 21:14, 15); 3) that the Spirit would empower their witness (Luke 24:49, Acts 1:8); and 4) that they would be baptized in the Holy Spirit (as the Father had earlier promised through John the Baptist, Acts 1:4, 5). These promises begin to be filled on the post- Easter Day of Pentecost when Jesus poured out his Spirit of prophecy upon the company of about 120 disciples (Acts 2:1-21). What happened on the Day of Pentecost is a transfer of the Spirit from Jesus Himself, to his disciples (Acts 2:33). By this transfer of the Spirit Jesus' disciples became a community of Spirit-baptized, Spirit-empowered, and Spirit-filled prophets (Acts 1:5,8; 2:4,17-21).[11]

(B_1) Theophany: Jesus departs from Mt. Ascension (Luke 24:50-53, Acts 1:9-11)

Two theophanies, which we may describe as the "Cloud of His Presence," bracket Jesus' "On the Road" ministry. The first, on Mt. Transfiguration (Luke 9:28-35), has recommissioned Jesus to be the prophet like Moses; the second concludes his ministry on earth. However, the second theophany not only concludes his "On the Road" ministry, but also effects his enthronement as Christ and Lord—specifically, his enthronement as the Davidic King (Acts 2:22-36). In this way, the Davidic Messiah theme of the infancy narrative (1:5-

---

[11] Jacob Jervell, *The Theology of the Acts of the Apostles* (Cambridge: Cambridge University Press, 1996). In particular see the section, "The People of the Spirit," 43-54.

2:52) and the prophethood themes of Jesus' ministry in Galilee and On the Road (3:1-24:49) finally come together. In other words, the one who was born to be King, and, yet, who ministered as the anointed prophet, is finally enthroned as the royal prophet.

Jesus' Followers Become a Nation of Prophets (Acts 1-28)

The three short years of Jesus' Spirit-anointed public ministry conclude with his ascension and the subsequent transfer of the Holy Spirit from Himself to his disciples (Acts 1:9-11, 2:33). This transfer is a far greater transfer of leadership responsibility and the complementary power of the Spirit than the earlier prototypical transfer of some of the Spirit from Moses to the seventy elders (Numbers 11:24-29). It is, in fact, the greatest transfer in the experience of God's people. Its unparalleled greatness is in the fact that just as the Spirit was earlier given to Jesus exclusively and fully, so, beginning on the Day of Pentecost, the Spirit is transferred fully to his disciples. Further, its unparalleled greatness lies in the fact that whereas the Spirit was transferred from Moses to the Seventy for their ministry to Israel, so beginning on the Day of Pentecost, the Spirit is transferred from Jesus to the disciples not only for their ministry to Israel, but also for their ministry to the nations (Acts 1:8).

Jesus pours out the Spirit of Prophecy (Acts 1:12-2:41)

The post-Easter Day of Pentecost advances the salvation history of the prophet like Moses from tragedy to triumph. Fifty tumultuous and traumatic days earlier this royal prophet was rejected by his citizens and crucified. Now this same royal prophet, having ascended to heaven and being exalted to God's right hand as co-regent (Acts 2:30-32, 13:30-36), baptizes his loyal followers in the same Spirit of prophecy which had earlier anointed and inaugurated his own prophet like Moses ministry.

In the old covenant God had founded Israel to be a nation of priests (Exodus 19:5, 6). Now with the coming of the prophet like Moses, beginning with the outpouring of the Holy Spirit on the Day of Pentecost, God transforms his people into a nation of prophets. When God established the old covenant he presenced Himself on Mount Sinai with awesome and dramatic signs; now on the day of Pentecost his presence is signified by the theophanic signs of "wind and fire" (Acts 2:2,3). The third sign on the Day of Pentecost, namely, the disciples spoke in tongues as the Spirit gave utterance (Acts 2:4), signifies the transformation of Israel into a nation of Spirit-filled prophets.

Moses' transfer of leadership and its complementary transfer of the Holy Spirit sees its greatest fulfillment on the Day of Pentecost. The covenant context for the former transfer is the Sinai Covenant; for the latter it is the new covenant. The public location of the first transfer is the Tabernacle; for the latter transfer it is the Temple. The occasion for the first transfer was that Moses was to share his leadership with the elders of Israel; for the second transfer Jesus passes his prophetic ministry on to his disciples. In the time of Moses, the Spirit was transferred from one to a group of seventy. Similarly, on the Day of Pentecost the Spirit of prophecy is transferred from Jesus to a group, namely, the 120 disciples. Finally, in the time of Moses the sign that the transfer has taken place was that the elders prophesied. Similarly, on the Day of Pentecost the sign that the Spirit has been transferred from Jesus to the disciples was that they prophesied. Therefore, just as in the generation when the covenant was given to God's people at Mount Sinai the elders became the prophets of the covenant, so now, on the Day of Pentecost Moses' earnest desire that all God's people might be prophets continues toward fulfillment as the 120 disciples become the prophets of the new covenant.

The outburst of prophecy on the day of Pentecost, therefore, is an implicit fulfillment of Moses' earnest desire about a nation of prophets (Numbers 11:29). It is also an explicit fulfillment of an oracle of the prophet Joel. In an example of what is called "charismatic exegesis"[12] Peter, now himself a Spirit-filled prophet, explains the experience of Pentecost to the amazed and bewildered crowd. Applied to the experiences of Pentecost Joel's oracle, which Peter prophetically updates, five points are made. One, the *eschatos* or "last days" have arrived. The corollary of this is that the Messiah or Christ has already come. Two, this outpouring of the Spirit is about "prophesying". Three, this prophesying is (potentially) universal.[13] Everyone, male and female, young and old,

---

[12] Aune, *The Westminster Dictionary of New Testament & Early Christian Literature & Rhetoric*, 83.

[13] In a review essay of *The Prophethood of All Believers*, "Does Luke Believe Reception of the 'Spirit of Prophecy' Makes All 'Prophets'? Inviting Dialogue with

and [free] and bondslaves are included. No one is disqualified or excluded. And, as we have observed, this outpouring of the Spirit extends that earlier outburst of prophesying which Luke had reported in his Infancy Narrative about John and Jesus. Four, the Pentecost outpouring of the Spirit is attested by "wonders in the sky above" (2:2, 3, wind and fire) and "signs on the earth beneath" (2:4, "tongues-speaking"). Five, it is not a day of judgment, rather it is a great and glorious day—a day of blessing. And in these ways, then, the outpouring of the Spirit on the Day of Pentecost is a new stage in the fulfillment of Moses' earnest desire that the nation of priests would become a nation of prophets.

2.1.22 The growth and spread of the nation of prophets (2:42-12:25)

The outpouring of the Spirit on the Day of Pentecost established the disciples as a fledgling nation of prophets. It also inaugurated their Holy Spirit-baptized, Spirit-empowered and Spirit-filled witness about Jesus. As a result, that very day about three thousand Pentecost pilgrims who had gathered in Jerusalem from the ends of the earth were added to the church (Acts 2:9-11, 41). From this day onward the number of disciples, a.k.a. believers, not only grows in Jerusalem but soon spreads to the provinces (Samaria and Judea) and ultimately to the ends of the earth (Rome). Luke's reports about this numerical growth and geographic spread illustrates that the messengers who preach the good news are prophets and that those who believe are established as prophetic communities.

As Luke reports it, in Acts everyone who preaches the good news about Jesus is a prophet. This begins with the 120 disciples on the Day of Pentecost. Soon, over five thousand believers (Acts 4:4) are filled with the Holy Spirit and speak the word of God with boldness (Acts 4:31). In addition to Luke's special emphasis on the apostles as prophets, Luke also emphasizes the role of two "full of the Holy Spirit" deacons—Stephen in Jerusalem and Philip in Samaria and elsewhere (Acts 6:8-8:40). At this

---

Roger Stronstad" Max Turner challenges this interpretation. JEPTA, Vol XX 2000, 3-24. In the context of the prophetic gift David Hill observes, " . . . in the book of Acts that Christian prophecy, as an eschatological power of the Spirit, is a possibility for any Christian—else what would the fulfillment of Joel's prophecy mean?" David Hill, *New Testament Prophecy* (NFTL Atlanta: John Knox Press, 1979), 99.

point in his narrative Luke turns his attention back to Peter, who, having ministered in Jerusalem, next ministers in Samaria and then embarks on an evangelistic tour throughout some of the cities of western Judea (Acts 9:32-11:18). Finally, Luke focuses his narrative on Paul, who was filled with the Holy Spirit as early as his visit to Damascus (Acts 9:17). Paul's so- called three missionary journeys are misnamed by the church. They are, like Peter's earlier evangelistic tour (Acts 9:32-11:18), also evangelistic tours. Thus, the first thing which Luke informs his readership about Paul (and also Barnabas) at the beginning of the first evangelistic tour is that Paul and Barnabas are prophets (Acts 13:1). Similarly, the first thing we learn about the second evangelistic tour is that Paul and Silas, the new team, are also prophets (Acts 13:1, 15:32). These examples illustrate that in New Testament times it is Spirit-filled, Spiritful prophets who do the work of evangelism. This does not surprise Luke's readership, for early in his narrative he reported that the two prophets, John and Jesus, preached the good news (i.e., evangelized) to Israel (Luke 3, 4).

The nation of prophets spreads throughout the Empire (Acts 13:1-28:28)

On the Day of Pentecost Jesus established the disciples as a community of prophets. Before Luke turns his attention to the spread of the Gospel to the provinces he reports that the five thousand believers are filled with the Spirit and give prophetic witness in Jerusalem (Acts 4:4, 31-33). Luke will now identify the Christian community as the "church," that is, as the "nation" of prophets (cf. Deuteronomy 4:10, 9:10, 18:16; LXX). In addition to this rapid, exponential growth in the number of disciples in Jerusalem to full prophetic nationhood, Philip's "full of the Holy Spirit" ministry in Samaria results in a community of believers (Acts 8:12), who subsequently receive the Spirit as a result of a visit from Peter and John (Acts 8:14-17).[14] Sometime later the Lord will lead Peter

---

[14]In his commentary on Acts John Calvin insists that the Samaritans, the Household of Cornelius, and the Ephesian Twelve (Acts 8, 10, 19) were all "regenerate" (i.e., converted-initiated) *before* they subsequently received "the excellent graces of the Spirit," John Calvin, *The Acts of the Apostles* (Grand Rapids, MI: Baker Book House), 338-39, 407.

to a house church of righteous, God-fearing Gentile believers in Caesarea, i.e., Western Judea (Acts 10:1-11:18), who as a result are baptized in the Holy Spirit with the same sign as the disciples experienced on the Day of Pentecost, namely, speaking in tongues (Spirit-inspired "prophetic" speech). In addition, Luke reports the example of a group of about twelve disciples or believers in Ephesus who subsequently receive the Spirit when Paul returns to that city (Acts 19:1-7).[15] The result is that, as with the earlier examples in Jerusalem and Caesarea (Acts 2:4, 10:46), these Ephesians also speak in tongues, that is, they prophesy (Acts 19:6).

The Witness of John

Luke wrote his two-part history to *teach* his readership about the origin and spread of the Gospel (Luke 1:1-4). In contrast John wrote to *evangelize* his readers: "that you might believe that Jesus is the Christ, the Son of God; and that believing you may have like in his name" (John 20.31). Nevertheless, both Luke and John identify the theophany which begins the public ministry of Jesus to be his anointing for his prophet like Moses ministry. Thus, there is significant unity in their reports about the rebirth of prophecy when God anointed Jesus. But there is significant diversity as well. For example, for Luke the work of the Holy Spirit, whether for Jesus or his followers, is exclusively vocational. In contrast, for John, the work of the Holy Spirit may be either vocational or soteriological. In general, in his Gospel John begins with the prophet like Moses theme, transitions to the inward renewal theme, and concludes with the transfer of leadership—transfer of the Spirit theme.

Jesus: The New Fountainhead of Prophecy

According to John's Gospel, the public ministries of John the Baptist and his successor, Jesus, herald the fulfillment of the two complementary Moses as fountainhead of prophecy streams. On the one hand, Jesus is the prophet like Moses. On the other hand, just as the Spirit was earlier

---

[15]Though Luke's report about events in the early church continues for another nine chapters, Ephesus is, in fact, the last city which Luke reports to be evangelized.

transferred from Moses to the elders, so the Spirit will also be transferred from Jesus to his disciples.

Jesus is the Prophet like Moses[16]

For Luke the primary, most essential, fact about Jesus is that he is "the Son of God." Similarly, for John the most important fact is that Jesus is, "the Son of God." Because Jesus is the Son, he is God in the beginning (John 1:1). He, therefore, is the creator, and the life and the light (John 1:1-13). He was God's eternal Word who, in Jesus, became flesh; that is, the only begotten of God (John 1:14,18). Jesus' predecessor, John the Baptist, bore a twofold witness about him; namely, Jesus is both, "the Lamb of God," and, "the Son of God" (John 1:29, 34). In fact, nothing more needs to be observed about John the Evangelist's identification of Jesus than that he is the only begotten, the beloved son of God (John 3:16).

In addition to reporting that Jesus is, "the Son of God," John also reports that Jesus is the ultimate, exclusive fulfillment of Moses' prophecy about his successor. John emphasizes this by contrasting the status or identity of John the Baptist and Jesus. At the height of John the Baptist's ministry, priests and Levites from Jerusalem ask him, "Who are you?" (John 1:19). John denies that he is the Anointed One (John 1:20). When his interrogators continue to press him about his identity he denies that he is the eschatological Elijah, whose coming had been prophesied by Malachi (Malachi 4:5), and also denies that he is "the Prophet" (like Moses). Rather, the Baptist insists, he is merely the

---

[16]Interpreters draw different conclusions about the prophet like Moses theme in John's gospel. For example, Howard M. Teeple, *The Mosaic Eschatological Prophet* (JBLMS, Volume X, Philadelphia: Society of Biblical Literature, 1957), 120, claims, "The Fourth Gospel presents Jesus as *the* Prophet of the Hellenistic miracle-worker type, the bringer of *gnosis*, with prophetic knowledge of the past, present, and future." However, six years later T. Francis Glasson, *Moses in the Fourth Gospel* (Studies in Biblical Theology, London: SCM Press Ltd, 1963), 21 observes, "The importance of this Moses/Messiah parallelism has not always been sufficiently recognized in interpreting the New Testament." The John 6 Passover pericope self-evidently presents Jesus as *the* Prophet after the pattern of Moses and not after the pattern of the Hellenistic miracle-worker. See also Urban C. von Wehlde, "The Role of the Prophetic Spirit in John: A Struggle for Balance," in *Prophets and Prophecy in Jewish and Early Christian Literature*, edited by Joseph Verheyden, et al. Wissenschaflich Untersuchungen zum Neuen Testament 2. Reihe 286. (Tubingen: Mohr Siebeck, 2010), 211-242.

eschatological Messenger about whom Isaiah had prophesied (John 1:22, 23; Isaiah 40:3).

At this point John the Evangelist shifts the focus of his narrative from John the Baptist, and the questions about his identity, to his successor, who is also his superior (John 1:25-28). John identifies the Baptist's successor to be a certain Joshua, a.k.a., Jesus (John 1:29). The juxtaposition of these three introductory pericopes (John 1:19-24, 1:25-28, 1:29-34), implicitly shows that not John, but, rather, Jesus is the Christ, anointed by the Spirit (1:29-34, 41); not John but Jesus is the prophet like Moses. Therefore, though ultimately Jesus is more than the Prophet—he is the Son of God (John 1:1,18, 34) —he is never less than the fulfillment of Moses' prophecy about a successor prophet like himself (Deuteronomy 18:15).[17]

The descent of the Holy Spirit upon Jesus at his baptism by John the Baptist both anoints him and inaugurates his public ministry. John the Evangelist emphasizes that this anointing is permanent. The Baptist reports that he was able to identify his successor not only because the Spirit descended upon Jesus but also because the Spirit would remain on him (John 1:33). Further, the Evangelist emphasizes that the gift of the Spirit to Jesus is exclusive and unlimited, for, as he reports, God gives the Spirit to Jesus without measure (John 3:34). It is for this reason, namely that he is the exclusive bearer of the Spirit, that Jesus must ultimately "go away," for unless he does so the Paraclete will not come to them (John 16:7). By ascending to the Father, and sending the Paraclete, Jesus fulfills John the Baptist's prophecy that his successor will baptize his disciples in the Holy Spirit (John 1:33).

Jesus is recognized to be the prophet like Moses in a variety of different contexts or settings throughout his ministry. Ironically, it is the woman of Sychar in Samaria, rather than the Jews, who first recognizes that Jesus is a prophet. "Sir, I perceive that You are a prophet," she observes (John 4:19). Shortly thereafter, once Jesus has travelled through Samaria into Galilee he attested the principle, "that a prophet has no honor in his own country" (John 4:44). Later, John's Passover narrative (John 6:1-71) with all of its Moses-Exodus typology, reports that after

---

[17]Similarly, T.F. Glasson, *Moses in the Fourth Gospel*, 40 observes, "There can be little doubt that the way in which Christ is presented in the Fourth Gospel is intended to indicate that he is the fulfillment of Deut. 18:15- 19."

Jesus fed the 5,000 in the Wilderness the crowd affirm, "This is of a truth the Prophet who is to come into the world" (John 6:14). John follows the Passover narrative with a "Feast of Tabernacles" or exodus narrative (John 7:1-8:59). Echoing Moses' supply of "living" water from the rock (Numbers 20:8-13), Jesus offers streams of living water (John 7:37-39). Some in the festival crowd conclude, "This certainly is the Prophet" (John 7:40). Finally, John reports that the man who was born blind, whom Jesus has healed, identifies his healer to be a prophet (John 9:17). Clearly, these data show that in Samaria, Galilee and Judea, throughout his ministry Jesus not only identifies Himself to be a prophet, but others identify him to be a prophet. This is particularly the case in John's Passover and Feast of Tabernacles narratives, where in Galilee and in Judea the crowds identify him to be the Prophet like Moses (John 6-8).

Jesus commissions his disciples (John 17:18, 20:19-23[18]; Acts 2:1-4)

After reporting some preliminary considerations John opens his Gospel with a report that Jesus receives the Holy Spirit (John 1:29-34). Similarly, bookending his Gospel narrative (the principle of *inclusio*) John reports that Jesus transferred the Spirit to his disciples (John 20:19-23). By this act Jesus, Himself the Spirit-anointed prophet like Moses, initiated the fulfillment of the second prophetic stream of which Moses is the fountainhead. Upon receiving the Spirit Moses' ancient desire that all God's people might be prophets, specifically, that God would put his Spirit upon them begins to be fulfilled in the experience of the disciples.

Of necessity, the transfer of the Spirit from Jesus to the disciples had to await the conclusion of Jesus' own public ministry as the anointed prophet. This is because, as we have already observed, Jesus is the exclusive bearer of the Spirit from his anointing through to his resurrection—the entire span of his ministry. But though the Spirit is not given to the disciples until after his resurrection, neither do they begin their ministry as witnesses to Jesus until after his death and resurrection.

---

[18]For a full discussion of the recent interpretation of John 20:22 to the year AD 2000 see James McDonald, "Understanding John 20:22 as the Power and the Promise of the Spirit" (ACTS, 2001). He concludes, "There can be no question that John 20:22 represents the empowering of the disciples for proclaiming the words of Christ with authority and power, and that this empowering takes place on the day of Pentecost," 58.

Jesus begins to promise his disciples that co-operatively the Father and the Son will soon give them the Spirit-Paraclete, who is his *alter ego*. Thus, Jesus will ask the Father and he will give the disciples the Paraclete, who, unlike Jesus, will not go away (John 14:15). The Spirit-Paraclete will ensure that the disciples will "remember" everything necessary for their witness (John 14:26). Further, the gift of the Spirit-Paraclete is for the disciples' witness about Jesus (John 15:26, 27). Ultimately, through the true witness of the disciples the Spirit-Paraclete will glorify Jesus (John 16:13, 14). Clearly, according to this data the Spirit-Paraclete will soon be given to the disciples as Jesus' companions to enable them to be knowledgeable, truthful, effective witnesses about Jesus.

Jesus transferred the Holy Spirit to his disciples after the resurrection. This transfer signals the end of his own public, Spirit-anointed ministry. But this transfer is one episode in a complex series of events. These events are historically separated and spread over a period of about seven weeks. The first event is Jesus' *prayer* of commissioning (John 17:18).[19] On the night before his crucifixion Jesus prayed for his disciples, "As Thou didst send Me into the world, I have also sent them into the world" (John 17.18). This prayer is followed by the **act** of commissioning on the evening of resurrection day. At this point Jesus came to his disciples, saying, "Peace *be* with you; as the Father has sent Me, I also send you" (John 20:21).[20] John then reports, "And when he said this, He breathed on them and said, 'Receive the Holy Spirit'" (John 20:22). Advancing from John's Gospel to the episode of the outpouring of the Holy Spirit on the Day of Pentecost is the *power* and *sign* of

---

[19]For a detailed discussion of Jesus' pre-crucifixion prayer as "prophetic intercession" see Sukmin Cho, *Jesus as Prophet in the Fourth Gospel* (Sheffield: Sheffield Phoenix Press, 2006), 121-130.

[20]Based on apparent echoes between Jn 20:22 ("Jesus breathed") and the creation account, Gen 2:7 ("God breathed") there is a long-standing tradition among one school of interpreters that this episode (Jn 20:19-23) is about new life, i.e., being born again. For example, Dunn, *Baptism in the Holy* Spirit, 173-82, interprets John 20:22 to be an experience of regeneration. But a random sampling of recent commentaries written from within various traditions illustrates that the text itself is about commissioning for mission and not about new birth: C.K. Barrett, *The Gospel According to St. John*, second edition (Philadelphia: The Westminster Press, 1978); Barnabas Lindars, *The Gospel of John*, NCB (Greenwood, S.C: The Attic Press, Inc., 1972); J. Ramsey Michaels, *The Gospel of John*, NICNT (Grand Rapids: Wm. B. Eerdmans, 2010); Leon Morris, *Commentary on the Gospel of John*, NICNT (Grand Rapids: Wm. B. Eerdmans, 1971). Note: while these and other interpreters write about "commissioning" and "mission" in general, I interpret this commissioning more specifically to be about prophetic vocation.

commissioning (Acts 2:1-4). This commissioning of the disciples, then, separates what in Jesus' own earlier commissioning/anointing had been one event: prayer, the tangible gift of the Spirit, and the resulting empowering of the Spirit.[21]

The commissioning of the disciples has the same meaning for them as the earlier commissioning of Jesus. Thus, just as Jesus was earlier consecrated for ministry by being anointed, so Jesus consecrates his disciples to be prophets like Himself. Also, just as the Father sent Jesus for the prophet like Moses' vocation, so Jesus, in turn, sends out his disciples into the world to witness. Therefore, the gift of the Spirit to the disciples after the resurrection constitutes them to be heirs and successors to Jesus' prototypical prophetic ministry.

In addition to his Gospel John also wrote three letters and a book of prophecy, namely, the Revelation of Jesus Christ. These other writings are consistent with, and also extend, the implications of the commissioning scene which concludes his Gospel narrative (John 20:19-23). For example, when he writes his first epistle John assures his readership that it is they, and not the self-appointed teachers, with their message of sinless perfection (1 John1:5-10), who have the anointing (of the Holy Spirit, 1 John 2:20). He also assures them that this anointing comes from God and is true and is not a lie, as is the teaching of the self-appointed teachers (1 John 2:27). Therefore, those teachers listen to the Spirit of error and are false prophets, whereas John's readership listens to the Spirit of truth, that is, the Spirit of God and, by implication, true prophets such as John, himself (1 John 4:1-6).

In addition to this general description of his readership, who are a community of prophets who have been anointed by the Spirit of Truth,

---

[21]Recently, Cornelis Bennema, "The Giving of the Spirit in John 19-20," in the Spirit and Christ in the New Testament and Christian Theology, edited by J. Howard Marshall, Volker Rabens and Cornelis Bennema (Grand Rapids: Wm. B. Eerdmans, 2012), following the lead of Felix Porsch (1974), observes two complementary facts: 1) Jesus' glorification is a process, involving his death, resurrection, and ascension, and 2) the Spirit is given in ways that parallel this glorification process (86-104). According to Bennema, the three stages of the giving of the Spirit include: 1) the Symbolic giving of the Spirit at the cross (John 19:30), 2) this giving is as the Spirit of salvation (20:22), and 3) the giving of the Spirit as Paraclete at a later time (e.g., Pentecost) (87). However, Bennema's soteriological interpretation is nullified by the observation that John 20:19-23 has many direct linguistic and thematic parallels to Luke 24:36-47; Acts 1:8, which are about Jesus commissioning his disciples for witness (i.e., vocation).

John, when he writes the book of the Revelation of Jesus Christ, is conscious of prophetic inspiration.[22] He identifies this experience by the formula, "in the Spirit" (Revelation 1:10, 4:2, 17:3, 21:10). Therefore, on the principle of *inclusio*, he insists from first to last that "this book" is words of prophecy which must be heeded and which must not be altered (Revelation 1:3; 22:7, 18). Further, what is true in his experience is also true of the experience of his readership. Thus, it is by the "Spirit of prophecy" that they testify or witness about Jesus (Revelation 19:10).[23] This means that from the time after the resurrection when Jesus transferred the Spirit to his disciples (John 20:19-23) until the end of the first century when John identifies his readership as communities of prophets (1 John 2:20, 27; 4:6; Revelation 19:10), the number of prophets has grown from the original Twelve to an early approximation that "all the LORD's people were prophets, that the LORD [had] put His Spirit upon them" (Numbers 11:29).

The Spirit and Inward Renewal (Salvation)

In addition to what John writes about Jesus as the prophet like Moses and his disciples as a fledgling nation of prophets, John also writes about the Spirit and inward renewal. This soteriological emphasis is found in several tributary streams, such as, but not limited to, the prophecies of Isaiah and Ezekiel, and is reported by John—particularly in his narrative about Nicodemus and Jesus.

Jesus' teaching about discipleship and prophethood is given to his inner circle of companions and is, apparently, given privately. In contrast, his teaching about the Holy Spirit and inward renewal, like John the Baptist's teaching on the same subject, is given to outsiders and even strangers. Therefore, when he teaches about inward renewal he draws his language from those Scriptures which form a common heritage between

---

[22]George Johnston, *The Spirit-Paraclete in the Gospel of John.* (Society for New Testament Studies Monograph Series 12, Cambridge: Cambridge University Press, 1970), Johnston observes, "[The Revelation of John is] the longest and most obvious example of prophecy in the New Testament," 139.

[23]F.F. Bruce supports this interpretation in his essay, "The Spirit in the Apocalypse," in *Christ and Spirit in the New Testament: Studies in Honor of Charles Francis Digby Moule*, edited by Barnabas Lindars and Stephen S. Smalley (Cambridge: Cambridge University Press, 1973). Bruce observes, "In Rev. 19.10, however, it is through *Christian* prophets that the Spirit of prophecy bears witness," 337.

*Chapter 8 The Rebirth of Prophecy: Trajectories from 181
Moses to Jesus and His Followers*

Himself and his audience. This common heritage includes promises about cleansing by water and purification by the Spirit of judgment and of burning (Isaiah 4:4); the pouring out of lifegiving water and Spirit (Isaiah 44:4) and cleansing and a new heart and a new Spirit (Ezekiel 36:25, 26). There are many variations on these themes in the prophets, but it is this conjunction of water and Spirit in Isaiah and Ezekiel which is the heritage common to Nicodemus and Jesus.

Early in his Gospel John introduces a certain ruler of the Jews, named Nicodemus, into his narrative. Nicodemus initiates an encounter between himself and Jesus. This is a meeting between two prominent teachers. Nicodemus is "the teacher of Israel" and Jesus is the anointed teacher (John 3:10, 3:2). Their meeting leads to a clash between the Rabbi as the teacher of tradition (Nicodemus) and the Rabbi as charismatic prophet (Jesus).

Nicodemus begins the meeting complimenting the Rabbi, whom John's readers know has been anointed by the Spirit (John 1:29-34). Jesus immediately brushes this compliment aside and affirms authoritatively, "... I say to you, unless one is born again he cannot see the Kingdom of God" (John 3:3). Nicodemus attempts to deflect Jesus' assertion, asking rhetorical absurdities: "How can a man be born when he is old? He cannot enter a second time into his mother's womb and be born, can he?" (John 3:4). Ignoring these absurdities Jesus insists, again authoritatively (I say to you), "unless one is born of water and Spirit, he cannot enter the Kingdom of God" (John 3:5). Thus, to be born again is to be born of water and Spirit. In other words, Jesus teaches about two orders of birth or existence, namely, the physical and the spiritual, for, "that which is born of the flesh is flesh and that which is born of the Spirit is spirit" (John 3:6). Marveling at Jesus' teaching Nicodemus asks, "How can these things be?" (John 3:9). Jesus rebukes him for his lack of understanding, "Are you the teacher of Israel, and you do not understand these things?" (John 3:10).

Jesus rebukes Nicodemus as teacher because his knowledge of the prophets with their prophecies about cleansing and inward renewal by water and Spirit, is the common ground between the two of them. But, because Nicodemus has failed to understand the prophets it does not surprise John's readers that he also fails to understand Jesus, the Spirit-anointed prophet (like Moses). In spite of this, before long Nicodemus is defending Jesus (John 7:45-53), and by the time of Jesus' crucifixion he, along with a certain Joseph of Arimathea, seems to be a secret disciple (John 19:38-42). These latter two references to Nicodemus imply that because of his earlier encounter with Jesus he has been born again, born of water and Spirit, born of flesh and Spirit (John 3:3-6). For Nicodemus, this is a triumph of prophecy over tradition.

Summary

The above discussion of The Witness of Luke (2:1) and The Witness of John (2:2) illustrates that Luke's perspective of prophethood is more focused than is John's.

That is, he focuses on just the two streams of prophecy of which Moses is the fountainhead—Jesus as the prophet like Moses and Jesus' disciples as a growing nation of prophets. Luke is not only more focused than is John but he is also more comprehensive. He not only reports the transfer of the Spirit to the disciples but he also gives an extensive narrative in which he reports their developing prophetic ministries (Acts 2-28).

John reports these same two streams of prophethood of which Moses is the fountainhead. For example, like Luke he devotes his Gospel narrative to reporting about Jesus' ministry as the prophet like Moses. Like Luke, he also reports that Jesus transfers the Holy Spirit to his disciples for their service or vocation, but unlike Luke, he does not report about their subsequent and ongoing prophetic ministry. Therefore, in the "historical" sense the narrative subject of Acts is as much the sequel to John's narrative as it is to Luke's Gospel. In addition to this shared emphasis with Luke about the Spirit and the prophetic vocation, John also reports that Jesus also teaches about the Spirit and inward renewal or salvation. This is a theme from the Prophets which John does not have in common with Luke but which he does have in common with Paul.

The Witness of Paul

Readers of the New Testament recognize that for all of the significant differences between the Gospels of Luke and John, they have in common the theme of Jesus as the *NEW* fountainhead of prophecy, fulfilling that of which Moses is the original. Similarly, readers also quickly recognize that John has an additional emphasis, namely, the Spirit and salvation. In turn, readers of Paul's letters recognize that in his own way Paul, along with Luke and John, also emphasizes the Spirit and prophetic service, and along with John, he also emphasizes the theme of the Spirit and salvation. Further, Paul has an additional, unique emphasis – the theme of the Spirit and sanctification. Therefore, the theme of the Spirit and prophetic service can, with profit, be compared between the writings of Luke, John, and Paul. Similarly, the theme of the Spirit and salvation can be compared between John and Paul. Finally, Paul's theme of the Spirit and sanctification stands alone. In other words, with his emphasis on the complementary themes of the Holy Spirit and service, salvation and sanctification Paul's written doctrine of the Holy Spirit is much more complex than the doctrines of the Spirit which are to be found in either Luke's writings or John's writings. The following chart illustrates the distribution of the service, salvation, and sanctification themes among Luke, John, and Paul.

The Unity and Diversity of Holy Spirit Themes			
Theme	Luke	John	Paul
Service	☒	☒	☒
Salvation		☒	☒
Sanctification			☒

The Spirit and Prophetic Service

In the Acts of the Apostles Luke reported nothing about the apostle John's post-Pentecost prophetic ministry, except in those settings where he is found to be a companion of the apostle Peter (e.g., Acts 3:1-9, 8:14-17). In contrast, Luke reports extensively about Paul's ministry. In fact, along with Peter, Paul is one of Luke's great exemplars of a Spirit-filled prophetic ministry.

Paul's prophetic service in Acts[24]

The study of Luke-Acts shows that Peter is Luke's first and greatest hero in the fledgling nation of prophets. In Luke's narrative Peter, in fact, is the prototype prophet and Paul's ministry is validated by the standard of Peter's.[25] Paul, therefore, is Luke's second and great hero in the fledgling but rapidly growing nation of prophets.

The Christophany which a certain Saul of Tarsus experienced when he was en route from Jerusalem to Damascus effected radical changes. These changes include a new relationship with Jesus (from enemy to servant), a new vocation (from Pharisee to prophet), a new attitude toward Gentiles (from exclusion to inclusion in God's covenant people). Within three days of this transforming encounter a disciple in Damascus, Ananias, is sent to Saul to commission him to bear the name of Jesus to Gentiles, kings and the people of Israel (Acts 9:15). For this task Saul will be filled with the Holy Spirit (Acts 9:17). Immediately, Saul, now a Spirit-filled prophet, begins in Damascus to proclaim that Jesus is, "the Son of God" (Acts 9:21).

When Christians think about Paul and his ministry they almost always think about him as an apostle and/or his three missionary journeys. But these are not Luke's perspectives. For Luke, Paul is first and foremost a prophet and his so-called missionary journeys are actually prophetic or evangelistic tours.[26] Thus, Luke makes it explicit that the leaders of the first two journeys are the prophets Barnabas and Paul, and then Paul and Silas, respectively (Acts 13:1, 15:32). These itinerant tours fulfill the Old Testament prophetic mandate to be the "light to the Gentiles; that [they should] bring salvation to the ends of the earth" (Acts 13:46, 47; Isaiah 49:6). Indeed, Luke reiterates this prophetic mandate for

---

[24]F.F. Bruce, "Paul in Acts and Letters," in *Dictionary of Paul and His Letters*, edited by Gerald F. Hawthorne, Ralph P. Martin, Daniel G. Reid (Downers Grove, IL: InterVaristy Press, 1993.) Bruce observes, "If the author of Acts was, as seems most probable, an acquaintance and occasional companion of Paul, then Acts has claims to be recognized as a primary source of information about Paul," 680.

[25]A.J. Mattill, Jr., "The Purpose of Acts: Schneckenburger Reconsidered," in *Apostolic History and the Gospel*, edited by W. Ward Gasque and Ralph P. Martin (Grand Rapids, MI: William B. Eerdmans, 1970), 118.

[26]Jacob Jervell, *The Theology of the Acts of the Apostles*, 82-94. Jervell identifies the Paul of Acts, as a visionary, charismatic preacher, healer and miracle worker (13:8ff., 14:2ff., 16:16ff., 19:11ff., 20:7ff., 28:1ff.)," 92.

Paul, concluding his narrative about the spread of Christianity, reporting, "that this salvation of God has been sent to the Gentiles; they will also listen" (Compare Deuteronomy 18:15). And so, on the principle of *inclusio* from first to last (Acts 13:46, 47; 28:28), Paul and his companions minister about Jesus to the Gentiles, kings, and the sons of Israel as Spirit-filled prophets.

Paul the Prophet and Apostle[27]

In the nature of the case—Paul writes circumstantial letters—Paul identified himself in terms of apostleship (e.g., Romans 1:1, I Corinthians 1:1, etc.). This is for at least two reasons. One, he came to their cities and towns as one "sent" (*apostello*) to them, and, two, in more than one of the churches which he founded in these cities he later had to defend the authority and/or authenticity of his "sent" (apostolic) ministry. However, he does include himself among the "foundation," apostles and prophets (Ephesians 2:20) and among the "holy apostles and prophets" (Ephesians 3:5, compare I Corinthians 12:28). The phrase "apostles and prophets" is likely a hendiadys, meaning one group, i.e., apostles who are prophets,[28] rather than meaning two groups, i.e., "apostles" and "prophets."

As an "apostle and prophet" Paul's ministry—on his own reckoning—had a twofold emphasis. He understood himself to be a

---

[27]Recent interpreters handle Paul's data about the Spirit and prophecy differently. For example, at one end of the spectrum, Anthony C. Thistleton, *The Living Paul: An Introduction to the Apostle's Life and Thought* (Downer's Grove, IL: InterVarsity Press, 2009, 63-65) minimizes both the gifts of the Spirit and the supernatural. At the opposite end of the spectrum is Wayne Grudem, *The Gift of Prophecy in the New Testament and Today* (Revised Edition, Wheaton, IL: Crossway Books, 2000). In between these two extremes see Ben Witherington III, *The Paul Quest: The Renewed Search for the Jew of Tarsus* (Downers Grove, IL: InterVarsity Press, 1998), who gives a succinct discussion entitled, "Paul The Eschatological Prophet," 132- 35. In spite of its many fine insights it is a surprisingly truncated discussion for it is limited to Paul's prophetic words. But Paul's own letters make it plain that Paul's ministry often (if not always) included prophetic works (Galatians 3:1-5; I Thessalonians 1:5; 2 Corinthians 12:12; Romans 15:18, 19).

[28]E. Earle Ellis, "The Role of the Christian Prophet in Acts," in *Apostolic History and the Gospel*, Edited by W. Ward Gasque and Ralph P. Martin (Grand Rapids, MI: William B. Eerdmans, 1970). Ellis quotes E.G. Selwin, "who argued that 'apostles' were 'prophets' on circuit", explaining, "an apostle is simply a prophet who is sent (*apostello*) as a missionary," 64.

prophet in "word and deed" (Romans 15:18, compare Luke 24:19). Both of these dimensions—word and deed—are charismatic, for he ministered, "in the power of signs and wonders, in the power of the Spirit" (Romans 15:19). Indeed, as a prophet Paul ministered by the same Spirit-empowered signs and wonders, such as healing the sick and raising the dead, as did Peter. For example, when Paul writes to the Galatians he asks, rhetorically, "Does He then, who provides you with the Spirit and works miracles among you, do it by the Law, or by hearing with faith?" (Galatians 3:5). Also, Paul reminds the church of the Thessalonians that his witness came to them, both, "in word . . . [and] in power and in the Holy Spirit (1 Thessalonians 1:5). Later, Paul ministered to the Corinthians, "by signs and wonders and miracles" (2 Corinthians 12:12). This evidence by itself, and more so when supplemented by the relevant data in Acts about Paul's prophetic ministry (e.g. Acts 13:1-19:10), illustrates that from first to last Paul was one of those "apostles and prophets" who were mighty or powerful in the "deeds" of the Spirit.

Paul not only ministered in powerful "deeds" of the Spirit, but he also ministered in powerful "words" of the Spirit. The implications of Romans 15:18 are clear and far reaching, specifically, that *all* of Paul's witness about Jesus was prophetic and that *all* of Paul's letters are also prophetic. But in addition to this general fact Paul occasionally draws attention to specific words of prophecy in his letters. For example, in his letter to the Thessalonians Paul actually prophesies to the church, writing, "We say this by the word of the Lord" (1 Thessalonians 4:15).[29] Near the end of his life Paul prophesies to his son Timothy, "the Spirit explicitly says that in latter times some will fall away from the faith" (I Timothy 4:1).[30] Of course, Paul's letters also make it plain that prophecy is not limited to his own ministry, but the churches, themselves are prophetic communities. This is especially evident from what Paul writes to the church at Corinth (especially 1 Corinthians 12-14). But Paul hints about this reality in other letters, such as to the Ephesians, writing,

---

[29]David Hill, *New Testament Prophecy*, New Foundations Theological Library (Atlanta, John Knox Press, 1979). Hill offers an alternative explanation, namely, "that Paul goes back, not to a single saying of Jesus but to his apocalyptic teaching as a whole in order to validate his message and clarify the issues which agitated some of his correspondents," 130.

[30]See also Ben Witherington III, *The Paul Quest*, for a fuller discussion of Paul's prophetic utterances.

". . . be filled with the Spirit, speaking to one another in psalms and hymns and spiritual songs, singing and making melody with your heart to the Lord" (Ephesians 5:18, 19).

Paul may be expressing his prophetic consciousness when he writes to the Corinthians about his ministry to them, ". . . in the Holy Spirit, in genuine love, in the word of truth, in the power of God" (2 Corinthians 6:6-7). But, however this self-characterization is to be understood, Paul was a prophet. Of course, he was more than a prophet. He was, variously and overlapping, a prophet who was an apostle, an evangelist, and a pastor and teacher (Ephesians 4:11). In other words, he was, variously and overlapping, one sent out with good news who was also to shepherd and teach those who responded to the word of the Lord by faith. In all of this it appears valid to conclude that the ministry of prophets, and the prophetic communities which Paul established, were co-extensive with the spread of the Gospel.

The Spirit and Salvation

With the exception of one or two of his letters, such as Ephesians, which appears to be an extant copy of a circular letter, Paul's letters are all occasional or circumstantial letters. This means that whatever the circumstances which elicit the letter are the primary subjects of the letter. For this reason, Paul writes very little about the experiences of the Spirit and salvation to the churches which he addresses. However, when he writes to the church at Corinth he reminds them that by the Spirit they have been, "baptized into one body" (1 Corinthians 12:13) and that God has "placed the members, each one of them, in the body" (1 Corinthians 12:18). This experience of salvation is often termed conversion-initiation.[31] From Corinth itself he writes to the church at Rome that Christians are, "in the Spirit, if indeed the Spirit of God dwells in [them]" (Romans 8:9). Thus, those who have been justified by faith are "indwelt" by the Spirit, or have the Spirit resident within them. Therefore, Paul can observe that for Christians as individuals, "[their] body is a Temple of the Holy Spirit, who is in [them]" (1 Corinthians 6:19). Not only are individuals "indwelt" by the Spirit, but the entire body of Christians is as

---

[31] See Dunn, *Baptism in the Holy Spirit*, 90ff.

well (1 Corinthians 3:16). Developing this Temple imagery more fully Paul explains that, "the whole building, being fitted together is growing into a holy temple in the Lord; in whom you also are being built together into a dwelling of God in the Spirit' (Ephesians 2:21, 22). Therefore, in Paul's teaching about salvation all Christians have been incorporated into the body/church and individually and collectively are the dwelling place of God.

Paul emphasizes the "assuring" work of the Spirit in salvation in addition to the conversion-initiation work of the Spirit. For example, Paul writes, "God has sent forth the Spirit of His Son into our hearts, crying, 'Abba! Father!'" (Galatians 4:6) and Christians, "have received the Spirit of adoption as sons by which we cry out, 'Abba! Father!'" (Romans 8:15). Therefore, "the Spirit Himself bears witness with our Spirit that we are the children of God" (Romans 8:16). When he writes to the church in Corinth he explains that God "establishes" Christians in Christ. God does this, having anointed them, having sealed them, and having given them the Spirit as a pledge (2 Corinthians 1:21, 22). This word cluster, which explains that God establishes his people, means that God anoints his people with the Spirit to consecrate them for service; God seals his people with the Spirit to empower them for service, and that God gives the Spirit as a pledge obligating Himself to complete the work already begun. And so, either singly or as a cluster these experiences of the Spirit are God's witness of salvation to Christians.

The Spirit and Sanctification

The sanctifying work of the Holy Spirit is both an initial experience and an ongoing process of transformation. Paul writes about this sanctifying work in a number of texts. For example, using priestly language he writes that Gentile Christians are his "offering," sanctified by the Spirit (Romans 15:16). In other words, these formerly unclean people are now, by the Spirit, constituted a holy nation. Further, Paul reminds the Christians at Corinth, that with all of their ungodly background, "[they] were washed ... sanctified ... justified in the name of the Lord Jesus Christ, and in the Spirit of our God" (1 Corinthians 6:11). Later, when he writes to Titus, Paul observes that salvation is according to God's mercy, "by the washing of regeneration and renewing by the Holy Spirit whom He poured out on us" (Titus 3:5, 6). Clearly, it is this sanctifying work of the Spirit which is the basis for Paul identifying Christians as "saints" (Romans 1:7, 1 Corinthians 1:2, etc.). Paul's letters, however, show that "saints" do not always or inevitably live saintly lives. Walking in the Spirit will enable Christians to reduce the discrepancy in their lives between their status as saints and their lifestyle, which is all too often something less than saintly.

When Paul writes about sanctification he sometimes contrasts "flesh" and "Spirit."

His discussion in his letter to the Galatians is a vivid and extensive contrast (Galatians 5:16-26). Christians are to *walk* by the Spirit. As a result, those who do will not carry out the desire of the flesh = sinful nature (5:16). Spirit and flesh are not merely passive opposites. There is a war, indeed, mortal combat between the two (5:17). Paul identifies the flesh by its deeds: "immorality, impurity, sensuality, idolatry, sorcery, enmity, strife . . . and things like these" (5:19-21). The danger of these works of the flesh is that, "those who practice such things shall not inherit the Kingdom of God" (5:21b). But, in contrast to the deadly deeds of the flesh, the fruit of the Spirit includes: "love, joy, peace, patience, kindness, goodness, faithfulness, gentleness, self-control" (5:22,23). Since Christians have "crucified" or put to death the deeds of the flesh they, "live by the Spirit (5:25a). Therefore, Christians must not live by the flesh (as though they were still sinners) but must "walk by the Spirit" (5:25b). Paul makes a similar contrast between flesh and Spirit in his letter to the saints at Rome (Romans 8:1-13). He concludes his discussion, affirming, Christians are no longer, "in the flesh but in the Spirit" (8:9), and, therefore, Christians are obligated to put to death the deeds of the body = flesh by the Spirit (8:13). Herein is sanctification. It is walking by the Spirit. It is producing the fruit of the Spirit. It is living in the Spirit. Sanctification then is a matter of life or death (8:13).

Summary

Paul's theology of the Spirit is the most complex among the three major witnesses to the Spirit, namely, Luke, John, and Paul. For Paul, the Spirit is the active agent in salvation, incorporating converts into the body of Christ; the Spirit is also the active agent in sanctification, sustaining and transforming the lives of those whose initial experience of the Spirit has been conversion-initiation; and, finally, the Spirit is the active agent in charismatic service, both for Paul and for his converts, gifting each one with those graces/manifestations needed to serve God in the church and in the world. Obviously, Luke's single theme of the Spirit and prophetic service can be compared with Paul's emphasis on the Spirit and service, but not to Paul's themes of the Spirit and salvation and the Spirit and sanctification. Similarly, John's two themes of the Spirit and prophetic service and the Spirit and salvation can be compared to Paul's teaching on the same two themes. Therefore, in the end, Paul's most distinctive teaching about the Spirit is his teaching about the sanctifying work of the Spirit.

Reflection

God placed three anointed offices within Israel to lead the nation: 1) an anointed priesthood, 2) an anointed kingship and 3) an anointed prophethood. Jesus fulfilled all three of these anointed offices, but with surprising differences. For example, one difference is that Jesus' anointing is qualitatively superior, for unlike high priests, kings and prophets, who were anointed with oil, God anointed Jesus with the Holy Spirit. An equally important difference is that Jesus' kingship and high priesthood only take effect after his resurrection and ascension (Luke 19:11,12; Hebrews 8:4). In contrast to his anointed kingship and anointed high priesthood, Jesus' anointed prophethood, from first to last, takes place on earth (Luke 4:24, 24:29). This is significant for the subsequent ministry of the disciples.

Jesus' experience of Spirit-anointing, fullness and empowering (Luke 3:22; 4:1,14,18) is irrelevant for the disciples' experience of the Spirit if it is about messianic kingship or messianic high priesthood. Disciples, both then and now, cannot serve him as kings. Disciples, both then and now, cannot serve him as high priests. However, disciples who are Spirit-baptized, Spirit-empowered and Spirit-filled, both then and now, will extend and replicate Jesus' ministry as the Spirit-anointed, Spiritful, and Spirit-empowered prophet. Therefore, because Jesus ministered on earth as a prophet mighty in word and deed (Luke 24:19), and because Jesus transferred the Spirit of prophecy to his disciples (Acts

2:17, 33), his Spirit-baptized disciples, both then and now can also minister as prophets who are mighty in word and deed.

www.ingramcontent.com/pod-product-compliance
Lightning Source LLC
Chambersburg PA
CBHW050759160426
43192CB00010B/1570